The Inquiry in numbers

74   witnesses

24   days of evidence

90   seats available daily in the main court and annexe for members of the public

923,000   words of the hearing's transcripts published on the Hutton Inquiry's website

46 seconds   the duration of the telephone call David Kelly's line manager made to tell him his name was about to become public

21   names put to the Ministry of Defence by Michael Evans, defence editor of *The Times*, in order to have David Kelly's confirmed

£4.15   the expenses claim put in by Andrew Gilligan for the Appletise and Coca-Cola he and Kelly drank during their meeting at the Charing Cross Hotel

179   questions put to Kelly by MPs on the Commons Foreign Affairs Select Committee

787   documents submitted to the inquiry, comprising over 10,000 pages of evidence

3   pages withheld on national security grounds

19   years of Kelly's service to the government

£62,469   his final salary at the Ministry of Defence

8   computers belonging to or used by Kelly seized by police investigators holding a total of 41.5 gigabytes of information

£70   cost of the 740-pag̲ ̲ ̲ ̲ ̲ ̲ ̲ ̲ ̲ ̲d on 28 January 2004

'*What we've been told by one of the senior officials in charge of drawing up that dossier was that, actually the government probably erm, knew that that 45-minute figure was wrong, even before it decided to put it in. What this person says, is that a week before the publication date of the dossier, it was actually rather erm, a bland production. It didn't, the, the draft prepared for Mr Blair by the intelligence agencies actually didn't say very much more than was public knowledge already and erm, Downing Street, our source says, ordered a week before publication, ordered it to be sexed up, to be made more exciting and ordered more facts to be er, to be discovered.*'

Andrew Gilligan on the *Today* programme
BBC Radio 4, 6.07am, 29 May 2003

David Aaronovitch
Oliver Burkeman
Vikram Dodd
Jonathan Freedland
Tom Happold
David Hencke
Simon Hoggart
Ewen MacAskill
Richard Norton-Taylor
Polly Toynbee
Nicholas Watt
Matt Wells
Michael White
edited by **Simon Rogers**

The Hutton Inquiry and its impact

POLITICO'S
GUARDIAN BOOKS

First published in 2004
on behalf of Guardian Newspapers Ltd by
Politico's Publishing, an imprint of
Methuen Publishing Limited
215 Vauxhall Bridge Road
London SW1V 1EJ

Printed and bound in Great Britain by Cox and Wyman

A CIP catalogue record for this book is available from the British Library

ISBN 1 84275 106 9

10 9 8 7 6 5 4 3 2 1

Contents

Foreword
Alan Rusbridger

This is not the book we thought it would be. When the government
sent for Lord Hutton back in the hot summer of 2003 it was almost
universally assumed that this forbiddingly dry judge would evenly
and dispassionately drop forbiddingly dry judgements among the
cast of characters which had become unwittingly involved in the
tragedy of Dr David Kelly's death. As the deadline neared for the
verdict to be handed down the most eminent figures in Downing
Street, Whitehall and the BBC adopted a brace position. No one
could predict who would live and who would perish.

The impact, when it came, was softened by an extensive and
impressively accurate leak of the main conclusions in the *Sun*. But
even that leak was poor preparation for the singular narrative upon
which Hutton remorselessly embarked. At every turn the politicians, civil servants and spooks were exonerated. At every turn the
BBC journalists, managers and governors were damned.

There was an air of disbelief in the courtroom. Jonathan
Freedland reported: 'Several journalists began first to sniff, then to
snort and finally to chuckle their derision. Jeremy Paxman, for once
barred from asking questions, was shaking his head in bemusement
as each new finding of favour from the government came down
from the bench.'

The amusement didn't last for long. It didn't take much reflection to realise the report was a disaster for the BBC and
much-needed manna from heaven for the government. Within
hours the chairman of the BBC, Gavyn Davies, had resigned.
Within twenty-four hours the decapitation of the world's most

admired broadcasting organisation was complete, with the director general, Greg Dyke, being forced out as well. A small butterfly fluttering at 6.07 one May morning had wrought a hurricane.

The impact of Hutton? From the perspective of Westminster and Whitehall the temptation is to say none, except in the negative sense of all the things which didn't happen. The Prime Minister wasn't damaged. The Secretary of State for Defence didn't resign. There was no cabinet reshuffle, no reassessment of the interface between politics and intelligence, no soul-searching about spin, no wider post-mortem about how the intelligence on weapons of mass destruction was so wrong, nothing. With one bound they were all free – and it showed on their faces. Some of the major players neglected the wise lesson of Edmund Burke: 'Magnanimity in politics is not seldom the truest wisdom.'

For the BBC, the impact couldn't have been more serious. It was plunged into a very great and dangerous crisis. In the immediate run-up to the crucial renewal of its charter – due to coincide with the run-up to a general election – the corporation had been summarily been deprived of both its chairman and director general. It was led by a board of governors of mixed abilities, and who had hardly performed with distinction. Its enemies – political, commercial, journalistic and ideological – were swarming with increasing confidence.

Some defenders of the BBC consoled themselves with the thought that a more rigorous style of journalism would emerge as a result. Others feared long-term consequences for a proud tradition of robust, intelligent and – occasionally – trouble-making journalism.

More alarming still was Lord Hutton's apparent distaste for many of the recent hard-won advances in free speech. He seemed to think Dr Kelly had no business to be giving voice to his conscience in front of a journalist, and deserved no protection for doing so. He implied that news organisations had no business reporting the concerns of respected public servants unless they could independently satisfy themselves of the truth of their statements. He placed little emphasis on modern developments in the law of defamation which take some account of the right to be wrong. In other words, judges are required to consider the chilling effect on free speech if every journalistic slip is punished as the gravest of civil offences. Courts should now take into consideration whether the story was in the public interest, the nature of the source, the lengths to which the story was checked and so on. Judged by these criteria, the BBC journalist Andrew Gilligan got more right than he got wrong in the nineteen radio broadcasts on 29 May.

There were two other important lessons from Hutton. One was that it is possible for a government to release every single document, email and private diary entry – and still emerge without a blemish on its character. That, surely, should convince even the most hardened sceptics that there is little to fear from a liberal policy on freedom of information. And, finally, Hutton may have killed off the notion that judges – wrenched from the comforts of precedence and procedure – necessarily know best. A whitewash? Leave that for the headline writers. A more considered epitaph might be that Lord Hutton was simply naive. He knew little about the characters and events he was required to confront in this, his last case. Throughout most of the period in question he had been living on a different island in a different world. And it showed.

Preface

Simon Rogers

It was an unprepossessing location for an inquiry that would transform British political life. A cramped courtroom at the back of the Royal Courts of Justice on the Strand that was more *Changing Rooms* than *Rumpole of the Bailey*. Despite appearances, this was one of Britain's most powerful judicial hearings, and it stayed peculiarly British, right down to the B&Q-style bookshelves. It was about as far removed in grandeur from a US congressional hearing as is possible: legendary *Washington Post* reporter Carl Bernstein, one half of the duo which uncovered the Watergate scandal, described it as 'more like a dull classroom than a seat of judicial might: Swiss cheese ceiling, filthy carpet, empty bookcases and cheap chairs from some Office Depot outlet'.

That environment and the atmosphere of quiet and determined professionalism that Lord Hutton brought to his inquiry succeeded in something quite amazing: it stripped away the mystique of power. As Bernstein wrote in the *Mirror*, Tony Blair became Mr Blair, not Prime Minister Blair, when confronted by the judge. Figures unused to the spotlight, such as the MoD's Sir Kevin Tebbit, briefly became public names before disappearing back into powerful obscurity.

We had horrendous details from the Kelly family of the moments before the weapons inspector's disappearance and the tremendous hole his death had left in their lives. At the same time, we had the personnel management skills of civil servants taken apart in a gentlemanly but forensic manner. We were provided with more inside information about the inner workings of Britain's government than ever before.

But as it progressed, what really happened to David Kelly became less clear to all but the most assiduous followers of the action in court 73. The 74 witnesses, 923,000 words of transcript and 10,000 pages of evidence swamped the British media with what appeared to be incremental details of the smallest importance. It was the equivalent of a Sir Humphrey deluging his minister with red cases of documents: the story was in danger of getting lost. The fact that a decent and honourable man had died – one of the few people in the world who might have found elusive Iraqi weapons of mass destruction – seemed to disappear beneath a flood of information.

But for those who followed the minute details and understood their significance, the inquiry process was something else entirely. Its lessons built up over the weeks – and what seemed mysterious and cloudy at first became clearer as witnesses appeared and were recalled to explain their stories better.

The final report became just another controversial development. For the first time ever we, as members of the public, were able to hear and read the evidence, and come to our own conclusions. Was it just a charter to cherrypick whatever fitted our personal prejudices? Or was it treating us as adults, able to decide for ourselves what happened?

The death of Dr Kelly in a wood in Oxfordshire turned out to be just the beginning of a news story that reverberated around the world. We at the *Guardian* wanted to tell that story. Our attempt is to make clear what actually happened – and what it means.

What we have done is to provide as complete a guide to the inquiry as possible. The *Guardian*'s specialist reporters, who covered every fine detail over the weeks of the hearings and reported the final result, have pored over the evidence to produce the chapters you will find here, which are published for the first time. We have also analysed every day of the hearings, detailing each witness, each piece of background documentary evidence and each quote from which we thought there were relevant lessons.

In many ways, this book is about the awful word which has dominated recent British political history: spin. Andrew Gilligan's report, the government response and the fallout that followed were all about different interpretations of the details. Lord Hutton's final report is yet another interpretation of the evidence, as is this book itself.

It's been a long time since history was simply the version of events people decided to agree upon. And Hutton's inquiry and report, whatever their faults, were history – made before our eyes.

* * *

First thanks must go to Richard Norton-Taylor, for whose advice and expertise I am profoundly grateful. The other writers who made this book possible were the Hutton reporting team, who between them pored over the transcripts each day of the inquiry providing concise and accessible analysis. They were (in alphabetical order): Owen Bowcott, Vikram Dodd, Ewen MacAskill, Nick Watt and Matt Wells. Besides the exclusive pieces they have written for this book, their help in compiling the day-by-day guide was invaluable.

The *Guardian*'s engine room is the newsdesk – the newspaper wouldn't happen if they weren't there, six days a week. So, particular thanks must go to deputy editor (news), Paul Johnson for his advice, to home editor Ed Pilkington for lending me his personal office and his time and to Georgina Henry, the paper's deputy editor.

Thanks too to home news editor Andrew Culf, who made sure that I had the time to put the book together. For his early advice, I am indebted too to Julian Glover, the paper's assistant news editor (politics).

The *Guardian* is now a multi-format newspaper and the book benefited from the particular help of Tom Happold and Matthew

Tempest from *Guardian Unlimited*. The research department provided endless background material. In particular Richard Nelson, James Bisset, Tom Clare, Jo Anne Kennedy and Lucy Moffatt, who all helped with digging out cuttings. Liane Katz organised the transcripts into a more readable form and Davina Joseph and Rosemary Hammond's administrative help was indispensable.

That this book makes sense is down primarily to the sub-editing and proofreading skills of Anne Sacks and David Marsh, who never complained, despite enormous provocation.

The fact that this book has been published at all is down to the foresight of a few: Alan Rusbridger, the editor of the *Guardian*, set the tone and ensured it happened in the first place. Lisa Darnell, the *Guardian*'s book publisher, and Sean Magee at Politico's offered constant advice and expertise and never ever panicked about producing a book that would be out a week after the inquiry reported. They just calmly got us there.

To everyone else who helped out with the many bits and pieces that went in – thank you.

Finally, Liza made everything possible.

Simon Rogers
January 2004

Dramatis personae

Tony Blair
Prime Minister of the United Kingdom.

James Blitz
Political editor of the *Financial Times*.

Andrew Caldecott QC
Counsel for the BBC, a leading defamation specialist who had appeared in media libel trials including Naomi Campbell's battle with the *Daily Mirror*.

Alastair Campbell
Director of communications and strategy during the writing of the dossier and the aftermath of Andrew Gilligan's report.

Wing Commander John Clark
A friend and colleague of David Kelly who shared an office with the scientist at the Ministry of Defence.

Gavyn Davies
The chairman of the BBC board of governors.

Sir Richard Dearlove
Chief of MI6, otherwise known as C.

James Dingemans QC
A QC of one year's standing, he was selected by Lord Hutton to be senior counsel to the inquiry. Dingemans asked the majority of the questions in the neutral first stage of the inquiry, assisted by the junior counsel Peter Knox.

Dramatis Personae

Greg Dyke
Director general of the BBC.

Andrew Gilligan
Defence correspondent, *Today* programme, BBC Radio 4.

Jeremy Gompertz QC
Counsel for the Kelly family. A criminal and commercial practitioner and part-time judge, one of his most notable former appearances was for the police in the Stephen Lawrence inquiry.

Richard Hatfield
The MoD personnel director who interviewed Dr Kelly over his meetings with Gilligan.

Geoff Hoon
Secretary of State for Defence.

Martin Howard
Deputy chief of intelligence, MoD's Defence Intelligence Staff.

Lord Hutton
Lord Chief Justice of Northern Ireland for nearly ten years before he was appointed a law lord, one of twelve judges in the House of Lords, the UK's highest court, in 1997. He came to the inquiry with the reputation of a conservative and safe pair of hands.

Brian Jones and Mr A
Civil servants working in counter-proliferation and defence intelligence.

David Kelly
The UK's top scientific adviser on weapons of mass destruction in Iraq and weapons inspector.

Janice Kelly
David Kelly's widow. The two met at Leeds university in the 1960s and were married for 36 years.

Tom Kelly
The Prime Minister's official spokesman.

Peter Knox QC
A colleague of Dingemans at the 3 Hare Court barristers' chambers, the junior counsel to the inquiry specialised in commercial and business law but has also worked in the Privy Council.

Patrick Lamb
Deputy head of the Foreign Office's Counter-Proliferation Department, to which Dr Kelly was the senior scientific adviser.

David Lloyd Jones QC
Counsel for the MoD. A deputy high court judge, he had formerly acted for British soldiers challenging a ruling by the Bloody Sunday inquiry that they had to go to Derry to give evidence.

Sir David Omand
Coordinator of security and intelligence at the Cabinet Office, a post created in 2002 to coordinate the work of MI5, MI6 and GCHQ in the manner of the US homeland security secretary.

Jonathan Powell
The Downing Street chief of staff.

Heather Rogers QC
Gilligan's counsel. A media lawyer specialising in libel who represented Mohamed Al-Fayed against Neil Hamilton, she is also a colleague of Cherie Booth, the Prime Minister's wife, at Matrix chambers.

Nick Rufford
Sunday Times reporter, friendly with Dr Kelly, who interviewed the scientist over his garden gate the day after the MoD announced a potential source had come forward.

Richard Sambrook
BBC head of news who described the BBC's side of the row with the government and his correspondence with Campbell.

John Scarlett
Chairman of the Joint Intelligence Committee, the Cabinet Office body that prepares intelligence assessments for the government.

Jonathan Sumption QC
The government's QC. Previously represented the government when Jack Straw, then Home Secretary, employed him in 1999 to fight a challenge by General Pinochet to his extradition to Spain.

Richard Taylor
Special adviser to Geoff Hoon.

Pam Teare
The MoD's director of news.

Kevin Tebbit
MoD permanent secretary and one of the first people Tony Blair spoke to after David Kelly's death.

Susan Watts
BBC *Newsnight* science editor.

Bryan Wells
David Kelly's line manager at the MoD's Counter-Proliferation and Arms Control Secretariat.

Simon Jeffery

Timeline

3 September 2002
Tony Blair announces the imminent publication of a dossier spelling out why Iraq poses 'a real and unique threat to the security of the region and the rest of the world' to a press conference in his Sedgefield constituency.

5 September
A draft version of the dossier is circulated. Alastair Campbell says it needs a 'substantial rewrite . . . as per TB's discussion'.

10–11 September
A piece of intelligence suggesting that Iraq could launch chemical weapons within 45 minutes of an order being given makes its first appearance in the dossier.

24 September
The dossier, entitled *Iraq's Weapons of Mass Destruction: the assessment of the British government,* is published. The London *Evening Standard*'s headline reads: '45 minutes to attack'. Next day the *Sun* splashes 'He's got 'em . . . let's get him' across its front page. Iraq denounces the dossier as 'short-sighted, naive lies'.

8 November
The UN security council votes unanimously to deliver an ultimatum to Iraq to accept the unconditional return of weapons inspectors or face unspecified 'serious consequences'.

20 March 2003
War begins as air strikes are launched in and around Baghdad against what President George Bush calls 'targets of military opportunity'. Baghdad falls to US troops on 9 April.

1 May

Bush declares major combat operations over. No weapons of mass destruction are fired at invading troops or discovered in the advance on the main Iraqi cities.

22 May

Dr David Kelly, a Ministry of Defence biological weapons expert, meets BBC *Today* programme defence correspondent Andrew Gilligan in the Charing Cross Hotel in central London. The two talk about intelligence officers' concerns over the dossier, the likely extent of Iraq's chemical and biological weapons programmes, and weapons inspections then under way in Iraq.

29 May

Gilligan makes a series of reports on the *Today* programme and on BBC Five Live based on his meeting with Kelly. He says his source told him the dossier was made 'sexier' in the week before its publication, the classic example being the claim that weapons of mass destruction would be ready for use within 45 minutes. In one report he says the government 'knew that claim was questionable'.

1 June

Gilligan revisits the story in the *Mail on Sunday*. He says he asked his source how the transformation happened. 'The answer was a single word,' he wrote. 'Campbell.'

6 June

Campbell writes to Richard Sambrook, the BBC director of news, to complain the reports gave the impression the government took Britain to war on a false basis. He also uses a press briefing to highlight what he says are a series of inaccuracies in Gilligan's reports.

8 June

Gilligan *Mail on Sunday* article 'Hurricane Alastair and tropical storm Tony blew into my life' accuses Downing Street of briefing against him

19 June

The Commons Foreign Affairs Select Committee questions Gilligan about his reports and his source. He says it was 'one of the senior officials in charge of drawing up the dossier . . . easily sufficiently senior and credible to be worth reporting.'

25–26 June

Campbell faces the Foreign Affairs Committee. He says he takes the accusations contained in the Gilligan report – which he calls a 'lie' – very seriously. He writes to Sambrook demanding an apology.

27 June

Sambrook stands by the story and accuses Campbell of 'conducting a personal vendetta' against Gilligan. His recipient then makes a surprise appearance on that evening's *Channel 4 News*. Angry and wagging his finger at presenter Jon Snow, Campbell tears into the 'fundamental attack upon the integrity of the government'.

30 June

Kelly writes to his manager, Bryan Wells, admitting he had met Gilligan on 22 May.

3 July

Geoff Hoon, the Defence Secretary, calls Downing Street to say a possible source has come forward but that his account of the meeting does not back up all the details of Gilligan's story. Blair learns of the development on a visit to the North West.

4 July

A meeting is held in Downing Street to discuss Kelly's admission. Campbell writes in his diary that it would 'fuck' Gilligan if Kelly was indeed his source, due to the discrepancies between their two accounts.

5–6 July

Campbell writes in his diary that he spent much of the weekend discussing Kelly's admission with Blair and Hoon. He says he and the Defence Secretary wanted 'to get the source up' but the Prime Minister was nervous. Campbell also telephones Jonathan Powell, the Downing Street chief of staff, to warn him that they know of a possible source.

A report in *The Times* identifies Gilligan's source as a scientist working in Iraq and the BBC governors release a statement giving unconditional backing to Gilligan. Sir Kevin Tebbit, the MoD's senior civil servant, warns Blair that Kelly could be named imminently.

7 July

A second meeting takes place at the Prime Minister's office. Described by Jonathan Powell as a fast-paced running meeting that 'gets smaller and bigger and bigger and smaller', Tony Blair, Jack Straw and senior Whitehall and intelligence figures discuss whether to put Kelly before the Foreign Affairs Committee. Kelly is interviewed by Martin Howard, the MoD deputy chief of intelligence, Richard Hatfield, the MoD head of personnel, and Wells. He later tells *Sunday Times* journalist Nicholas Rufford that he was 'put through the wringer'.

8 July

A Downing Street meeting chaired by Blair decides to put out an MoD statement saying an official had admitted speaking to Andrew Gilligan after an earlier plan to disclose his existence in a letter to the Commons Intelligence and Security Committee falls through. Supplementary material is put together by the MoD after consultations with No. 10 to help press officers field follow-up questions. It is agreed at the meeting to confirm Kelly's name to journalists who guess it correctly.

9 July

Geoff Hoon writes to Gavyn Davies, the BBC chairman of governors, asking him to confirm whether Kelly was the source. The MoD press office later confirms to *Financial Times* journalist James

Blitz that the scientist admitted to meeting Gilligan. On the advice of the press office, Kelly drives from his Oxfordshire home to Cornwall to escape the media.

10 July

The *Guardian*, *The Times* and the *Financial Times* name Kelly as the source of Gilligan's allegations. Blair accepts that Kelly will have to give evidence to both the Foreign Affairs Committee and the Intelligence and Security Committee. Downing Street spokesman Tom Kelly sends an email to Powell reading: 'This is now a game of chicken with the Beeb.'

13 July

Rejecting the MoD's offer of a hotel in London, Kelly leaves his wife in Cornwall to stay with his daughter Rachel in Oxfordshire. She said she overheard her father on the phone saying that he was 'very depressed' by the media coverage, and that he would only read the sports sections of the newspapers.

14 July

Government officials brief Kelly ahead of his appearance before the Foreign Affairs Committee.

15 July

Kelly faces the Foreign Affairs Committee. Rachel Kelly later told the inquiry her father said that Andrew Mackinlay – who asked him if he was 'chaff' – was an 'utter bastard'. His colleague, Wing Commander John Clark, said he was thrown by a question from David Chidgey about his contact with Susan Watts, BBC *Newsnight* science editor.

16 July

Kelly appears in front of the Intelligence and Security Committee and returns that evening to Oxfordshire for a meal at his daughter's house before going to his own home. On the same day, Blair challenges the BBC to reveal Gilligan's source.

Timeline

17 July
Gilligan faces the Foreign Affairs Committee for a second time, and is branded an 'unsatisfactory witness'. At 3pm, Kelly leaves home, telling his wife he is going for a walk. When he fails to return home by 11.45pm, his family contacts the police.

18 July
Thames Valley Police find a body near to Kelly's home. It is later confirmed as Kelly. Journalists accompanying Blair on a flight from Washington to Tokyo are told by the Prime Minister's official spokesman that there will be an independent judicial inquiry into the circumstances surrounding his death. Lord Hutton, a Law Lord and Former Lord Chief Justice of Northern Ireland, is appointed to head an inquiry into the circumstances surrounding the death of Kelly.

20 July
The BBC confirms that Kelly was the source of both Gilligan's and Watts's reports.

1 August
Lord Hutton announces that Blair, Hoon, civil servants, BBC executives and journalists will be called to the inquiry. He also asks to see all letters, memos, reports and any other documentation that 'in any way related to Dr Kelly'.

11 August
The inquiry begins in earnest as the first witnesses give evidence.

13 October
Inquiry finishes with the MoD official Sir Kevin Tebbit testifying.

28 January 2004
Lord Hutton reports.

Simon Jeffery

Glossary

45-minute claim

The assertion, as expressed in the dossier, that Saddam Hussein's military planning allowed for 'some of the WMD to be ready within 45 minutes of an order to use them'.

Baha'i

Religion originating in a reformist movement in Iranian Islam that counted David Kelly among its followers.

Counter-Proliferation and Arms Control Secretariat

Kelly's main department, a MoD unit that deals with non-proliferation, weapons inspections and export controls. It employed Kelly as a biological weapons expert.

CPD

The Counter-Proliferation Department, the Foreign Office unit to which Kelly was seconded. As well as dealing in the full range of arms control issues and with the UN inspectors, it also drew up background material for the dossier.

Den, the

Office in No. 10 Downing Street where the Prime Minister conducts meetings with his most trusted advisers.

DIS

Defence Intelligence Staff. A unit within the Ministry of Defence that analyses raw intelligence and offers assessments to policy makers and military planners. Some DIS staff expressed concerns over the dossier.

DSTL

Defence Science and Technology Laboratory, the MoD department formerly known as Porton Down where Kelly began his government career in 1984, and continued to have a second line manager. An arms and defence research organisation, its 3,000 employees include the largest number of scientists and engineers in the public services.

FAC
Commons Foreign Affairs Select Committee. A cross-party body of MPs whose investigation into the Iraq dossiers saw Kelly, Andrew Gilligan and Alastair Campbell called to give evidence.

FCO
Foreign and Commonwealth Office, more commonly known as the Foreign Office.

Iraq Survey Group
US-led weapons inspection unit working in Iraq since the ousting of the former regime. Kelly was preparing to join it in the weeks before his death.

ISC
Commons Intelligence and Security Committee, a cross-party body that conducted a parallel investigation to the Foreign Affairs Committee into the intelligence used ahead of the Iraq. It also called Kelly and Gilligan to give evidence but, unlike the Foreign Affairs Committee, its hearings were behind closed doors.

JIC
The Joint Intelligence Committee, a Cabinet Office body made up of heads of the intelligence agencies that provides assessments to the Prime Minister.

MoD
Ministry of Defence.

MoD mole
Early reference to Kelly in the media when his identity was unknown.

pay grade

Where a civil servant fits on a salary scale and a reflection of seniority. Kelly asked for a rise in his grading, while Alastair Campbell dismissed the contributions of a junior, a No. 10 press officer, as being 'effectively above his pay grade'.

PMOS

Prime Minister's official spokesman.

running meeting

A lengthy meeting where participants come and go during a morning. Jonathan Powell, the Downing Street chief of staff, described it as one that gets 'smaller and bigger and bigger and smaller'.

senior civil servant

Description awarded to members of the civil service on the higher pay grades. The MoD said that while an undoubted expert in his field, Kelly was not a member of the senior civil service.

'sex up'

The central allegation against the government, that it had 'sexed up' intelligence, that emerged from Gilligan's reports. John Williams, the Foreign Office press secretary, told the reporter he had done 'great violence to the English language'.

SIS

Special Intelligence Services, better known as MI6. Its main role is to gather intelligence in support of the UK's security, defence, foreign and economic policies.

source

Refers to Gilligan's source for the 'sexing up' claims and the source for the 45-minute claim. Both were single-sourced (coming from one person) in areas – journalism and intelligence – where double-sourcing is preferred. Both the government and Gilligan claimed their sources were strong enough not to need collaboration.

two-way

A convention in radio and television news where a reporter will be interviewed by a presenter, answering, often unscripted, a series of questions on his or her story live on air. It was such an exchange that *Today* used to deliver Gilligan's report on the Iraq dossier.

Unmovic

The United Nations Monitoring, Verification and Inspection Commission set up in 1999 to assess the extent of Iraq's disarmament. It entered the country in late 2002 under Hans Blix.

Unscom

The United Nations Special Commission, the biological and chemical weapons inspection regime in place from 1991 to 1998 that counted Kelly among its number.

WMDs

Nuclear, biological and chemical weapons of mass destruction.

Simon Jeffery

Introduction

Richard Norton-Taylor

July 17, 2003, will be a day Tony Blair is unlikely to forget. In Washington, the US Congress gave him a rapturous reception, a reward for his decision to join America's invasion of Iraq. In Britain, Dr David Kelly, the government scientist and chief adviser on the state of Iraq's chemical and biological weapons programme went for a walk. The next day he was found dead, apparently having committed suicide. Elation fell to despair as Blair heard of the news which was to undermine trust in his government, open it up to unprecedented scrutiny and, potentially most damaging, question the Prime Minister's judgment and honesty on the most important decision facing the leader of any country – taking it to war.

The Prime Minister, flying from Washington for an official visit to the Far East, was thousands of miles away from his closest advisers, unable to judge at first hand the media and public reaction back home to Kelly's death. But he knew the opposition in parliament to the invasion of Iraq was growing, with MPs from all parties pressing for an inquiry into the accuracy and reliablity of the intelligence on which the government's dossier on Iraq's banned weapons programme, was based. In other words, did Britain go to war on a flawed, or false, prospectus?

Though the Kelly affair was about much more than this, that question was at the heart of it. It was a question, however, the government wanted to avoid. Shocked and looking drawn on his plane, Blair was in frantic contact with Whitehall, notably his old and trusted friend, Lord Falconer, Lord Chancellor and head of the new Department for Constitutional Affairs, and the top civil servant at the Ministry of Defence, Sir Kevin Tebbit. Blair quickly agreed to set up an independent judicial inquiry 'urgently to conduct an investigation into the circumstances surrounding the death of Dr Kelly'.

Blair and Falconer chose Lord Hutton, a Law Lord on the point of retirement, to conduct the inquiry hoping the former chief justice of Northern Ireland would be cautious, a safe pair of hands, interpreting his mandate narrowly, restricting himself to the personal treatment of Kelly and the allegation by the BBC Radio 4 *Today* programme reporter, Andrew Gilligan, that Downing Street had 'sexed up' the weapons dossier, inserting claims it knew were probably untrue.

The allegation, furiously denied by Blair, set off a chain of events which ultimately ended with Kelly's death. The question was who would be implicated and what would the inquiry unearth. At the time the decision to set up the Hutton Inquiry sent shivers across Whitehall and haunted the government throughout August and September – months when ministers and their close advisers take to the beaches and villas abroad. Their holidays were shattered daily with embarrassing, and potentially fatal, headlines and disclosures.

For Whitehall, and the intelligence establishment in particular, any independent inquiry delving into its secret world is always most unwelcome. A huge amount was at stake: the probity of the Prime Minister – accused, he said, by the BBC of lying about intelligence on the threat posed by Saddam Hussein – the reputation of the BBC, the credibility of the intelligence agencies, the Ministry of Defence 'duty of care' to Dr Kelly who was in its charge, and the ability of MPs to hold the government to account. Few could have guessed what it would uncover, how it would provide an unprecedented insight into the workings – and mindset – of Blair's inner circle in 10 Downing Street, including its relations with the intelligence agencies.

It may be too early for the full ramifications of Lord Hutton's report to have sunk into the body politic, but it is clear that it has huge implications for Downing Street, parliament, the intelligence agencies, the transparency of government, journalism, and the future of the BBC, plunged into the greatest crisis of its history with the resignation of Gavyn Davies, its chairman of governors, and Greg Dyke, the director general, two unexpected – and, to many, unjust – victims of Lord Hutton's report. None of these institutions will be the same again. The inquiry shook the government to its core, dealt a body blow to the intelligence services, and severely wounded the BBC just at the time its charter was coming up for renewal.

Hutton raised hopes, later to be dashed, when he insisted in his opening statement at the inquiry that he was in charge, and he alone would decide what matters were relevant. 'This Inquiry is to be conducted – and I stress it – by myself', he said. 'This means that all the decisions have to be taken by me. Let me indicate now, so that there need to be no misunderstanding, what are the implications of what I have just said. First of all, it is I, and I alone, who will decide what witnesses will be called. I also decide to what matters their evidence will be directed.' For the first time emails were produced as official documents in a public inquiry. Blair's instructions to Downing Street and the Cabinet Office were clear and reflected the old Whitehall adage: 'the cover-up is greater than the original sin'. In other words, give the inquiry anything you find relevant to its terms of reference.

On its side, in an unprecedented display of openness, the inquiry placed hundreds of documents on its website, including extracts from the diary of Alastair Campbell, the Prime Minister's communications director.

Evidence to the inquiry revealed just how far the row between Downing Street and the BBC over the allegations about the weapons dossier had penetrated the heart of government. 'It was grim for me and it was grim for TB [Tony Blair] and there is this huge stuff about trust', wrote Campbell in his diary, extracts from which were read out and released to the inquiry. The documents also revealed just how deeply involved Downing Street was in preparing the Iraqi weapons dossier.

A flavour came in an email from an official in the Joint Intelligence Committee to his colleagues on 11 September 2002, eight days before the drafting deadline. 'Dear All', he said, 'We have now received comments back from No. 10 on the first draft of the dossier. Unsurprisingly, they have further questions and areas they would like expanded'. The email continued: 'They want more details on the items procured for their nuclear programme – how many did they buy, what does this equate to in terms of significance to a nuclear weapons programme? . . . Can we say how many chemical and biological weapons Iraq currently has by type? If we can't give weapons numbers, can we give any idea on the quantity of agent available?'

The writer, whose name is blacked out, added wearily: 'I appreciate everyone, us included, has been around at least some of these buoys before . . . But No. 10 through the Chairman [John Scarlett, chairman of Whitehall's Joint Intelligence Committee] want the document to be as strong as possible within the bounds of available intelligence . . .' Jonathan Powell, the Prime Minister's chief of staff, in an email on 17 September warned Scarlett, Campbell, and Sir David Manning, Blair's foreign policy adviser: 'the document does nothing to demonstrate he [Saddam] has the motive to attack his neighbours let alone the west'.

Two days later, a worried Powell asked: 'What will be the headline in the *Standard* [London's *Evening Standard*] on day of publication? What do we want it to be?'

He added: 'I think the statement . . . that "Saddam is prepared to use chemical and biological weapons if he believes his regime is under threat" is a bit of a problem.' It backed up the argument, warned Powell, that Iraq did not pose a chemical and biological weapons threat and 'we will only create one if we attack him'.

He was commenting on a draft which stated: 'Intelligence indicates that as part of Iraq's military planning Saddam is prepared to use chemical and biological weapons *if he believes his regime is under threat*' (emphasis added.)

The dossier was changed to say: 'Intelligence indicates that as part of Iraq's military planning, Saddam is willing to use chemical and biological weapons.' Scarlett told the inquiry he dropped the qualification acting under 'delegated authority'.

This was a key issue, for one of Andrew Gilligan's main allegations, based on his meeting with Kelly, is that Downing Street 'sexed up' the weapons dossier.

Another key issue was the claim in the dossier – made most forcefully in the preface signed by the Prime Minister – that Iraqi forces could deploy chemical and biological weapons within 45 minutes of an order to do so. That claim was singled out by Kelly in his meeting with Gilligan, and later in conversations with the BBC *Newsnight* science correspondent, Susan Watts. Kelly's concern about that claim was shared by officials in the Defence Intelligence Staff. Scarlett told the inquiry that the 45-minute claim was meant to refer only to short-range battlefield weapons such as mortars, and not to long-range missiles able to strike at British bases in Cyprus, as the dossier implied. The admission further undermined the dossier. Asked why he had not put the record straight, Geoff Hoon, the Defence Secretary, replied that he found the task of trying to correct what appeared in the media time-consuming and frustrating. However, the evidence is that Downing Street was only too delighted at headlines in the press at the time warning of a 45-minute threat to Britain, not British troops invading Iraq. Another key issue was how Kelly came to be publicly identified in the so-called 'outing strategy', and the role of the Prime Minister in particular.

A few days after Kelly's death, Blair was confronted by journalists on his aircraft as it prepared to land in Hong Kong. 'Why did you authorise the naming of David Kelly?' he was asked. 'That is completely untrue,' replied Blair.

'Did you authorise anyone in Downing Street or in the Ministry of Defence to release David Kelly's name?' he was asked. 'Emphatically not,' responded Blair. 'I did not authorise the leaking of the name of David Kelly'. The Prime Minister added: 'Nobody was authorised to name David Kelly. I believe we have acted properly throughout.'

The clearest evidence that Blair was personally involved in the decisions which led to the Kelly's unmasking was provided by Sir Kevin Tebbit , the top civil servant at the Ministry of Defence, at his second appearance at the inquiry. He said the decisive meeting from which everything else flowed was chaired by the Prime Minister at 10 Downing Street on 8 July 2003.

'A policy decision on the handling of this matter had not been taken until the Prime Minister's meeting. It was only after that that any of the press people had an authoritative basis on which to proceed,' said Tebbit. The 8 July meeting was 'decisive'. Not only did it decide that the MoD should issue a press statement giving details of Kelly's background, it also led, Tebbit agreed, to the decision to prepare a question-and-answer briefing paper for the media which provided even more clues to Kelly's identity, including confirmation of his name to those journalists who had guessed it, in a procedure of which Kelly was totally unaware.

The impact of Sir Kevin's evidence was muted because it was given at a special late session of the inquiry well after the rest of the evidence. His cross-examination was delayed to enable him to recover from an eye operation. Hoon also appeared to point the finger at Downing

Street as witness after witness seemed to passed the buck, including blaming Kelly for talking to Gilligan in the first place.

The picture which emerged from the evidence was one where almost everyone was to blame and where exaggeration – by those drawing up the weapons dossier, Gilligan, and Kelly himself – was a central theme running through the whole ugly and, in the end, tragic, episode.

So when Lord Hutton's report was finally published on 28 January 2004 it fell on an astonished world, a genuine surprise even to ministers who could not believe their good fortune. Seasoned Whitehall observers said they expected a 'massively destructive week for the establishment'. Most expected the judge to spread the blame across the field, though criticising Gilligan more than most.

In the event, Hutton reserved his criticism, and it was harsh, for Gilligan and the BBC. He dwelt on the 'grave allegations' the BBC reporter had levelled at Downing Street, accusing it of inserting claims in the dossier it knew were probably untrue and against the wishes of the intelligence agencies, a report he made in the first of nineteen broadcasts on that fateful day of 29 May 2003. He sharply criticised what he called the BBC's 'editorial system' and the corporation's governors for the way they handled the affair. The Ministry of Defence came in for some mild criticism for not telling Kelly properly – only through a brief telephone call – that he had been identified by journalists. But even here, there were mitigating factors, said the report: 'Dr Kelly was not an easy man to help or to whom to give advice'.

Ministers and officials were exonerated from any wrongdoing, or in Hutton's mantra from anything 'dishonourable or underhand or duplicitous'. Hutton accepted Blair's argument that he approved the Ministry of Defence press release stating that an individual had admitted speaking to Gilligan because he did not want the government to be accused of a cover-up. Kelly's name, the Prime Minister said, would have anyway come out eventually.

Hutton's 740-page report consists largely of reproduced documents and extracts from the evidence which, more often than not, are left in the wind, passed over with no comment despite their significance – apparent to all during the inquiry. He did not consider evidence that Kelly was used by the government in its battle with the BBC, that he was 'coached' and told to avoid 'tricky areas' when he gave evidence in public to the Commons Foreign Affairs Committee – an ordeal from which he never recovered. Hutton does not comment on the evidence that Gilligan told members of the Commons committee that Kelly was the source of his BBC colleague, Susan Watts – information which, according to the evidence, seriously worried Kelly when he thought about the implications of his lying about meeting the BBC *Newsnight* reporter. Despite the evidence, Hutton exonerated Downing Street and Alastair Campbell from 'sexing up' the dossier, save only in the sense that the term meant the dossier was drafted in such a way 'as to make the case against Saddam Hussein as strong as intelligence contained in it permitted'. Scarlett, he said, may have been influenced by pressure from the prime minister, but only 'subconsciously' so.

He cleared government officials of trying to out Kelly by stealth through the media despite a series of articles, notably in *The Times* newspaper. Hutton did not consider the accuracy of MI6 intelligence which went into the government's weapons dossier because he said it was outside his terms of reference. He did not comment on the 45-minute claim – and what weapons it referred to – even though they were central to Kelly's case. He brushed aside criticism of the dossier by defence intelligence officials.

And Hutton did not address the escalating row between Alastair Campbell and the BBC, a serious dispute from which, the inquiry heard, it was difficult for either side to back down. The BBC governors, it was clear, believed that for Campbell – whose attack on the corporation's journalists went far beyond Gilligan – it was a fight to the death. After the inquiry, Campbell resigned. After the Hutton Report was published both Davies and Dyke resigned – too many scalps on one side, the public appeared to think.

So unbalanced did Hutton's report appear, that it ensured the debate will continue. Indeed, Hutton's approach may serve, ironically, to be against the government's interest. The day after the report was published, a letter appeared in the *Guardian*. 'As any inept DIY bodger could tell you, whitewash applied carefully and thinly will last years', said the writer. 'Too thick and it will flake off in no time'. Opinion polls immediately after the report's publication showed a significant majority critical of it and in support of the BBC.

Trust in the government, and Blair personally, declined as the evidence during the inquiry emerged. And the focus inevitably switched from all the different strands and players of the Kelly affair to the one question which Hutton said he did not even try to answer – the failure to find any weapons of mass destruction in Iraq. Their existence was the reason the government gave for going to war. 'We must ensure that he [Saddam] does not get to use the weapons he has', said Blair in his preface to the dossier. The government, as well as parliament and the public, may want an answer to why the Prime Minister was allowed to have that misleading sentence under his name. Though Hutton's report will continue to be pored over, not least by the BBC, attention is likely to switch now to the intelligence agencies.

The government responded to Lord Hutton's report by publicly insisting it wanted to draw a line under the whole affair. But the unrelenting reverberations make that a forlorn hope.

The dossier
Ewen MacAskill

Sinan Rasim Said, head of Iraq's biggest weapons manufacturing complex, al-Qa'qa near Baghdad, stood patiently in the sun watching a handful of British journalists exploring his plant. Behind him, adding a sinister element to the exercise, bright yellow smoke poured from a chimney. If Iraq was covertly building weapons of mass destruction (WMD), as the US and British governments claimed, al-Qa'qa fitted the bill. At the entrance to the complex, which covered 26 square miles and produced almost all the explosives and propellent fuel used by the Iraqi military, was a slogan: 'The heroes of military production say yes to Saddam Hussein.' No western journalists had previously been permitted to enter.

Sweating in the heat, the journalists – from *Channel 4 News*, the *Sunday Telegraph*, the *Independent*, the *Mirror*, a freelance film crew and myself from the *Guardian* – tried to look knowledgeable, inspecting rusty pipes and boilers and other unfamiliar machinery. It was 24 September 2002, the day the British government published its dossier, *Iraq's Weapons of Mass Destruction*. The dossier expressed concern that phosgene, a banned nerve agent, was being manufactured at al-Qa'qa. Said, smiling and seemingly unperturbed by the sudden and unexpected media attention, denied that he was manufacturing phosgene for use as a nerve agent. And, indeed, he could prove it. 'It is a pretty stupid mistake for the British to make,' he said. The journalists remained suspicious, used to Iraqi officials lying casually on an almost daily basis. The choice was between the word of an Iraqi weapons manufacturer and that of the Prime Minister Tony Blair, based on British intelligence. Given the record of Iraqi duplicity regarding its weapons programmes over the previous decade, it should have been no contest. And yet the Iraqi official's explanation was credible and he was able to prove he was telling the truth. On this occasion, the Iraqis were right and the British dossier on Iraqi WMD was wrong. And if the dossier, into which Downing Street and British intelligence had put so much effort, was wrong about phosgene at al-Qa'qa, what else was it wrong about?

Astonishingly, even some in the British intelligence community chose to take the side of Said against a dossier produced by their own government and their own security services. A British weapons expert, after reading an account of the trip to al-Qa'qa in the *Guardian*, sent an email to Dr David Kelly, a fellow weapons inspector, the day after the dossier was published. 'So all in all – having read page 2 of the *Guardian* – I'm with the manager of al-Qa'qa: it is a pretty stupid mistake for the British to make.'

That dossier has turned out to be one of the most infamous and divisive documents in recent British history. Such is its notoriety that only a few copies remained around Whitehall towards the end of 2003, and these were being taken home by Foreign Office diplomats and Ministry of Defence officials as souvenirs, a reminder of the arguments and acrimony that it has produced, and the consequences it has had for Blair's premiership – and for Kelly.

As well as al-Qa'qa, many of the other claims made in the dossier and attributed to British intelligence are now, at the very least, deeply suspect. The suspicion on the part of the anti-war lobby is that Blair used the dossier to prepare the British public for conflict by exaggerating the WMD threat posed by Saddam. The government refuses to accept this and stands by the entire contents of the dossier.

The genesis of the war – and the dossier – goes back to Florida in November 2000. The hung US presidential vote, after much recounting, finally came down in favour of George Bush. Until that point, US and British policy on Iraq had been unchanged almost since the end of the Gulf War in 1991. Saddam was rightly seen as a malign and volatile dictator, a constant source of instability in the region. The US, under George Bush's father, opted against invasion in 1991 and his successor, Bill Clinton, along with first John Major and then Blair, opted for containment, keeping Saddam weak through the stringent imposition of United Nations sanctions and through US and British fighters retaining control of the skies over southern and northern Iraq, the no-fly zones. The Foreign Office accepted that the policy was seriously flawed and that the Iraqi population was suffering from the sanctions – one UN estimate is of half a million Iraqi children dying. The Foreign Office knew it was losing the battle for international opinion. By the end of the 1990s, the US and British governments were forced to compromise, setting up a programme in which food was exchanged for Iraqi oil. Although the worry in the Foreign Office was that Saddam was covertly building a nuclear weapon, its assessment was that it would take years for Saddam to achieve that objective and in the meantime containment was the best, albeit flawed, policy available. The alternatives were seen to be much too risky. The Foreign Office did not want war, with all the uncertainties which that entailed.

That changed with Bush. Coming into office with him were a group of Republicans committed to radical change in the Middle East. Dismayed by the instability, lack of democracy and hostility towards Israel and the US, these neo-conservatives sought to alter dramatically the politics of the Middle East, and central to that policy was the removal of Saddam. Iraq was to become a model democracy, a beacon for the rest of the Middle East, which – Israel apart – had not a single democracy. The neo-cons pushed for an early war against Iraq. According to Blair and to US journalists covering the White House, Bush initially resisted this pressure for an Iraq war. But Paul O'Neill, at the time part of Bush's team as Treasury secretary, claimed that Bush was bent on war from the moment he took office.

Whatever the truth, Bush was intent on the removal of Saddam Hussein after the September 11 attacks on the World Trade Center and the Pentagon. Any perceived threat to the US round the world was now seen by Washington as a legitimate target, and Iraq was top of the list after Osama bin Laden's al-Qaeda and its Taliban supporters in Afghanistan.

Early in 2002, with the occupation of Afghanistan complete and well aware that Iraq was the new target, Downing Street recognised the need to prepare other members of the government, the Labour party and the public at large for the possibility of war against Iraq. There was a rare and tentative cabinet discussion in February 2002, recounted by Robin Cook, the former Foreign Secretary, in his autobiography, *Point of Departure*. The Home Secretary, David Blunkett, asked for a discussion on Iraq. Cook, then in the cabinet as Leader of the House of Commons, argued that the rest of the Arab world saw the Israeli Prime Minister, Ariel Sharon, rather than Saddam, as the problem, and would not understand the obsession with Iraq. 'Somewhat to my surprise this line provides a round of "hear, hearing" from colleagues, which is the nearest I heard to mutiny in the cabinet,' he said. It would not be heard again, other than by Cook and his colleague, Clare Short, the International Development Secretary, who also opposed war.

Downing Street was unfazed by the cabinet mood. No. 10 asked the Foreign Office to produce a dossier on the threat posed by WMD worldwide. It would deal not exclusively with Iraq but all four countries seen as a threat: Iraq, North Korea, Iran and Libya. The dossier was never published. The Foreign Office, refusing to accept the new mood in Washington, stood by containment and argued that while the threat posed by Saddam was serious, it was no greater than it had been the previous year. Downing Street was unhappy with this draft dossier. Alastair Campbell, at the time Blair's director of communications, later told the Hutton inquiry that the reason for non-publication had been that it 'wasn't a terribly good document overall'. In Washington and London, the threat from Iran, North Korea and Libya was for another day: the immediate problem was Iraq.

A Foreign Office source, asked after the war why Britain had abandoned containment, replied tersely: 'Washington.' And why had Britain gone to war? 'Washington.' That became clear in April 2002 when Blair went to see Bush at Prairie Chapel ranch at Crawford, Texas. There is a widespread belief that the decision to go to war was made there. A US official gave credence to this when he said in advance of the summit: 'What is at issue is timing and that is something that is going to be covered this weekend.'

Few other than the two men and their immediate advisers know for sure: the two met without note-takers. We do know that Blair argued in favour of dealing with the Israeli–Palestinian conflict before Iraq, arguing this was the best way to deal with Arab hostility towards the west. He also argued that if the US was intent on action against Iraq, the US should involve as much of the international community as possible by seeking UN legitimacy for action. He said as much in a speech that weekend at the George Bush Senior Presidential Library, pleading for the US to temper its instinct for global unilateralism. 'Like it or not, whether you are a utilitarian or a utopian, the world is interdependent,' the Prime Minister said.

Bush was prepared to go part of the way with Blair, and in subsequent speeches would speak about the need for a Palestinian state and would eventually explore the UN route on Iraq, though only as long as the UN was prepared to go along with US policy. And that policy, as Bush made clear at Prairie Chapel, was to end Saddam's rule. 'I made up my mind that Saddam needs to go. That's about all I'm willing to share with you,' he said. But Blair, though he too wished to see the end of Saddam, could not back regime change because it was contrary to international law, which Britain interpreted more strictly than the US. Blair's position with regard to the US was spelt out to the *Guardian* during a trip to West Africa earlier that year: if you want to have influence in the world, you have to be close to Washington. Blair was convinced the issue of Saddam could not be left unresolved indefinitely. The Prime Minister may have realised that war was probably inevitable at that point but still hoped to secure the backing of the UN and that, possibly but unlikely, Saddam may have been forced into compliance – allowing UN weapons inspectors to return to Iraq – without war.

The Iraq issue died down in Britain in the months after the Prairie Chapel meeting, partly because attention switched to Israel's ferocious drive into the West Bank, the intense fighting in Nablus and Jenin, and the siege of the Church of the Nativity in Bethlehem.

Bellicose noises about Iraq were heard from Washington in August 2002, and Blair and Campbell, returning from another trip to Africa, discussed again the need for a dossier, this time on Iraq alone. Blair, on 3 September, speaking from his Sedgefield constituency, promised that one would be published. In his diary that day, Campbell recorded questions that it would have to address. These were pertinent at the time he wrote them and remain pertinent today: 'Why Iraq? Why now?' An honest answer to Campbell's question was 'because Washington wants to'. That would not be good enough for the British public.

The Foreign Office produced a second draft dossier two days later, one devoted exclusively to Iraq. It was a typical Foreign Office document – cautious and dry. It saw Iraq as a threat but not an imminent one. There were a lot of caveats attached to the intelligence. Campbell, a former political editor of the *Daily Mirror*, with a tabloid instinct for the dramatic, did not like it and ordered a rewrite. John Williams, chief press officer at the Foreign Office and,

15

like Campbell, a former political editor of the *Daily Mirror*, offered to do the new version. Also offering was John Scarlett, head of the Joint Intelligence Committee, a group that has representatives from MI6, the foreign spy agency, MI5, the internal security agency, GCHQ, the communications and listening post, and the Ministry of Defence's Defence Intelligence Staff. Campbell removed responsibility from the Foreign Office and gave it to Scarlett. From then on, the Foreign Office had only a minimal role, as did the Ministry of Defence. The dossier was primarily the work of the intelligence services and Downing Street.

On 8 September, Blair made another visit to Washington, to the presidential retreat at Camp David. It was a crucial meeting at which the fate of Iraq was all but decided and yet, curiously, it was never mentioned at the Hutton inquiry, in spite of all the hours in the courtroom examining the minutiae of the dossier. The eventual thrust of the dossier was the result of the discussions and decisions taken at Camp David. Short, the International Development Secretary, was briefed afterwards by three senior members of the government to stop fretting about war because the decision had already been taken and there was nothing she could do about it. It is understood they were Sir Richard Dearlove, the head of MI6, Andrew Turnbull, the Cabinet Secretary, and Gordon Brown, the Chancellor of the Exchequer. War was to begin in February or March.

As Blair and Bush talked at Camp David, the US began moving a military headquarters to the Gulf along with thousands of tons of military equipment. At Camp David itself, British military personnel were briefed on the military options should Saddam fail to come into line, and Downing Street officials discussed with their Washington counterparts how to win round public opinion.

Blair was relieved at Camp David to find that Bush had overcome his ideological dislike of the UN and would make a speech at the UN headquarters in New York the following week to seek a resolution demanding that Iraq allow UN weapons inspectors back into the country and give them full cooperation. Journalists travelling back to Britain with Blair were left with the belief that the Prime Minister would now be able to argue that Saddam was being given a last chance but the journalists were also convinced that Downing Street thought it was unlikely that Saddam would comply with UN demands.

A *Financial Times* reporter noted: 'So while the diplomacy gets under way at the UN, Blair is turning his mind to how he can make the case for an eventual attack on Iraq to a sceptical British public.'

On return from Camp David, on 9 September, Campbell chaired a meeting of the Joint Intelligence Committee. It was unusual: Campbell was a press officer, not in any way related to intelligence, and it was yet another sign of the extent to which his power had expanded since arriving at Downing Street with Blair in 1997. The intelligence services were under pressure at the time because the earlier drafts had already been rejected but they had not come up with any significant fresh intelligence to indicate that Saddam was secretly developing WMD. The problem was that Iraq was an intelligence black hole. A British minister who regularly read intelligence reports said that in almost every other Arab country Britain was able to get detailed reports and he expressed amazement at the quality and speed with which it arrived, seeing accounts of discussions in the inner sanctums of the Arab world within days. By contrast, there was little available from Iraq, especially in the period after 1998. Before that, between 1991 and 1998, UN weapons inspectors working in Iraq had provided information about Iraq's WMD programme but this came to an end when the inspectors left in 1998 before a US-British bombing raid. A sign that the intelligence services were struggling came on 11 September when they issued an alert to all their agencies to hunt in the bottom of the cupboard for any evidence they might have missed on Iraq's

WMD. Realising the paucity of evidence of WMD, an unnamed government official sent an email to the secret services saying Downing Street wanted the dossier 'to be as strong as possible within the bounds of available intelligence'. The official, a member of Whitehall's Joint Intelligence Committee, said: 'This is therefore a last! call for any items of intelligence that agencies think can and should be included.'

The day before, on 10 September, Scarlett, with contributions from the various intelligence services and after discussion at the Joint Intelligence Committee, sent a draft of what was to become the final document to Downing Street. It was much stronger than the Easter draft: Saddam was portrayed as much more menacing, the threat current. And it included for the first time a claim that the Iraqi military could deploy chemical and biological weapons within 45 minutes. According to the Joint Intelligence Committee, the information had only become available on 29 August and was from a senior Iraqi officer via an intermediary. The government has never identified either the officer or the intermediary.

The next day Blair saw the draft for the first time. Campbell, in his diary, noted that he had had a further meeting with Scarlett, and claimed that, contrary to subsequent accusations that he had 'sexed up' the dossier, he had told him to avoid ramping up it up: 'The drier the better, cut the rhetoric.' But others in Downing Street were more exercised about it. Phil Bassett, a Downing Street adviser, expressed his unhappiness with the draft in an email to Campbell the same day in which he said 'it needs to be written more in officialese, lots of it is too journalistic as it now stands, with some of the opening chapter as a biog of Saddam reading like STimes at its worst, needs more weight, writing, detail.' He added: 'Crucially, though, it's intelligence-lite.' In a separate email about the same time, he said there was 'a very long way to go [with the dossier] I think. Think we are in a lot of trouble with this as it stands now.' Godric Smith, Campbell's deputy, was also concerned about the quality of the draft: 'I think there's material here we can work with, but it's a bit of a muddle and needs more clarity in the guts of it in terms of what is new/old.'

On 12 September 2002, Bush, finally making his address to the UN, warned Iraq to allow the UN weapons inspectors to return or face the consequences. The expectation in Washington and London government circles was that Saddam would refuse, even though there had been newspaper reports months earlier that in fact they would allow inspection access. On 17 September, that is exactly what Saddam did. That temporarily forced Washington and London off balance but they remained confident that even if the inspectors were allowed back, Saddam would not co-operate with them and would engage in the kind of obstructionist tactics used against the inspectors in the 1990s. War remained the likeliest outcome.

There was no sense among the many Downing Street emails at the time that the government was focused on the UN route and anxious to avoid war. Many of the Downing Street advisers were concentrating on producing a dossier that would justify war. No one anywhere disputed that Saddam had been a threat in the past and might be again in the future: the question was whether he presented a threat either at the time or in the immediate future. Downing Street advisers tried to address that. Danny Pruce, a Foreign Office diplomat seconded to the Downing Street press department, sent an email to a Foreign Office colleague: 'Can we insert a few quotes from speeches he [Saddam] has made which, even if they are not specific, demonstrate that he is a bad man with a general hostility towards his neighbours and the west?' He set out a course of action for bringing public opinion round: 'Much of the evidence we have is largely circumstantial so we need to convey to our readers that the cumulation of these facts demonstrates an intent on Saddam's part – the more they can be led to this conclusion themselves rather than have

19

to accept judgments from us, the better.' The idea that the UN inspectors may have done their job better than expected between 1991 and 1998 and actually successfully disarmed Saddam of most, and possibly all, his WMD was not a scenario being considered. In a separate email, Pruce said: 'Our aim should be to convey the impression that things have not been static in Iraq but that over the past decade he has been aggressively and relentlessly pursuing WMD while brutally repressing his own people.' He added that any reference to weapons should describe their destructive capacity, for example, that UN weapons inspectors between 1991 and 1998 'found enough chemical warfare agent to kill x thousand people or contaminate an area the size of Wales.' Campbell, when asked at the Hutton inquiry about Pruce's emails, played down his importance, saying that comments about what should be in the dossier were taken by staff acting above their pay grade.

Pruce, though, was not alone. Other Downing Street aides, more senior, were also throwing in suggestions along the same lines, contributing towards an alarming picture of the Iraqi threat. Tom Kelly, another Downing Street press officer, in an email to Campbell on 11 September, wrote that there was a need to demonstrate that Saddam had not only the capability to mount an attack but also the intent: 'We know that [Saddam] is a bad man and has done bad things in the past. We know he is trying to get WMD – and this shows those attempts are intensifying. But can we show why we think he intends to use them aggressively, rather than in self-defence? We need that to counter the argument that Saddam is bad, but not mad.'

Many of these proposals from Downing Street staffers went far beyond just the kind of cosmetic presentational changes they were supposed to be engaged in. Tom Kelly, for instance, wrote to Campbell's deputy, Godric Smith, expressing regret that the dossier could not talk up the nuclear threat. The MI6 assessment was that while Saddam wanted a nuclear capability, he did not possess one and was unlikely to do so for years to come. Tom Kelly reluctantly acknowledged this: 'The weakness, obviously, is our inability to say he could pull the nuclear trigger any time soon.'

That same day, the Joint Intelligence Committee and Downing Street worked in earnest to finish the dossier. Jonathan Powell, the Downing Street chief of staff, part of whose job was to pick holes, made the strongest criticism of the draft. He pointed out in an email to Scarlett what he regarded as a central weakness in the draft, which he said 'does nothing to demonstrate a threat, let alone an imminent threat from Saddam. In other words, it shows he has the means but it does not demonstrate he has the motive to attack his neighbours let alone the west. We will need to make it clear in launching the document that we do not claim that we have evidence that he is an imminent threat.' He added: 'If I was Saddam I would take a party of western journalists to the Ibn Sina factory or one of the others pictured in the document to demonstrate there is nothing there. How do we close off that avenue to him in advance?' It was a perceptive point. The western journalists did, in fact, go to the disputed sites, though not the Ibn Sina factory.

Campbell, who had been working on a foreword to the dossier to be signed by the Prime Minister, sent a series of questions that day to Scarlett about the document. Although Campbell insists he did not 'sex up' the dossier, it is open to debate whether the changes he suggested amounted to doing just that. He received a reply from Scarlett the next day, accepting some of the proposed changes, including that 'it would be stronger if we said that despite sanctions and the policy of containment, he [Saddam] has made real progress.'

A sentence was added to the text. The dossier in its final form reads that intelligence 'confirms that despite sanctions and the policy of containment, Saddam has continued to make progress with his illicit weapons programme'.

Campbell also proposed hardening the nuclear threat. An earlier draft said that as long as sanctions continued to hinder imports, Iraq would find it difficult to produce a nuclear weapon. It added: 'After the lifting of sanctions, we assess that Iraq would need at least five years to produce a weapon. Progress would be much quicker if Iraq were able to buy fissile material.' Campbell said the Prime Minister, 'like me, was worried about the way you have expressed the nuclear issue, particularly in paragraph 18. Can we not go back, on timings to "radiological device in months: nuclear bomb in 1–2 years with help; 5 years with no sanctions."' In a later memo to Scarlett, he suggested the wording: 'In these circumstances, the JIC (Joint Intelligence Committee) assessed in early 2002 that they could produce nuclear weapons in between one and two years.' The final document reads: 'Iraq could produce a nuclear weapon in between one and two years.'

On the nuclear issue, the dossier also claimed that 'there is intelligence that Iraq has sought the supply of significant quantities of uranium from Africa.' This claim has since been seriously undercut – and even rejected by the CIA, which accepts that Iraq did not after all try to get uranium from Niger. The claim appears to have originated from discredited diplomatic sources in Rome. The British government continues to insist it is true, and that its information came from an alternative, independent source.

The 45-minute claim gained a life of its own, gathering momentum with each new draft. Blair's foreword to the dossier contained the strongest version, saying Saddam's military planning allowed for some of his WMD 'to be ready within 45 minutes of an order to use them'. In the executive summary, the 45-minute claim in early drafts was presented as Iraq 'could deploy' or 'could be ready'. In the final version, this was hardened up to 'are deployable'.

When the dossier was published, the 45-minute claim was one of the few new bits of information in it and parts of the media immediately latched onto it, under the impression that it meant Saddam could deliver WMD on medium-range missiles, possibly as far as

Cyprus. Scarlett, when questioned during the Hutton inquiry, disclosed that, in fact, it referred not to WMD being fired on medium-range missiles but to their use as battlefield weapons. This was a significant admission. Instead of Saddam posing a threat by raining down missiles on other states, including the British base in Cyprus, Scarlett was admitting that the Iraqi army would only use the weapons in self-defence: in response to invasion. Campbell took the draft, complete with the WMD reference, home to read on 11 September and insists that was the first time he saw the mention of the 45-minute claim. This matters because it runs counter to the report made after the war by the BBC reporter, Andrew Gilligan, that the Downing Street director of communications had inserted it, not the intelligence services. Campbell told the Hutton Inquiry he did not know where the claim had come from, other than from the Joint Intelligence Committee and that he never asked for the source of this raw material. 'I had no input, output or influence upon them [the Joint Intelligence Committee] at any stage in the process,' Campbell told the inquiry.

As the dossier neared completion, there were serious misgivings within parts of the intelligence community. The Defence Intelligence Staff – the Ministry of Defence intelligence arm – expressed concern about the way that the intelligence was being handled. They were unhappy at the precedent of intelligence being put into the public arena in this fashion and unhappy at the way it was being distorted. Brian Jones, a former analyst with Defence Intelligence Staff, claimed it was being overegged. Another weapons analyst, known at the Hutton Inquiry only as Mr A, who took part in the discussions of the Defence Intelligence Staff, says he suggested making four changes while Kelly, also present at the talks, recommended twelve alterations, mostly for reasons of 'language'.

Mr A said he and Kelly were generally supportive of the dossier: 'Both of us believed that if you took the dossier as a whole it was a reasonable and accurate reflection of the intelligence.' But Mr A said the perception was there had been interference from outside the intelligence community in the dossier. Mr A, in an email to Kelly the day after the dossier was published, blamed the 'spin merchants of this administration' for the specific blunder over the al-Qa'qa claim. Mr A told the inquiry the dossier's language was hardened for political ends: 'The perception was that the dossier had been round the houses several times in order to try to find a form of words which would strengthen certain political objectives.'

Others questioned the motive of the source of the 45-minute claim, wondering if his purpose was to influence rather than inform. Kelly, who was involved in these discussions and described as 'risible' the idea that WMD could be deployed in 45 minutes. Kelly believed that Saddam had WMD and posed a threat, and that this WMD could be deployed in days or weeks, but not 45 minutes. Mr A said all the 10 people at the Defence Intelligence Staff meeting were worried by the 45-minute claim. Asked by Lord Hutton what Kelly's view of the claim was, Mr A said: 'All those of us without access to that intelligence immediately asked the question: well, what does the 45 minutes refer to? Are you referring to a technical process? Are you referring to a commander control process? And if your assessment causes you to immediately ask questions, then we felt that it was not perhaps a statement that ought to be included.'

On 24 September 2002, the dossier was published. Blair, in the foreword, is categoric about the threat being faced, in spite of the various uncertainties and doubts expressed in the private debate within Downing Street and the intelligence community. 'I am in no doubt that the threat is serious and current, that he [Saddam] has made progress on WMD and that he has to be stopped.' The London *Evening Standard* carried the headline that day: '45 Minutes to attack'.

In Baghdad, British journalists gathered round a computer in the

Rashid Hotel to access the Downing Street website to obtain a copy. Days earlier, the journalists had asked the deputy prime minister, Tariq Aziz, if they could visit any site mentioned in the dossier and he said he would think about it. He said that allowing journalists to have a look around would not make any difference, as the US was intent on war. Permission was granted.

The problem was that the dossier had very little specific information. It did name four sites being of concern: the Castor oil production plant at Fallujah, where the castor bean pulp could be used to make the biological agent ricin; the al-Dawrah foot-and-mouth disease vaccine institute, which had been involved in biological weapons production before the Gulf War in 1991; the Amariyah Sera and Vaccine Plant at Abu Ghraib, which had been involved in biological weapons storage and research and which had recently expanded its facilities; and the al-Qa'qa complex.

Of the latter, the dossier said: 'Of particular concern are elements of the phosgene production plant at al-Qa'qa. These were severely damaged during the Gulf war and dismantled under Unscom (the UN weapons inspectors operating in Iraq in the 1990s) supervision, but have since been rebuilt. While phosgene does have industrial uses, it can also be used by itself as a chemical agent or as a precursor for nerve agent.'

The journalists, after discussion among themselves, opted to visit Amariyah, which was in Baghdad, and al-Qa'qa, less than an hour's drive from the capital. Both places were vaguely sinister and rundown, but at neither location was there any obvious evidence of WMD. The journalists admitted among themselves they could have been standing beside WMD and would not have had the expertise to recognise it. But they could test the claims in the dossier. The expanded area at Amariyah that concerned British intelligence did contain fridge-freezers that could have been used to store biological agents but all had been switched off and showed no sign of having been used recently.

Said, the manager at al-Qa'qa, said that the disputed machinery was used to make munitions and a by-product of that was phosgene. The UN weapons inspectors in Iraq 1991–98 had inspected the machinery and accepted it had a legitimate use, and that phosgene was an unavoidable by-product. They tagged it to make sure the phosgene had not been removed, and made regular return trips to ensure it had not been tampered with. Said offered what appeared to be conclusive proof: a small, silver-coloured metal tag, fixed to the machinery by United Nations weapons inspectors years earlier. If Iraq had been engaged in illegal activity at al-Qa'qa by using the machinery to produce nerve agent, as British intelligence suspected, that tag would have been broken. It was intact.

At the time of our visit, the UN weapons inspectors were due to return to Iraq within the next few months. If the manager was lying about the tag, they would have known as soon as they visited the site. They found nothing untoward at either al-Qa'qa or Amariyah.

Nor did the US-led Iraq Survey Group, the 1,100-strong group of scientists and weapons specialists who searched Iraq for six months after the war was officially declared over by Bush. They reported in autumn 2003 their failure to find any of the WMD named in the dossier. David Kay, head of the Iraq Survey Group, delivered to the US Congress his findings and concluded that Saddam had taken no steps to revive his nuclear weapons plan since 1998, and had abandoned any large-scale chemical weapons programme more than a decade ago. 'We have not found, at this point, actual weapons.'

In January 2004, David Kay resigned from the Iraq Survey Group. He told a Senate hearing that failures had become too apparent in the US's intelligence-gathering capabilities. 'We were almost all wrong, and I certainly include myself here,' he said.

The September dossier was not the only one the British government produced in the run-up to the war. There was one on human rights from the Foreign Office in December. That caused minor embarrassment. While no one disputed that Saddam's regime had an appalling human rights record, one of the Iraqi victims fielded for the press at the launch of the dossier revealed he had been tortured by British equipment. And there was another dossier early in 2003, the so-called dodgy dossier, based on the work of a research student.

But it is the September dossier that was crucial, and the one that has done untold damage to the credibility of the British intelligence service. Crucially, perhaps, it has done more than any other document to make an already sceptical public even more wary of politicians.

Mr Said appears to have been right about the innocent use of phosgene at al-Qa'qa. He was certainly right in his assessment of US intentions. Six months before the war began, standing with the British journalists in the scrubland of his military complex, he suggested conflict was inevitable, regardless of what the Iraqis did. 'The way the Americans are talking, they are very aggressive. They need a war always,' Mr Said said.

The first two months of 2003 were marked by tortuous discussions at the United Nations that the US and Britain eventually abandoned, blaming French intransigence. UN weapons inspectors operating in Iraq pleaded for more time, but never got it.

On 20 March 2002, US forces, acting on what turned out to be faulty intelligence, launched a dawn raid on a villa in a southern suburb of Baghdad in the mistaken belief that Saddam was there. Over the next twenty-four hours, US and British tanks went over the Kuwaiti border into Iraq, the British heading for Basra and the US striking out on the long, bloody road to Baghdad.

The story of the story

Matt Wells

Unnoticed by the thousands of Kent commuters who spill into the Strand each morning, the Charing Cross Hotel is a quiet monument to the past glories of Britain's faded railway network. But for a short encounter on 22 May 2003 – exactly a week after its 138th birthday – this grand Victorian terminus stopover would have remained as anonymous as any of the others in the chain that now runs it.

At about 4pm that day, just as the rush was beginning for the evening trains out of the grimy station beyond, two men emerged within a few minutes of each other from the crowds in the cobbled forecourt. Each pushed through the revolving glass doors, past the reception desk and up the sweeping marble staircase to the discreet first floor bar above. It was not their first meeting, but it was to be their most significant; what they discussed in the course of the next hour or so, in the comfort of the bar's green leather armchairs, would lead ultimately to the death of one and the vilification of the other. Gilligan recalls that he was about 10 or 15 minutes late; Dr Kelly, a punctual sort of character, was already there. For what turned out to be such an auspicious meeting, the drinks order now seems decidedly lacking in drama or glamour; one had a Coke, the other a glass of Appletise. The bill came to £4.15: not bad for a scoop that would rock the government and plunge its relations with the BBC into crisis.

The meeting was instigated by Gilligan, who had spent some weeks reporting from Baghdad on the aftermath of the war in Iraq. (His stint in the Iraqi capital had already made waves; almost as soon as President George Bush had declared victory, Gilligan asserted on the radio that for many people, life in liberated Baghdad was worse than ever.)

Now back in London, he wanted to ask Kelly, who was regarded as Britain's foremost expert on weapons of mass destruction, about why he thought such weapons had not been discovered as soon as Saddam had fallen six weeks previously, given the certainty with which their existence had been proclaimed by the coalition leaders before the war. For his part, Kelly was passionately interested in Iraq, and relished the opportunity to question closely anyone who had spent some time there. The pair had met before – Gilligan thinks this was their third encounter, although in a lapse of memory that contributed to his image at the inquiry as something of a shambolic figure, he could not be sure. (Adding to the image of someone lacking in order, he had lost his 2001 appointments diary, which would have confirmed whether he had seen Kelly on a fourth occasion.)

The reporter had not expected the meeting to elicit a scoop; rather, he was hoping to use any information provided by Kelly to add weight to his post-conflict reports for the *Today* programme about the situation in Iraq. Gilligan recalls that they spent an hour and a half together, although Kelly said before he died that the meeting lasted half that time. At first, the conversation was relatively mundane. It began, says Gilligan, with a discussion about the state of the railways: the reporter blamed his delay on a late train – Charing Cross is a short 20-minute train ride up the line from the tranquil London suburb of Greenwich, where he lives. 'It was like our other meetings, in that it was intended as a general discussion of issues around Iraq,' Gilligan said later in his evidence to Lord Hutton's inquiry. Soon, however, it would turn to matters of more substance. Half an hour into the conversation, said Gilligan, the pair reached the topic of the September dossier. When it was published in 2002, Kelly had told the journalist that there was nothing significantly new in it, and Gilligan reported as much in his broadcasts for the *Today* programme at the time. But Gilligan claims that this time Kelly said the atmosphere had turned febrile in the week before the dossier was published. 'Until the week before,' Gilligan quoted him later as saying, 'it was just like I told you. It was transformed the week before publication, to make it sexier.'

Gilligan, who has been described by friends and colleagues as having a tabloid reporter's nose for a story, was startled by this unexpected revelation, and asked Kelly if he could take notes. But unlike most journalists, who rely on the old-fashioned notebook and pen, Gilligan used a Sharp electronic organiser (often misdescribed as a Palm Pilot, which is the brand leader). As he tapped away, Kelly poured out an extraordinary story of how statements in the dossier had been boosted to give them more impact in the battle to convince a sceptical country and mutinous Labour Party of the case for war against Iraq. The most obvious example concerned the claims around Iraq's weapons of mass destruction, said Kelly, as quoted by Gilligan in a newspaper article after his *Today* programme broadcast. 'The classic was the statement that WMD were ready for use in 45 minutes. One source said it took 45 minutes to launch a missile and that was misinterpreted to mean that WMD could be deployed in 45 minutes. There was no evidence that they had loaded conventional missiles with WMD, or could do so anything like that quickly.' Gilligan says he asked Kelly how this transformation came about. 'The answer was a single word:

"Campbell."

"What? Campbell made it up?"

"No, it was real information. But it was included against our wishes because it wasn't reliable."

This is the account of the conversation that Gilligan gave in a colourfully written article for the *Mail on Sunday*, three days after he reported the story on the *Today* programme. Giving evidence to the Foreign Affairs Committee, Kelly insisted he had said nothing of the sort. And it emerged at the Hutton inquiry that Gilligan suggested the phrase 'to make it sexier', which Kelly repeated back to him. It was also claimed during Lord Hutton's inquiry that Kelly initially refused to name names in connection with the 'sexing up' of the dossier and only acceded when Gilligan put Campbell's name to him. Whatever the precise details, there are few who now dispute that Kelly said the substance of what Gilligan reported him as saying. And Gilligan knew that what Kelly said was potentially explosive. It was, in journalistic parlance, a cracking story.

* * *

The first thing that Gilligan did, he says now, was to compile a full manuscript note of the meeting – recalling the questions, the answers, fleshing out the sentences from the fragmented notes on his electronic organiser. Displaying a carelessness that was to be held against him at the inquiry later, he has now lost the manuscript. But at the time it was the most comprehensive note of what Kelly had said.

Gilligan knew he had a significant story. As defence and diplomatic correspondent of the *Today* programme, he knew inside out the background to the government's tactics for persuading Britain of the case for war. He had been reporting on the issue for more than a year, documenting every twist and turn. In essence, Kelly was suggesting that the basis on which the British government had taken the country to war was false, that it had pulled the wool over the eyes of the electorate, and that the intelligence community was, to put it mildly, unhappy about it. The trouble was, Kelly was only one source. Certainly, he was a pretty reliable one – he was a believer in getting things right, in accuracy of language, and in fair dealing. But it was not in his interests to undermine the government; in fact, he was a supporter of the war and knew from first-hand experience the extent of Iraq's old WMD programmes. So Gilligan knew that Kelly alone would not be good enough, and that he would need corroborative material to get the story on air. If nothing else, the BBC's producer guidelines – the rules by which all the corporation's journalists must abide – say stories based on single anonymous sources can only be run in exceptional circumstances. So Gilligan sought to stand up the story independently of Kelly.

Over the next few days, he contacted two senior government contacts, whose names he has never disclosed. He told both of them what Kelly had said – that the September dossier had been transformed in the week before it was published, and this transformation was carried out at the behest of Alastair Campbell. Irritatingly for Gilligan, neither of them would confirm the story – but intriguingly neither of them denied it either. One told Gilligan to 'keep digging'. Gilligan compared the September dossier to others produced by the Joint Intelligence Committee, and found its language to be much more assertive. He looked at the resignation speech given by former Foreign Secretary Robin Cook in the run-up to the war, who said weapons of mass destruction would not be found in the commonly understood sense of the term. He also took into account the government's dossier 'form' – it had already admitted plagiarising a PhD thesis in a previous 'dodgy' dossier on Iraq. There was still nothing concrete to corroborate Kelly's assertions, but there was now plenty of circumstantial evidence. At this stage, some more cautious journalists might have filed the story under 'work in progress' – one BBC colleague who had similar information thought it unworthy of broadcast. But Gilligan, with his tabloid nose and his brief to cause trouble, thought he could make something of it.

But Gilligan's word alone would not get the story on air. First, he had to get it past his editors. The *Today* programme's team works in two shifts: the day team and the night team. The day team works to set up the next morning's programme, and hands over at 8pm to the night team which takes care of any loose ends or overnight news developments before the programme goes on air at 6am. The overall programme editor, Kevin Marsh, oversees both teams.

Because the story was based largely on a single anonymous source, allowed by the BBC producer guidelines only in exceptional circumstances, Marsh was involved in the decision-making process. It was decided that, as Kelly was such a senior and reliable source, his position as a former Unscom weapons inspector and the 'expert of choice' when it came to weapons of mass destruction made his views worth reporting. The day editor on 28 May was Miranda Holt, and she included the WMD story on the 'master prospects' – the list of confirmed items that the day team would pass on to the night shift at 8pm. She noted that a request had been lodged with the Ministry of Defence to interview the Armed Forces Minister Adam Ingram on another story – about the controversial use of cluster bombs in Iraq – and that the 'bid' had been extended to cover Gilligan's WMD story. Gilligan, too, was in contact with the MoD that night, but its press office would later claim that he did not give any detailed warning about the story that he would report the next day. There is no dispute that Downing Street was not contacted in advance, even though Gilligan would make damning claims about No. 10's involvement in the dossier.

Perhaps there was a systems failure, perhaps it was just that the *Today* programme failed to see the significance of the story. Certainly the cluster bomb issue was regarded as more important, and was placed higher up the prospects list. The *Today* team evidently thought it sufficient that Ingram had been asked to respond to Gilligan's story when he appeared in the prestigious 8.10am slot, the most listened-to portion of the programme.

Holt summarised Gilligan's story thus, noting that he would introduce the story to listeners via a live interview with one of the programme's presenters before Ingram's interview. 'The dossier on Iraq which the government produced last September,' Holt wrote, 'was jazzed up at the last minute to include new information based on dubious sources, including the claim that chemical and biological weapons could be deployed at 45 minutes' notice. Live 07.00–07.30 Andrew Gilligan illustrated two-way. Gilligan has got this from a senior source who shall remain anonymous.'

By now, the journey of the story to air was under way.

* * *

There is a story about Gilligan from his days at the *Sunday Telegraph*, where he worked before joining the *Today* programme, which illustrates his unorthodox working practices. The unexpurgated version is that the newspaper's editor, Dominic Lawson, was concerned when he arrived for work one morning that his office had been disturbed. He asked security staff to investigate and an examination of closed-circuit camera tapes found that Gilligan, after working late into the night, had curled up on the sofa in Lawson's office.

Gilligan's working practices, it seems, have not much changed over the years. Back at his home in Greenwich, south-east London, he spent much of the night of 28 May preparing the dossier story. After further discussions with the *Today* programme team, based on the other side of London at the BBC's news department in Television Centre, White City, it was decided that Gilligan would appear twice in the programme to discuss his story: once at 6.07am in an unscripted conversation with presenter John Humphrys, and again at 7.32am in a scripted version that would include a sample of Kelly's key quotes, voiced by one of the programme's backroom staff. Crucially, the quotes would not finger Campbell directly for the dossier's 'transformation'.

Typically, the first hour of the *Today* programme consists of straightforward reports from correspondents and is intended as a 'news briefing' for early risers. Only later does the programme delve deeper into the background to the stories in the news, and consequently more effort is invested in later stories. It is a distinction that would be lost on Lord Hutton, but it meant that the initial 6.07am version of the story would receive less attention from the programme team – and, as it turned out, Gilligan himself – than the 7.32am outing.

In fact, the first mention of the WMD story on *Today* came even earlier than 6.07am. Gilligan had deemed it worthy of consideration for inclusion in the half-hourly news summaries that punctuate the programme, but which, in a quirk of BBC tradition, are edited separately from the *Today* team by the radio news department's bulletins section. Gilligan was logged in to the BBC's editorial system ENPS at home, and submitted a draft script for a short report to that night's bulletins editor, Dave Treanor. In the draft, submitted by Gilligan on ENPS's internal messaging facility, he wrote: 'One senior British official has now told us that the original version of the dossier produced by the intelligence services added little to what was already publicly known. But one week before publication, said this official, the dossier was "transformed" on Downing Street's orders. The now infamous "45-minute" assertion was one of several claims added – against the wishes of the intelligence services, who said it was from a single source which they didn't necessarily believe.' Treanor's assistant, Paul Deal, accepted the story but suggested an alteration. 'I just wonder whether "infamous" is a bit strong,' he replied. Gilligan agreed: 'Fair enough – will delete infamous,' he said.

The BBC's bulletins department, which also produces the regular news summaries for Radios 2, 3 and Five Live, is often regarded as stuffy and lacking in verve. But on this occasion, its caution seems well judged, in hindsight at least. For while Gilligan's scripted summary could be justified on the basis of the facts – Kelly was certainly a 'senior official' and members of the Defence Intelligence Staff have testified to their disapproval of the September dossier – in his live broadcasts on the *Today* programme he threw traditional BBC caution to the White City winds. His first live appearance in the programme at 6.07am proved to be the weakest link in the BBC's defence at the Hutton Inquiry.

Many BBC correspondents now have the facility to broadcast from their homes. An ISDN line with a headset and microphone can be connected into a bedroom or study, enabling the reporter to speak in broadcast-quality sound without needing to be in the studio. This is particularly useful for early morning or late-night broadcasts, or for stories that break when the reporter is not near a studio. (At least one senior BBC correspondent has admitted addressing the nation on the *Today* programme in his pyjamas.) Gilligan has such a facility, and was sitting at home ready when the studio dialled him up just after 6am on 29 May. His lack of sleep was obvious to listeners; he was hesitant, his voice gravelly. He said: 'What we've been told by one of the senior officials in charge of drawing up that dossier was that, actually the government probably knew that that 45-minute figure was wrong, even before it decided to put it in.'

He went on: 'Downing Street, our source says, ordered a week before publication, ordered it to be sexed up, to be made more exciting and ordered more facts to be er, to be discovered.'

This was the first time that Gilligan had made the assertion on air that the government knew the 45-minute claim was wrong before the dossier was produced. It may even have been the first time that his editors had heard it. Gilligan does little to disguise a suggestion that Downing Street acted in bad faith; little wonder that No. 10 was incandescent. By the time the story came around again at 7.32am, the government's early shift press officers, employed specifically to monitor every word of the *Today* programme, had put out a denial. Humphrys told Gilligan: 'Let me just quote what they said to you:

"Not one word of the dossier was not entirely the work of the intelligence agencies." Sorry to submit you to this sort of English but there we are. I think we know what they mean.'

Gilligan then broadcast his prepared text, illustrated with recordings of Kelly's quotes. It is a much more considered piece than the 6.07am version: he waters down the assertion that the government knew the 45-minute claim to be wrong – instead, he says merely that it was 'questionable'. He also stresses that his source believes it was '30% likely' that Saddam Hussein had a chemical weapons programme in the six months before the war. The accusation of bad faith, however, remains. But in this broadcast, it is Humphrys' own introduction that comes back to haunt the BBC. His assertion that the September dossier was 'cobbled together at the last minute' was not an off-the-cuff remark. Humphrys scripted it himself, before the start of the programme at 6am. It was to be the subject of serious criticism from no less a figure than the BBC chairman Gavyn Davies, who said later that Humphrys' tone was frequently 'inappropriate'.

Finally, at 8.10am, the Armed Forces Minister Adam Ingram came on to defend the government's position. Ingram answered questions about the issue of cluster bombs first, before launching into a bad-tempered exchange with Humphrys over Gilligan's WMD story, during which he denied that No. 10 had exerted any pressure on the security services to slant the document in a particular way.

But the end of the interview with Ingram did not signal the end of the story for Gilligan. Other BBC news outlets were interested in the story, and were rebroadcasting it. Gilligan's pre-recorded piece for BBC radio bulletins was airing on other BBC networks – a little-known quirk of this tale is that the story was first aired on the 5am news on Radio 2 and Five Live – and misunderstandings were already beginning to creep in. The bulletin compiler who had written the introduction to Gilligan's report for the Radio 2 and Five Live news summaries made what was to become a common slip. The script read: 'BBC News has learned that intelligence officials were unhappy with the dossier published by the government last September, which claimed that Iraq had the ability to launch weapons of mass destruction in 45 minutes.' Gilligan had been careful not to call Kelly an 'intelligence official' because he was not one. He was merely an official attached to the Ministry of Defence, who had access to intelligence material, albeit highly classified. (In fact, Gilligan said later, he had asked Kelly how he would like to be described, offering him two options: 'One of the senior officials involved in drawing up the dossier or the senior official in charge of drawing up the dossier.' Kelly, he said, approved both; Gilligan used the second, stronger version in his 7.32am *Today* broadcast.)

By the end of 29 May, Gilligan had appeared on the BBC nineteen times. But Gilligan's tale presented a problem that is unique to the BBC. Because it is such a large organisation, with 40 hours of news for every hour of the day, journalists tend to be allocated to different programmes or networks. An editor of a television news bulletin on BBC1 would not normally have access to Gilligan, who is attached to the *Today* programme. Exclusive stories run by one section of the organisation often have to be independently corroborated before another part of the empire is prepared to run them. A simple analogy would be to regard the separate programmes as different newspapers within the same media group: journalists on *The Times*, for example, would be unlikely to run, without caveats, an exclusive controversial story from the *Sun* without corroborating it independently first, even though the two newspapers are located in the same building.

So the editor of the *Ten O'Clock News* on BBC1 put one of his own correspondents onto the story. Gavin Hewitt is one of the BBC's most experienced journalists, a former reporter on the current affairs series *Panorama* and known to have good contacts in the field of diplomacy and intelligence. Without knowing Gilligan's source, he turned for help to Tom Mangold, an old colleague from

Panorama. Mangold, author of *Plague Wars*, a seminal book on biological warfare, immediately suggested Kelly as a potential contact, and gave Hewitt his numbers.

By this time Kelly was on official business in New York, but found time to talk to Hewitt on his mobile telephone. Hewitt quoted him directly, although anonymously, at the conclusion of the report he produced for that night's *Ten O'Clock News*: 'I have spoken to one of those who was consulted on the dossier. Six months' work was apparently involved. But in the final week before publication, some material was taken out, some material put in. His judgment: some spin from No. 10 did come into play. Even so, the intelligence community remains convinced weapons of mass destruction will be found in Iraq. Only then will all the doubts go away.'

Unknown to Gilligan, another BBC journalist was also following the story with particular interest. Susan Watts, the science editor of BBC2's *Newsnight* programme, which sees itself as an arch rival to *Today*, had spoken to Kelly some time before Gilligan. She recognised some of what he had said to her, in Gilligan's report, and wondered whether she had committed that cardinal journalistic sin: missing the story. Watts knew Kelly well: as *Newsnight*'s science specialist, her brief was to cover biological weapons. As the foremost expert on the subject in Britain, Kelly was a key contact. The pair had met some years previously, and talked periodically. One such conversation had taken place on 7 May 2002 – two weeks before his encounter with Gilligan.

Watts's shorthand note records Kelly as saying about the 45-minute claim: 'A mistake to put in, Alastair Campbell seeing something in there, single source but not corroborated, sounded good.' But Watts, who was preparing a briefing for a *Newsnight* interview with Robin Cook, did not seize on the significance of Kelly's remark. Indeed, she dismissed it as a 'gossipy aside'. She talked to Kelly again on 12 May, but still did not act on his dossier comments. Only after Gilligan's report was Watts alerted to the potential significance of his views. She called Kelly on 30 May, the day after Gilligan's story hit the airwaves; by now it was all over the newspaper front pages. This time, she recorded the call.

'What intrigued me, and which prompted me to ring you,' she says, 'was the quotes yesterday on the *Today* programme about the 45 minute part of the dossier.'

'Yep,' replies Kelly, 'we spoke about this before of course.'

'We have,' says Watts.

'I think you know my views on that.'

'Yes. I've looked back at my notes and you were actually quite specific at that time – I may have missed a trick on that one.'

Watts, sounding somewhat sheepish on the tape, proceeds to question Kelly in more detail about his views, and uses his material in reports for *Newsnight* on 2 and 4 June. The Hewitt and Watts reports were later to be used by the BBC in its evidence to the Hutton inquiry as important corroboration to Gilligan's story. At the time, however, none of the three journalists knew for sure that Kelly was the source for each of them. Two things were clear: that the story was not going away, and that it had seriously rankled the government. Marsh, Gilligan's editor on the *Today* programme, was pleased.

* * *

'Statement of the obvious, I guess, but it's really good to have you back here in the UK. Great week; great stories, well handled and well told. 'Course it's meant *Today* has had a great week too . . . and that's lifted everyone. We still have to have that conversation – but since you're entirely nocturnal while I'm a normal human being, we don't seem to meet too often. Maybe you could creek [*sic*] the coffin lid open next week during daylight hours??? Anyhow, it's great to have you back on your beat. Talk soon. K'.

In the weeks ahead, Marsh and Gilligan were to have plenty of conversations. Unfortunately, none of them were to be of the nature that Marsh originally intended. For while the story might have eventually faded into the background of some other controversy – the easily bored media are always on the lookout for the next big row – one thing ensured it would remain at the top of No. 10's priority list. As well as reporting for Radio 4, Gilligan was a regular contributor to other (mostly right-leaning) publications, notably the *Spectator* magazine and the *Mail on Sunday*. The *MoS*, never slow to pick up on a story with potential to bate the government, commissioned Gilligan to write a review of how his dossier report had set the news agenda that week. Usually, BBC journalists' 'freelance' work is vetted by their line managers. But this vital article would slip through the net.

Marsh gave Gilligan permission to write it, but said he would be out of contact at the weekend and said other arrangements should be made to have the text approved. Gilligan submitted a draft of the piece to the *Mail on Sunday*, which judged it rather dry, and asked for it to be rewritten. This first draft did not mention Campbell's name, and the newspaper insists that it did not suggest that Gilligan refer to him.

But the second draft did indeed feature prominently the Prime Minister's confidant. Typically for Gilligan's written work, it was strongly self-serving, but – the reference to Campbell aside – did not go much further in essence than his 29 May broadcasts.

But Gilligan had no control of the presentation of the piece. In classic tabloid style, the design of the page put a sharp top spin on the text of the piece. Alongside an unflattering picture of Campbell, the heading – masquerading as a quote from Gilligan – ran: 'I asked my intelligence source why Blair misled us all over Saddam's WMD. His response? One word . . . Campbell.'

It sent Downing Street's fiery communications director into a blue rage. That one headline, more than anything else, set the course for the firestorm that followed.

The firestorm breaks

Nicholas Watt

In the shadow of a tacky fresco depicting a reclining maiden, which adorned the walls of Saddam Hussein's opulent Basra lair, Alastair Campbell was in a grumpy mood. As Tony Blair played the part of a war hero, with a rousing speech of thanks to British troops weeks after the liberation of Iraq, the British media were once again refusing to concentrate on a historic moment. Ignoring the Prime Minister's address from the heart of Saddam's palace, the gaggle of reporters huddled round the Downing Street director of communications and strategy to quiz him about an early morning broadcast back home by Andrew Gilligan, the *bête noire* of Downing Street.

With a weary look, signalling his contempt for the man dubbed by No. 10 as 'gullible Gilligan', Campbell emphatically denied the central charge of the explosive report broadcast on the *Today* programme at 6.07 that morning, 29 May. Downing Street had not 'sexed up' its arms dossier of the previous September by inserting a key claim about Iraq's banned weapons – that they could be fired within 45 minutes – knowing the intelligence to be wrong. Proud of his 'nose' for a story, the former tabloid hack told his former confreres they were missing the 'big picture' and should concentrate on the sight of the first world leader to visit Iraq since the fall of Saddam.

Sadly for Campbell, newsdesks back in London took a different view, as he soon came to realise. By that night, on a flight to Poland after visiting British troops in southern Iraq and Kuwait, Blair and Campbell put in place a fightback that came close to consuming the entire Downing Street machinery for four months. The normal business of government, which was meant to focus on core domestic issues after the end of the war, was cast aside as senior figures from the Prime Minister downwards attempted to blow apart Gilligan's report. Campbell, who was already locked in an ongoing fight with the BBC over its reporting of the war, became so absorbed in his final battle with Gilligan that he had to be told by the Prime Minister to pipe down. Downing Street's obsession with the issue rebounded on the Prime Minister in the late summer when opinion polls showed a dramatic collapse in his personal support. Trust, Blair's greatest commodity since his coronation as Labour leader nearly 10 years before, had also plummeted.

When wall-to-wall coverage of the Hutton inquiry finally drew to a close at the end of September, ministers were left wondering how a broadcast at 6.07am had come close to derailing a government. The Blair circle were in no doubt. Campbell, who had come to develop a pathological hatred of what he perceived as the BBC's condescending metropolitan manner, believed they had reported a downright 'lie' which was given legs because of the corporation's refusal to back down. Others outside the immediate circle, including ministers normally well disposed to Blair, wondered whether Downing Street had lost a sense of perspective.

* * *

The voice of an anxious junior press officer back in London was the first sign of trouble for the Blair circle on the morning of the broadcast. As he waited on the tarmac of a Kuwaiti military airfield to board an RAF C130 Hercules aircraft to Basra, Tom Kelly, the Prime Minister's official spokesman, groaned as he heard the two words dreaded by Downing Street crackle down his mobile phone: Andrew Gilligan. Clicking his phone off, the veteran Belfast journalist turned government spokesman immediately turned to his boss Alastair Campbell to alert him to the 'severe charge' in the Gilligan report. In a rushed conversation in the stifling desert heat, the two men agreed that instructions should be issued to the press office back in London to release a firm denial.

As he was led up to the 'Herc' by Kuwaiti government dignitaries, Tony Blair knew nothing about the BBC report. During an uncomfortable flight up the Shatt al-Arab waterway to Iraq's second city of Basra, Campbell and Kelly left the Prime Minister in blissful ignorance because the incessant noise of the plane made conversation impossible.

After arriving at Basra airport, where the Prime Minister was greeted by the heavily guarded US administrator Paul Bremer, the Downing Street aides removed their earplugs and alerted Blair to the crisis brewing back home. Action had already been taken because a letter had been fired off to the BBC by Anne Shevas, the most senior press officer on duty in London, who declared: 'We categorically deny the allegations made.'

While Campbell may have tried to fob off journalists at Saddam's palace, Blair was in no doubt of the gravity of the charge, admitting later to the Hutton inquiry in melodramatic terms that he would have been forced to resign had Gilligan been proved right. 'This was an attack that went to the heart of not just the office of prime minister but also the way our intelligence services operated. It went in a sense to the credibility, I felt, of the country, never mind the Prime Minister. It was a very, very serious charge,' he told Lord Hutton.

To underline the depth of his concern, Blair told the inquiry that he ordered a classic piece of Downing Street 'news management' to quash the allegations. On a flight from Kuwait to Poland on the evening of the broadcast, after his tour of southern Iraq, Blair and Campbell agreed the Prime Minister would have to deny the allegation in person with the full authority of John Scarlett, the chairman of the Joint Intelligence Committee who had been in charge of drawing up the dossier. Later that night, after clearing the Prime Minister's proposed statement with Scarlett, Campbell recorded his sense of frustration when he wrote in his diary of how Blair's post-war tour of Iraq had been overshadowed by a 'ghastly story, claiming intelligence services not happy with dossier'.

As an accomplished Whitehall operator Scarlett did try to improve Campbell's mood by mocking their relationship. In his diary Campbell recorded Scarlett as telling him over the telephone: 'You are the brutal political hatchet man and I am the dry intelli-gence officer and we have been made to live up to our stereotypes. It is not very nice.'

But Scarlett offered strong support. He went on to say: 'I assure you it [the leak] is not coming from the top.'

* * *

On a perfect east European spring day, which came as a relief to the travelling party after the sweltering heat of the Gulf, Blair attempted to shut down the issue when he appeared before the press after meeting his Polish counterpart in Warsaw. Coming close to breaching diplomatic protocol, Blair cantered through the usual niceties before pre-empting the travelling journalists by declaring: 'The idea that we authorised or made our intelligence agencies invent some piece of evidence is completely absurd.'

The Prime Minister's circle hoped that such a clear statement would put the issue to rest, allowing Blair to enjoy the tercentenary celebrations of St Petersburg on the evening of Saturday 31 May. They had not reckoned with Gilligan, who responded to the Downing Street denial with an explosive *Mail on Sunday* article the next day, 1 June, in which he claimed that his source had pinned the blame on one person: Campbell. Later that night, by which time the

Blair party had moved on to the French Alpine lakeside resort of Evian for the G8 summit, Campbell had grown fearful. 'It was grim for me and it was grim for TB and there is this huge stuff about trust,' he wrote in his diary. Just days into what Blair later described as a 'raging storm', Campbell had put his finger on the most damaging aspect of the saga.

Blair was equally worried, as he made clear to the inquiry when he declared that Gilligan's decision to place Campbell in the frame was tantamount to placing 'booster rockets' on the original allegations. His analogy raised curious questions about Downing Street's sense of perspective. To accuse the Prime Minister of taking the country to war on a false basis appeared to be a grave offence. But to lay the blame on an unelected official appeared, by the Prime Minister's logic, to be unforgivable. Even admirers wondered whether Blair's admission showed that too much trust had been placed in the hands of Campbell, whose fixation with the BBC was the driving force behind the government fightback.

Amid the increasingly agitated mood among the Downing Street circle, Blair kept up appearances at the G8 summit as he attempted to mend fences with President Jacques Chirac after their rows over the war. As he attended his final dinner on the night of 2 June, however, the BBC struck again. Shortly after 10.30pm the earnest figure of Susan Watts, the respected science editor of BBC2's *Newsnight*, popped up to offer her interpretation of Gilligan's story. Despite these differences Watts corroborated Gilligan in one key area. Reporting on a conversation with David Kelly, whose identity she protected, she said her source had made clear that 'the government's insistence that the Iraqi threat was imminent was a Downing Street interpretation of intelligence conclusions'. Watts did not repeat Gilligan's most serious charge – that Downing Street had inserted intelligence knowing it to be false – but she did make clear that No. 10 was guilty on the 'sexed up' charge.

Much to the anger of Watts, who made little attempt to hide her contempt for Gilligan's style of journalism, her report later took centre stage at the Hutton inquiry as BBC managers tried to use it to show that the *Today* reporter had been right all along. On the night of 2 June, however, her report appeared not to register in Downing Street, a fact later seized on by critics of the government, who used this as evidence of a vendetta against Gilligan. Campbell, who was attending a funeral in New York on 2 June, later told the inquiry that he did not complain about the report because Watts said the crucial 45-minute claim had been inserted into the dossier with the support of the intelligence agencies. Although he missed the report, his mood was gloomy at the time.

On 3 June he wrote in his diary of a 'sense of a firestorm developing which was causing considerable difficulty with MPs, with the press and by now with the media right around the world'. The dramatic language in Campbell's compelling diary, which was published in limited form by the Hutton inquiry, showed a deeply troubled figure fighting the battle of his life to clear his own and his boss's name. Night after night he would repair to his room, wherever he was in the world, to report the 'grim' lows and the ecstatic highs which, at one point, led him to believe that he would be able to 'fuck' Gilligan.

* * *

Tired after his whirlwind tour of five countries in almost as many days, Blair returned to Downing Street on 3 June to prepare for hostile questions in the Commons the next day. As he was 'prepped' for his grilling in his Downing Street office, known as 'the Den', the pugilistic leader of the Commons, John Reid, laid down an awkward trap for the Prime Minister when he blamed 'rogue elements' in the intelligence services for creating the furore. Reid's intervention in *The Times* guaranteed a bruising encounter in the Commons the next day when the Tory leader Iain Duncan Smith accused the government of maligning the entire intelligence community. The Prime Minister soldiered on to put across his central message – that the secretive parliamentary Intelligence and Security Committee would examine the allegations.

Disdainful of Duncan Smith's attempts to make capital out of the government's woes after being an enthusiastic supporter of the war, Campbell turned his attention to the matter dominating his mind on his return from New York: his battle with the BBC. For months Campbell had been writing letters to the corporation, sometimes on a daily basis, to rail against its coverage of the Iraq war. At times the BBC climbed down and confessed to errors. Most of the time, the BBC vigorously defended its journalism because senior managers described the Campbell letters as belonging to the 'green ink brigade'.

Amid this background, Campbell wrote his first letter of complaint about the 'sexed up' report on Friday 6 June. The angry tone gave a taste of what was to turn into the most ferocious row between any government and the BBC, dwarfing even Norman Tebbit's attack on Kate Adie's reporting of the 1986 bombing of Tripoli. 'On the word of a single, uncorroborated source you have allowed one reporter to drive the BBC's coverage. We are left wondering why you have guidelines at all, given that they are so persistently breached without any comeback at all,' Campbell wrote. For good measure he included a transcript of Gilligan's original 6.07am broadcast on 29 May.

Satisfied that he had the BBC banged to rights, Campbell headed home where his mood darkened during a weekend of dismal headlines. On his return to work on Monday 9 June he cheered up when the parliamentary Intelligence and Security Committee, a secretive body of MPs and peers appointed by the Prime Minister to oversee the intelligence services, published a report that endorsed the production of the contentious September 2002 arms dossier. Believing that this undermined Gilligan, Campbell was able to turn his attention to Gordon Brown's long-awaited assessment of the five euro tests that day. The atmosphere was surprisingly buoyant in Downing Street because the Prime Minister and Chancellor had ended months of bickering to cut a deal where Blair would accept a 'not yet' verdict in exchange for Brown talking up the single currency and holding out the possibility of a referendum before the next general election.

The mood quickly changed two days later on 11 June when the BBC replied to Campbell's letter with a strong defence of Gilligan. Richard Sambrook, the corporation's director of news, wrote: 'We have not suggested that the 45 minute point was invented by anyone in Downing Street against the wishes of anyone in the intelligence community. We have suggested that there are pertinent and serious questions to be asked about the presentation of the intelligence material.'

Raging at the 'utterly disingenuous' letter, Campbell composed a reply on 12 June which pointed out that the parliamentary Intelligence Committee had just confirmed Gilligan's story to be wrong. With the BBC firmly in his sights, Campbell might have been expected to lock horns with his tormentors when a group of its senior executives trooped into Downing Street for lunch that day. The atmosphere at the meal, which was designed to encourage the BBC not to lose sight of domestic issues, was surprisingly friendly as the corporation's loquacious political editor Andrew Marr held court.

Some of the guests seemed surprised at the Prime Minister's relaxed mood given that he was in the middle of carrying out a cabinet reshuffle, after the ultra-Blairite Alan Milburn had shocked the political world by resigning as Health Secretary to concentrate on his home life.

The Gilligan row did not pass completely unnoticed, however. As the lunch broke up Tom Kelly approached Sambrook, an old colleague from his time at the BBC, to warn him that this time Downing Street was serious about its complaint. As they walked down the historic No. 10 stairs, past the black and white photographs of previous prime ministers and down to the imposing black front door, Sambrook was equally adamant that the BBC genuinely believed Gilligan to be right. As the door closed on the BBC guests, the Downing Street officials returned to the Prime Minister's 'Den' to put the finishing touches to the cabinet reshuffle.

* * *

On a warm, clear summer's evening in a tatty room at the top of a turret overlooking the Thames, the Westminster lobby was growing impatient. A promised briefing on that day's cabinet reshuffle had been endlessly delayed and deadlines were slipping. By the time the briefing eventually kicked off shortly after 6pm, the famously slick No. 10 spinning machine struggled to explain the intricacies of the cabinet changes, which heralded the end of 1,400 years of history with the demise of the post of Lord Chancellor. Downing Street's hesitation led to days of hostile coverage of the 'botched' reshuffle and raised questions about whether No. 10 was losing its grip as it engaged in war with the BBC.

Any hopes of a respite in that battle were dashed when the BBC sent its response to Campbell's latest letter four days later on Monday 16 June. Rejecting his objections, Sambrook suggested that Campbell might like to raise the matter with the BBC's programme complaints unit. Showing that he never leaves a single stone unturned when he goes into battle, Campbell declined the offer after carrying out research which showed that the unit rarely upholds complaints.

Frustrated by the BBC's refusal to concede any ground, Campbell had to endure the sight of his arch enemy Gilligan giving evidence three days later on 19 June to the commons Foreign Affairs Select Committee which had decided to carry out its own inquiry. Gilligan's insistence to the MPs that his source had blamed Campbell for having 'sexed up' the arms dossier, convinced MPs on the committee to issue a second summons to the Downing Street communications director.

Blair was determined to prevent Campbell giving evidence. But his mood changed when a rare event occurred. During six years in Downing Street Blair had hardly bothered to heed the concerns of backbench Labour MPs whose instincts, he believed, had guaranteed electoral oblivion in the 1980s. But on Sunday 22 June the loyal, if slightly obscure, Labour backbencher Eric Illsley struck a chord in Downing Street when he told the *Independent on Sunday* that Campbell faced censure after his office had plagiarised an academic thesis for a second arms dossier published in February. Within 24 hours Downing Street duly announced that Campbell would give evidence before the committee.

As a troubled soul, who throws himself into every challenge with an intensity bordering on the obsessive, Campbell spent hours preparing for his joust with MPs on the committee. By the time he marched into into parliament's brand new Portcullis House on the afternoon of Wednesday 25 June, Campbell was in confident mood as he denounced the BBC for reporting 'lies'.

Fearful that he might lose his cool during the committee hearing, Campbell pressed a pin into his hand which meant that specks of blood squirted onto a sheaf of documents in front of him. Playing to the television cameras, which were broadcasting his appearance live, Campbell ended with a dramatic flourish when he said: 'I simply say in relation to the BBC story: it is a lie, it was a lie, it is a lie that is continually repeated and until we get an apology for it I will keep making sure that parliament, people like yourselves and the public know that it was a lie.' Believing that he had scored a minor triumph, Campbell recorded his most positive thought in months in his diary later that night when he wrote that he had 'opened up a flank' with the BBC. The strength of his performance on live television would, he believed, force the corporation to explain the 'indefensible' in public.

Once again the BBC showed it had no intention of caving in when Sambrook made the highly symbolic move of appearing on the *Today* programme the following morning to condemn Campbell for having 'seriously misrepresented' the corporation. 'He said we were trying to suggest the Prime Minister had led the country into war on a false basis. We've never suggested that . . . He said we've not apologised. Well that is true because we have nothing to apologise for,' Sambrook said.

Enraged by this response, Campbell immediately fired off a letter to the BBC. This took the form of 12 questions, to which Campbell demanded simply yes or no answers by midnight. The key question asked: 'Does it [the BBC] still stand by the allegation . . . that both we and the intelligence services knew the 45-minute claim to be wrong and inserted it despite knowing that? Yes or no?'

Within 24 hours a familiar ritual ensued as the BBC sent back its reply, refusing once again to concede any ground. In what will probably be remembered as one of the toughest letters from the BBC to any government, Sambrook wrote: 'We have to believe that you are conducting a personal vendetta against a particular journalist whose reports on a number of occasions have caused you discomfort.'

* * *

The immaculate courts of the All England Lawn Tennis and Croquet Club, nestling at the bottom of a small hill close to gentrified Wimbledon village, are an oasis of calm. But on 27 June, as the first week of the annual tennis tournament drew to a close, the club witnessed an outburst which resonated beyond John McEnroe's notorious 'you cannot be serious' attack on a hapless umpire in the early 1980s.

Enjoying his status on the celebrity circuit Campbell had taken his son to watch the tennis, only to be interrupted on his mobile by Downing Street with news of the BBC reply. Furious with the corporation, Campbell dictated a statement which condemned the BBC for 'weasel words and sophistry'. He then left Wimbledon early to drive back to Downing Street where his mood darkened even more as his listened to 6pm radio news, which he later described as 'a press release against the government'.

Raging at the BBC's stubbornness, Campbell broke the cardinal rule of spin doctoring – which is never to become the story – when he stormed into Channel 4's studios to denounce the corporation live on the 7pm Friday evening television news. The first that the veteran presenter Jon Snow knew of the interview was when a producer shouted 'Alastair Campbell has entered the building' into his earpiece four minutes into the bulletin. Within minutes a thunderous-looking Campbell was sitting opposite Snow, jabbing his finger and mixing his syntax as he called on the BBC to 'just accept for once they have got it wrong'.

His performance, which the Tories seized on as proof that Campbell had 'completely lost the plot', raised alarm bells in Downing Street. Campbell himself recorded in his diary that night that his response was 'probably too angry', while the Prime Minister urged him the following day to calm down. On 29 June Campbell declared a partial ceasefire with the BBC when he wrote to the corporation: 'Given how far apart we remain, I see little purpose in continuing our exchanges in advance of the Foreign Affairs Committee report . . . I reserve the right to pursue my case further.'

When Campbell and Blair returned to Downing Street after the weekend, an exasperated Prime Minister asked whether they would ever shake off the row and return the media's attention to the bread and butter issues that decide elections.

* * *

A little over 100 miles away, as Blair and Campbell spoke on 30 June, a troubled government scientist was sitting down in his Oxfordshire study to compose a letter which would trigger a series of tragic events unimagined by any of the characters involved. Alarmed by the reports about Gilligan, Kelly wrote to his line manager Dr Bryan Wells to admit that he had met the BBC journalist a week before his report appeared on the *Today* programme. But he insisted that he could not be Gilligan's source.

Blair's first inkling that events would take a different course came on Thursday 3 July, during a visit to his wife's home city of Liverpool when he was told by his chief of staff Jonathan Powell that an unnamed scientist had come forward. His immediate instinct was a textbook example of how to respond: 'I said we had to proceed with caution. We needed proper information; and I said to keep the information to ourselves at that point.'

If Blair acted calmly, Campbell could not contain his excitement at what he saw as a key breakthrough which would finally clear Downing Street. In colourful language, which he came to regret when it was published in the cold of light of day by the Hutton Inquiry, Campbell recorded how his elation was shared by the Defence Secretary Geoff Hoon when they spoke on 4 July. In the most notorious passage of his diary, he wrote: 'GH [Geoff Hoon] said his initial instinct was to throw the book at him [Kelly], but in fact there was a case for trying to get some kind of plea bargain. Says he'd come forward and he was saying yes to speak to AG [Gilligan], yes he said intel went in late, but he never said the other stuff. It was double-edge but GH and I agreed it would fuck Gilligan if that was his source. He said he was an expert rather than a spy or full-time MoD official.' His earthy language came back to haunt him and Hoon, who both had to embark on a lengthy explanation to try to convince Lord Hutton that the MoD had not tried to broker a plea bargain with Kelly.

As Hoon and Campbell celebrated the breakthrough, Kelly was facing the first of two interviews with Martin Hatfield, the MoD's director of personnel. In a sign of how the Whitehall machinery had turned its powerful gaze on the diffident weapons expert, Blair was faxed details of the interview within hours at Chequers, the Prime Minister's official country residence in the Chilterns, just outside London.

The Blairs had fallen in love with Chequers the moment they set eyes on the tranquil retreat that offers a respite from the chaotic pace of Downing Street. But on Friday 4 July – US independence day – and for the rest of that weekend the Chequers fax machine rarely stopped work as the Kelly affair entered its final stages. In his report of the scientist's first interview Sir Kevin Tebbit, the MoD's most senior civil servant, concluded that there was not enough information to decide whether it would be right to pass on Kelly's details to the parliamentary Intelligence Committee.

Nerves became frayed the following day, Saturday 5 July, when *The Times* published crucial details about the as yet unnamed scientist. This was regarded with particular significance because Campbell knew that Sambrook, who had visited *The Times* for lunch the previous day, was the most likely source for the information which increased their fears that Kelly's name would be uncovered imminently.

These concerns were expressed in a second letter from Sir Kevin, faxed to the Prime Minister, who was still at Chequers, which also indicated that Kelly was the most likely source for the BBC story.

Determined to try and clarify once and for all whether Kelly was the source the Prime Minister instructed Sir David Omand, security and intelligence coordinator at the Cabinet Office, to ask 'for a deeper analysis' of what the scientist had said.

Fearing that the media net was closing in on Kelly, an increasingly anxious Campbell tried to persuade Blair that he should pre-empt the BBC by writing to the corporation's governors ahead of a meeting that weekend. The great and the good who sit on the BBC board should be told that Downing Street 'may' know the identity of the source, who was not a spy and who had not been directly involved in drawing up the arms dossier. Blair was initially tempted by this idea, but ruled it out, as Campbell recorded in his diary on Sunday 6 July. 'GH, like me, wanted to get it out that the source had broken cover to claim that AG misrepresented him . . . TB was fine [about writing to the BBC governors] but backed off after speaking to Omand, who felt the guy had to be treated properly and interviewed again. GH and I felt we were missing a trick . . . GH said he was almost as steamed up as I was. TB said he didn't want to push the system too far. But my worry was that I wanted a clear win not a messy draw.'

As Campbell expressed frustration at Blair's caution, the Prime Minister was tying himself up in knots about how to deal with what he later called a 'quandary'. Pacing the corridors and grounds of Chequers that weekend, Blair knew that the timing could not have been worse. Within days the Foreign Affairs Select Committee was due to publish its report which would rule on whether Downing Street had 'sexed up' the arms dossier. To withhold details about Kelly, who at that stage remained unnamed, would open Downing Street up to charges of a cover-up. To pass on the information to MPs would, on the other hand, leave Downing Street vulnerable to charges of failing to protect a respected civil servant – the very issue at the heart of the inquiry.

Unsure which way to turn, Blair opted for the safe option and called in as many senior civil servants as he could muster to give him protection by ensuring that he acted 'by the book'. The list amounted to a roll-call of some of the grandest figures in Whitehall: John Scarlett, Sir Kevin Tebbit, Sir David Manning, Blair's then chief foreign policy adviser, and Sir David Omand. The Whitehall knights, plus Scarlett, who has yet to receive his gong, virtually took up residence in Downing Street from the next day at the start of the most crucial week which would see Kelly outed, and raise questions about whether Downing Street had improperly helped to flush out his name.

The final countdown began in chaotic fashion at No. 10 on the morning of Monday 7 July when Blair popped into a working breakfast with IT experts at around 8.30am. With his mind on other matters – he had to deliver a major speech on criminal justice reform at the nearby Queen Elizabeth II conference centre – Blair slipped out of the breakfast to ask Powell to summon the top brass: Sir David Omand, Sir Kevin Tebbit and John Scarlett. In a sign of Campbell's power, the Prime Minister was asked to wait because some of them were attending a separate meeting with the communications director to discuss with Jack Straw his response to the Foreign Affairs Select Committee report which was due out within hours. The report cleared Campbell of the central charge of having 'sexed up' the dossier, but did nothing to change the BBC's position because Labour MPs used their majority to carry the report after a split on party lines.

Irritated by what Campbell had called in his diary 'a messy draw', Straw, the Blair aides and senior civil servants piled into the Prime Minister's 'Den' for the first of a series of seemingly endless meetings to discuss what to do about Kelly.

Powell gave a vivid account of the frenetic pace in Downing Street when he recalled the rolling meetings which were held on such an ad hoc basis that no notes were kept and officials darted in and out. Asked at the inquiry whether the first meeting on Monday became bigger, Powell said: 'It gets smaller and bigger and bigger and smaller, yes.'

The discussion quickly turned to the key issue: should Kelly appear in public before MPs, a prospect that alarmed the Prime Minister who asked whether the scientist's views on weapons of mass destruction would embarrass the government. Sir Kevin warned that Kelly might have some 'uncomfortable' views. Determined to uncover whether the scientist was indeed the source, and whether he would embarrass the Prime Minister, the highly political John Scarlett left the meeting to dictate a note that would later come back to haunt him. The scientist, he ruled, should be subject to a 'proper security-style interview'.

With his mind, as ever, on damaging headlines Campbell was growing nervous about the Prime Minister's appearance before the cross-party liaison committee of senior backbench MPs the following day. It would be five days since Downing Street had been alerted about Kelly and surely, he feared, news might have reached an MP who could inflict severe damage on the Prime Minister by springing a surprise question.

At around 6pm Godric Smith, the Prime Minister's second official spokesman, wandered into Campbell's office to hear him suggesting to Hoon over his speakerphone that details about Kelly should be leaked to a favoured newspaper. This idea appeared to be welcomed by Hoon who, according to Campbell's diary that night, 'wanted to get up the source'. Smith insisted the idea should be shelved.

Campbell kept his counsel, leaving it to Blair to throw caution to the wind. In a private conversation earlier on 7 July with Gavyn Davies, the BBC chairman, the Prime Minister became the first person in government to brief details about Kelly to an outsider. Acting against the advice of civil servants, who wanted to say nothing about Kelly at that stage, Blair told Davies that there 'may be someone who has come forward as a source'. Davies stood his ground, insisting that the Gilligan report had been corroborated by Susan Watts on *Newsnight*.

Blair had now placed himself at the heart of the government's contentious 'naming strategy', a convoluted process which outed Kelly within two days. The first stage came the following day, 8 July, when the Ministry of Defence announced that an 'unnamed individual' had come forward to say he met Gilligan. The final, and most contentious, stage came on 9 July when the MoD confirmed the scientist's identity to journalists who came up with his name.

Derided by critics as an example of Downing Street's cynical use of the media, the naming process became one of the key elements of the Hutton Inquiry. Had Kelly's name been released purely as a tool in the government's battle with the BBC, the inquiry asked, or had No. 10 acted in a sensitive manner to cope with the inevitable naming of the scientist?

Less than twenty-four hours after Kelly's second interview, the process swung into action on Tuesday 8 July when a familiar cast gathered in the Prime Minister's Den after his appearance before backbench MPs. Sir David Manning reported that Kelly had confirmed suspicions that he was indeed the BBC's source – making it more likely that he would be named. A proposal to release details about Kelly in the form of a letter to Ann Taylor, the chair of the parliamentary Intelligence Committee, was ditched after she refused to be 'bounced'.

Learning that they had been rebuffed by a normally loyal backbencher, the Blair circle decided that the MoD should release a statement that would make the announcement about Kelly and Gilligan, without naming the scientist and providing few biographical details. After lunch the cast, minus the Prime Minister, converged on Godric Smith's room where his computer contained an early draft of the MoD statement. Within a few hours they finally settled on a text that Sir Kevin took back to the MoD for final amendments. At 5.45pm the MoD released its statement, which announced in bald terms that an 'unnamed individual' had come forward. As newspapers seized on the statement, Downing Street's mood improved amid hopes that the BBC would find it hard to hold the line. Within hours the BBC had taken issue with the MoD statement.

With the corporation refusing to budge, and newspapers determined to unmask Kelly, Downing Street moved to the next stage of the process the following day, 9 July. Powell instructed Hoon to implement plans to write to the BBC's Gavyn Davies with the name of Kelly and asking him to confirm whether he was Gilligan's source. The BBC refused to play ball, much to the frustration of Campbell, who recorded in his diary that night: 'BBC story moving away because they were refusing to take on the source idea. There was a big conspiracy at work really. We kept pressing on as best we could at the briefings but the biggest thing needed was the source out. We agreed that we should not do it ourselves, so didn't but later in the day the *FT*, *Guardian*, after a while Evans [defence editor of *The Times*] got the name.'

* * *

As a former journalist who made his name reporting on the intricacies of Northern Ireland politics, Tom Kelly is an astute spokesman who often leaves journalists frustrated as he fends off awkward questions. It therefore came as a surprise on 9 July when he provided vital clues to Westminster journalists at their morning briefing about the mysterious 'unnamed individual'. His titbits of information were interpreted as a sign of Downing Street's desperation to give journalists enough information to identify Kelly while allowing No. 10 to say that its hands were clean. Tom Kelly later explained that he had merely tried to counter the BBC statement of the night before which had contradicted the MoD by releasing inaccurate information about Dr Kelly.

With journalists sensing they were closing in on the scientist, Tom Kelly provided more clues at his afternoon briefing. These proved helpful to journalists who, under the final stage of the process, were given crucial pieces of biographical information by the MoD if they asked the right questions. By the early evening, Kelly's identity was in the open amid farcical scenes which involved *The Times* providing 21 names to the MoD before having the name confirmed.

Believing they were in the clear – the MoD had told No. 10 that Kelly had not expected to remain anonymous – Downing Street turned its attention the following day to Kelly's inevitable appearance before MPs and how that would undermine the BBC. Tom Kelly wrote in colourful terms how the scientist had now become a crucial element in No. 10's battle with the BBC. 'This is now a game of chicken with the Beeb. The only way they will shift is [if] they see the screw tightening,' he wrote in an email to Powell on 10 July.

Fearing that Kelly's appearance was fraught with danger, the government started making elaborate preparations. Hoon took the rare step of directly overruling his most senior civil servant when he rejected Sir Kevin's idea for the scientist to be spared the ordeal of a public grilling at the hands of the Foreign Affairs Select Committee. Warned four days earlier by Sir Kevin that Kelly may have 'uncomfortable' things to say, Hoon also told the Foreign Affairs Committee that the scientist would appear on the understanding that he was not questioned on the areas where he was likely to be outspoken – 'the wider issues of Iraq's WMD' and on the preparation of the arms dossier. Donald Anderson, the chairman of the committee, agreed, although this was ignored by other MPs on the committee when Kelly gave evidence three days later on Tuesday 15 July.

* * *

On one of the hottest days during one of the hottest summers on record an anxious-looking figure, with the air of a distinguished don, walked at a lightening pace up to St Stephen's entrance, the main pedestrian route into the House of Commons. Surrounded by television cameras, Kelly had finally emerged from the shadows to answer his summons by MPs.

Seated at a wooden table in front of the MPs, who sat at a horseshoe table in the Victorian committee room in the heart of the gothic Palace of Westminster, a clearly troubled Kelly could barely be heard as he murmured his answers in the uncomfortably hot committee room. In scenes that were heartbreaking to watch after his death, Kelly insisted that he could not have been Gilligan's only source. 'I believe I am not the main source,' he whispered. 'From the conversation I had with him I don't see how he could make the authoritative statements he was making from the comments I made.'

MPs, who appeared oblivious to his discomfort, pulled no punches. At one point the blunt-speaking Labour MP Andrew Mackinlay added to Kelly's unease when he intervened to declare that he had been used by the government to divert MPs from their inquiry. In remarks repeated endlessly on television, the MP asked: 'Have you ever felt like the fall guy? You have been set up, haven't you?' His face reddening with anxiety, Kelly could just about be heard as he replied: 'I accept the process.'

His clear unease cut little ice with Campbell, who was more interested in how Kelly's appearance had done little for the government. 'GS [Godric Smith] . . . and I predicted it would be a disaster and so it proved,' Campbell wrote in his diary that night.

Believing that Downing Street should now 'sort of put this behind us and forget', Campbell's thoughts turned to his own appearance in private before the parliamentary Intelligence Committee early on the morning of Thursday 17 July. Within hours of his grilling, he was safely on board the Prime Minister's chartered British Airways Boeing 777 for one of the main highlights of No. 10's year: Blair's speech to a joint meeting of both houses of the US Congress.

* * *

For weeks the Blair circle had been working on the Prime Minister's speech, which would mark his entry into a distinguished club as he became only the third British prime minister since Winston Churchill to address Congress. All saw the speech as a key moment for Blair to stamp his mark on the world in a way which would put an end to charges that he was President Bush's 'poodle'. In a sign of nerves in the Prime Minister's circle, Blair declined to make his traditional tour of the plane during the transatlantic flight as the former Washington diplomat Jonathan Powell put the finishing touches to the speech.

As the plane touched down at Andrews Air Force base outside Washington, the atmosphere lightened when news reached the Blair party that Gilligan had just been declared an 'unsatisfactory witness' by MPs on the Foreign Affairs Select Committee after a second appearance. Emerging into the intense Washington heat, the Prime Minister beamed with delight as he was whisked off in a lengthy motorcade to Capitol Hill. Senior members of Congress lined up to meet the visiting hero, who was given the first of nineteen standing ovations when he took his place in front of Washington's great and good on the podium where Churchill, Clement Attlee and Margaret Thatcher had stood before him.

Casting aside the domestic rows, Blair declared that history would judge the Iraq war favourably.

When ecstatic members of Congress eventually stopped their applause, Blair was whisked off to the White House for a press conference with President George W. Bush. By then the media's attention had turned to the fate of two Britons, imprisoned at the US military base in Guantanamo Bay, who were facing the prospect of the death penalty. By the end of the evening, following a dinner with the Bushes, the Prime Minister had secured a deal which would spare the lives of the two Britons. As he flew back to Andrews Air Force with the President, who was flying home to Texas on Air Force One, the Prime Minister could have been forgiven for thinking he had scored a major triumph. A good night's sleep on his 14-hour flight to Tokyo would clear his mind to allow him to put the finishing touches to another landmark speech in which he would signal his willingness to challenge Brown's veto on British membership of the euro.

As the Prime Minister's party experienced the strange sensation of waking up at around 8.30am London time the following morning to find the sun setting over the Bering Strait, one of the secure satellite telephones rang with news that was to bring an abrupt end to the euphoria of Washington: Dr David Kelly had gone missing. Within hours, the worst was confirmed. Knowing that his premiership could now be in grave peril, the Prime Minister embarked on a round of telephone calls to colleagues back in London which lasted for most of the remaining seven hours of the flight.

The sight of suction pads, fixed to the windows of the Prime Minister's cabin, showed this was no ordinary flight. Attached to the pads were mini aerials which picked up a secure satellite signal to allow the Prime Minister to speak in private. As his plane raced over the international dateline and south towards Tokyo, the Prime Minister spoke to Hoon, Sir Kevin Tebbit, Campbell and to his old flatmate, the new Lord Chancellor, Lord Falconer. In one of the most crucial conversations of the day – or night depending on who was talking – the two lawyers threw around a series of names of judges to chair the inquiry into Kelly's death. The Prime Minister was understood to have taken a shine to Lord Mackay of Clashfern, the last Tory Lord Chancellor, on the grounds that appointing a political opponent would show the inquiry would be genuinely independent. Although Lord Mackay is widely respected as an impartial figure, this suggestion was ruled out by key No. 10 officials. Lord Hutton, a highly respected former Chief Justice of Northern Ireland who had shown he was no lackey of the state in his highly sensitive position, was eventually chosen.

Blair took so long to finalise the details of the inquiry that his spokesman, Godric Smith, emerged only minutes before the plane landed in Tokyo to give Downing Street's first reaction to Dr Kelly's death. Amid a flurry of activity from junior No. 10 officials, Smith swept aside the thick curtain shielding the Prime Minister's first-class cabin to walk to the back of the aircraft, where he apologised that the briefing would have to be short. As the plane swayed from side to side as it prepared to land at Haneda airport, Smith was urgently recalled by a Downing Street clerk. A few minutes later Smith reappeared to grab one of the aircraft's internal speaker-phones to conduct his briefing. Moments later, with the plane descending rapidly, Smith was ordered into an economy class seat where, with the cord of the speakerphone stretched to its limit, he spoke of the Prime Minister's 'distress' at the news from home. Speaking for a few minutes, before he had to rush back to the Prime Minister's cabin for the landing, Smith announced that a judicial inquiry would be set up to examine the circumstances leading up to Kelly's death. As news of the inquiry was beamed back to London, Blair's anxiety showed on his face as he left the aircraft shortly before 3pm London time, accompanied by his wife Cherie.

From that moment on, the trip was entirely overshadowed by the Kelly affair, a point that was rammed home when the Prime Minister's euro speech the next day received barely any mention in the papers back home. Downing Street hoped the judicial inquiry would provide some cover for the Prime Minister, who fended off questions about Kelly by calling on everyone to show 'restraint and respect' and to await the findings of the inquiry. Even when one reporter asked Blair whether he had 'blood on his hands', he refused to budge.

Sensing that he was leaving himself vulnerable to charges of culpability, the Prime Minister eventually spoke out when he made his first appearance before the travelling press pack on the plane. As his 777 came in to land at Hong Kong the following Tuesday, 22 July, Blair swept down the plane to declare that he had 'emphatically' not ordered the leaking of Kelly's name.

An approaching typhoon provided a convenient excuse for Blair to return home early the following day, amid criticism at his lengthy round-the-world trip. Throughout the flight, which was nearly aborted at the final moment as wind and rain lashed the aircraft, Blair remained cocooned in his cabin. Back in London, he deflected questions on Kelly at his final prime ministerial press conference the following week.

As he enjoyed his summer holiday at Sir Cliff Richard's Barbados home, however, the Prime Minister had one more painful moment when a Whitehall official described Kelly as a 'Walter Mitty' fantasist. Downing Street initially denied responsibility for such a deeply insensitive slur. It quickly became apparent that Tom Kelly, the first member of the Blair circle to learn about the Gilligan story, was responsible. Within hours he issued an apology as he explained that he had been outlining in private a series of possibilities the inquiry might like to examine.

The stage was set for some bruising encounters at the inquiry which opened a week later.

The walk

Vikram Dodd

On his last morning alive Dr David Kelly could still not find any peace.

It was 17 July 2003 and finally he was back at his Oxfordshire home after being forced to flee when he was named as the suspected source for Andrew Gilligan's reports on the *Today* programme.

The shy civil servant had hoped that testifying before two committees of MPs over the preceding two days would end his ordeal. It had not.

On top of the fallout of his time in the glare of publicity which menaced every aspect of his life, he faced domestic trouble as well. His wife Janice, disabled through arthritis, was upset after their dash from home at ten minutes' notice to avoid a feared media scrum after he was outed.

As the day dragged on, he knew that none of this had gone away.

His bosses were pressing him for details of his media contacts to answer questions from MPs left unanswered by his appearance before them.

Hanging over his head was a threat that he would be disciplined if information emerged that he had not been frank with them.

Also he had told a parliamentary committee on live television that he was not the source for a BBC *Newsnight* story about the September dossier. He was.

By 3.20pm he left his Oxfordshire home to go for a walk. He took with him a small bottle of mineral water, a packet of 30 powerful painkillers belonging to his wife, his mobile phone and a knife. For the weapons inspector, the political had become all too devastatingly personal.

* * *

Little in Dr Kelly's background suggested that he was the sort of person to rock the boat.

When he was not looking for weapons of mass destruction in Iraq, he lived the typical lifestyle of middle England. On rare days off work he tended the garden and in the evening went to the village pub to play crib. Friends and family testified to Lord Hutton that he had seemed relaxed and happy in the months before his death.

His worries concerned having enough money for his retirement, a year away, and believing his bosses did not value his expertise. He was also exasperated by the bureaucracy which surrounded his work.

The questioning of his conduct that Kelly faced on that last day lay in vivid contrast with the praise showered upon him in his professional life. He was hailed as the 'weapons inspector's inspector', earning the honour Companion of St Michael and St George for his work hunting weapons in Iraq and in the former Soviet Union.

His bosses had held him in such high regard that they encouraged Dr Kelly to talk to the media, and he briefed journalists from news outlets across the world.

He had once been trusted to use his discretion to put the government's case about weapons of mass destruction. Now every crevice of his professional life was being poked into.

In mid June Kelly's bosses had their first doubts about his dealings with the media.

He spoke to an *Observer* reporter about trailers found in Iraq that the US and British governments, increasingly desperate to find evidence to support their reason for war, were touting as mobile laboratories for weapons of mass destruction. During a visit to Iraq the scientist had inspected the trailers and concluded they were harmless, giving the *Observer* a story it published on 15 June 2003. An unnamed British official was quoted as rubbishing claims that trailers found in Iraq were mobile production units for chemical and biological weapons. It said the source had seen the trailers, a detail narrowing the list of suspects to four, and placing Kelly under suspicion. When on 16 June his immediate boss Dr Bryan Wells rang Kelly, the scientist denied being the source.

Throughout June the row between the government and the BBC raged on, and in Britain's intelligence community the hunt was on for Gilligan's source. By 19 June, Martin Howard, deputy chief of defence intelligence, had heard that Kelly had talked to Gilligan and wanted the weapons expert interviewed.

That information had come from a friend of Kelly's, Patrick Lamb, head of counter-proliferation at the Foreign Office.

He said that Kelly had told him days before the controversial *Today* broadcast that he had spoken to Gilligan. The significance did not register with Lamb until he saw the *Observer* article, for which he thought Kelly was the mole: 'At that point it began to gel in my mind that he might be the source of Gilligan's piece,' Lamb said. At a party on 17 June at MI5's headquarters Lamb told Howard of his suspicions.

Kelly had also been one of several people suspected of leaking a classified document to Gilligan, an incident that was the focus of a police investigation. On that occasion he was not the mole.

For the people closest to him, the first change anyone noticed in Kelly was in late June.

His wife noticed that he was withdrawn and worried. One day at home he suddenly got up from his chair, went upstairs and dressed 'rather smarter than he would normally be at home, rather smarter than he would normally be if he were just popping down to the local pub for a game of crib or something like that.' He said he was going for a walk, telling his wife he had 'to think something through'.

Mrs Kelly said: 'I was immediately worried, the way he said it. 'I was actually quite worried about him at this time and I was really getting quite anxious.'

On 19 June, Andrew Gilligan testified to the Foreign Affairs Committee, giving more details about his source. Kelly's friend Olivia Bosch, herself a weapons inspector, said they led her to think it was Kelly.

She told him as much at a conference and within days Kelly had written to the MoD admitting to meeting Gilligan.

It is still far from clear what Kelly's gameplan was when he wrote his 30 June letter to Wells. His friends say that Kelly never anticipated the super-heated row that would erupt around him. With gossip filling Whitehall's corridors about the source, with the row between the government and BBC blazing away, did Kelly come forward because he feared his bosses would get to him first?

In his 30 June letter to Wells, he admitted meeting Gilligan but denied being his source. He wrote that he 'most certainly [had] never attempted to undermine government policy in any way' and that he had backed the war because a decade of work left him in no doubt of 'the menace of Iraq'. The letter continued: 'I have never made a claim as to the timing of when any part of the dossier was included. I have never acted as a conduit to release or leak information. I do not feel "deep unease" over the dossier.' If Gilligan had quoted Kelly accurately, the scientist had done exactly what he had denied in the letter.

Wells passed on Kelly's letter to Howard, who was leading the Whitehall hunt for Gilligan's source. On 4 July Kelly was interviewed for the first time by Richard Hatfield, the MoD head of personnel, with Wells taking notes. Hatfield pressed Kelly on whether he had told them the truth about his meeting with Gilligan, suggesting the reporter may have taped the conversation.

The meeting ended with Hatfield saying there would be no disciplinary action but Kelly would get a written reprimand. Hatfield added: 'The possibility of disciplinary action could of course be reopened if further facts came to light that called his account and assurances into question.' Wells said the weapons expert had been composed through the interview although he looked uncomfortable at times.

The next day there was another noticeable change in Kelly. His daughter Rachel, aged thirty, told the inquiry about a walk with her father through the Oxfordshire countryside on Saturday 5 July, the weekend before he was named. Ms Kelly, who works for the Royal Society for the Protection of Birds, said it was during that walk that she had become 'extremely concerned' about her father. She noticed that he was quieter than usual and asked if his mood was linked to the row raging between Alastair Campbell and the BBC, which was dominating the headlines.

Mr Campbell had gone on to *Channel 4 News* days earlier to launch his 'intemperate' attack on the BBC. Rachel recalled, 'On our way back I asked him if the situation in the media about Alastair Campbell was affecting him and his reaction alarmed me greatly. It was not that he jumped, but he said no, and he added "Not really", and I felt that I had intruded and he was very quiet, very pale and he just seemed to have the world's pressures on his shoulders. He seemed under severe stress. I did not want to cause him distress so I again tried to distract him.'

Rachel Kelly said she was 'very close' to her father, who had been 'very relaxed' just a few weeks before he became involved in the storm between the BBC and the government.

Monday 7 July was the last time a day started with any normality for Kelly. He was due to go to RAF Honnington for training ahead of his deployment to Iraq to join the hunt for WMD. Instead he was summoned back to London for a second interview.

Martin Howard, deputy chief of intelligence of the Defence Intelligence Staff, joined the interview. Kelly was told the reason for another grilling was to clear up 'discrepancies' between what he had told officials and what Gilligan had told MPs. Howard told the inquiry he had seen correspondence saying the Prime Minister wanted 'more detail' about the differences between what Gilligan had told the Foreign Affairs Committee about his source, and what Kelly had told officials, before 'we decided on the next steps'.

In the interview, Kelly held to his position that he could not have been Gilligan's source. The second interview did not satisfy Kelly's bosses.

That same day, John Scarlett, head of the Joint Intelligence Committee, sent a memo to Sir David Omand, the government's security co-ordinator, saying that Kelly appeared to be the source: 'Conclusion: Kelly needs a proper security-style interview in which all these inconsistencies are thrashed out . . .' Kelly was allowed back to RAF Honnington to resume his training.

On 8 July the Prime Minister chaired two meetings to decide what the government should do about the scientist.

As Kelly was driving home his mobile phone rang. It was the MoD's personnel director Richard Hatfield with the news that the MoD was going to issue a statement.

It took Hatfield 3 minutes, 49 seconds to run through the statement, which had been crafted in Downing Street, while Kelly sat in his car in a lay-by. Hatfield did not tell Kelly that his name would be confirmed if journalists guessed it.

That evening, Mrs Kelly told the inquiry, the couple watched *Channel 4 News*: 'We had a meal and then we went in to sit and watch the news. He seemed a little bit reluctant to come and watch the news.

The main story was a source had identified itself. Immediately David said to me: "It's me." My reaction was total dismay. My heart sank. I was terribly worried because the fact that he had said that to me, I knew then he was aware his name would be in the public domain quite soon. He confirmed that feeling, of course.'

Only at this point, nine days after writing his letter, did those closest to Dr Kelly get a sense of what he had been dealing with.

Mrs Kelly told the inquiry how her husband seemed 'desperately unhappy about it, really really unhappy about it. Totally dismayed. He mentioned he had had a reprimand at that stage from the MoD but they had not been unsupportive, were his words . . . I said: Would it mean a pension problem, would it mean you having to leave your job? He said it could be if it got worse, yes.'

She said he was in 'total dismay' at the prospect of his name becoming public. At that point there was only a day to go.

On 9 July Kelly cancelled plans to go to London, choosing instead to work on his vegetable patch in his garden at home. At sunset the couple sat outside after dinner drinking coffee.

At 7.03pm Kelly got a call from Wells, his line manager. He was told the press office had confirmed his name, but as Wells was on a train, the call lasted only 46 seconds. Kelly now knew the storm he had feared was about to break. The first taste came within minutes when Nick Rufford, a *Sunday Times* reporter, turned up on his doorstep.

Kelly had been a long-standing contact of Rufford, and the journalist told how the scientist, looking tired and pale, admitted: 'I have been through the wringer.'

Rufford told the inquiry: 'I asked him whether he knew his name was going to come out and he said: "I am a bit shocked. I was told it would all be confidential."'

After Rufford heeded Dr Kelly's demand he leave, the MoD press office called confirming the news his name was out. They suggested he may want to leave his home as the press would be on their way.

At ten minutes' notice the distinguished scientist threw together some clothes and with his wife he fled; fugitives from their own home, outed by a government he had served.

Kelly was 'very taut' as they raced down the M4 motorway. Both were desperately tired. At 7.54pm Wells called again. They were heading to Cornwall, where Mrs Kelly had a friend they could stay with, but by 9.45pm, too tired to carry on, they decided to stay the night in Weston-super-Mare.

Rachel told the inquiry she had had a call from her mother saying her parents were fleeing because the press had identified her father. She said her mother 'sounded very upset, very distressed' and she promised to look after her parents' cats.

The next morning Dr Kelly took one of the newspapers whose headlines he was dominating, and after managing a small breakfast, the couple set off for Cornwall.

They arrived in time for lunch, and Mrs Kelly remembered how she tried to lift her husband's darkening mood. 'I could not comfort him. He seemed to withdraw into himself completely. I decided that the best I could do, and I made a policy thing then, that I would keep him properly fed, good food, attractive food, and then keep him occupied as pleasantly as possible.'

On Friday 11 July Kelly took a call telling him he was going to have to testify before MPs. Later he was told that the Foreign Affairs Committee hearing would be televised: 'He was ballistic,' Mrs Kelly said. 'He felt it would be a kind of continuation of a reprimand in the public domain.'

Mrs Kelly took her husband to tourist sites to try and provide him with a sliver of solace.

Trips to the Lost Gardens of Heligan and the Eden Project did next to nothing to help the scientist's despair. Mrs Kelly told the inquiry: 'It was a very grim time for both of us. I have never, in all the Russian visits and all the difficulties he had in Iraq, where he had lots of discomforts, lots of horrors, guns pointing at him, munitions left lying around, I had never known him to be as unhappy as he was then.'

The couple scraped through Saturday and by Sunday Dr Kelly was hurt by remarks in a newspaper 'belittling' his status. It added to his dismay. Just before midday, he headed back towards Oxfordshire to prepare for the Foreign Affairs Committee hearings and decided to stay at Rachel's home, arriving by 5pm. Mrs Kelly had to make her own way home.

Rachel told how one look from her father, the first time she had seen him since the furore had erupted, left her worried that he felt humiliated: 'There was a really strong expression on his face that really shocked me and I was actually quite distressed to see the hurt that I could see in his face. It was a particular look. There was a lot of distress and anxiety, perhaps a bit of humiliation. I was aware that he seemed very gentle, more childlike. I was very conscious that our roles seemed to be reversing, that I needed to look after him and he needed to be looked after.'

Father and daughter talked about the week to come. Rachel Kelly said the appearance in public before the Foreign Affairs Committee weighed heaviest on his mind: 'I could see he was really very, very deeply traumatised by the fact that the second one would be televised live.'

Rachel said her father seemed nervous and tired, especially before a session on Monday 14 July for government officials to 'brief' him for his evidence to MPs. He went to London to meet Wells and Howard. They said the session was to familiarise Kelly with the workings of the Foreign Affairs Committee and the Intelligence and Security Committee and to discuss possible questions.

Kelly, if asked about his views on the Iraq war, would say it was a matter for ministers. At the end of the session, Wells handed him a reprimand letter. James Dingemans QC, counsel for the inquiry, asked Mr Howard: 'Was the effect of this discussion that Dr Kelly was being given a certain steer as to how his evidence should go?' Howard replied: 'No, certainly not.' Dingemans asked: 'Do you think he might have interpreted it that way?' Howard denied this: 'I started off by saying we must not feed you departmental lines.'

The plausibility of Howard's answer is tempered by a note of his about the session with certain topics listed under the heading 'tricky areas'.

Kelly said he would deny to MPs that he was Gilligan's source for the 45-minute claim. Howard, who at the time believed Kelly was the source, told him that he must answer questions 'according to your conscience'.

A MoD note recorded Howard as saying: 'Kelly is apparently feeling the pressure and is not handling it well.'

* * *

That evening, back in Oxfordshire, father and daughter went for a walk. Kelly was silent, 'lost in his thoughts' and 'transfixed by the water' as they strolled. 'He just seemed under an overwhelming amount of stress,' Rachel said. She overheard her father on the phone saying he was 'very depressed' by the media coverage, and would read only the sports sections of the newspapers.

Throughout this period Kelly managed to sleep relatively well, although he was still suffering from fatigue. On 15 July Kelly was to face the Foreign Affairs Committee. It was also his thirty-sixth wedding anniversary.

Wing Commander John Clark, a colleague and friend who accompanied Kelly to the parliamentary committee hearings, told the inquiry that before the FAC hearing he asked Kelly if he thought his 30 June letter would lead to his being exposed to 'the full glare of the press'. 'He said under no circumstances had he felt when he submitted his letter . . . that he would have ended up in that position.'

Kelly told a colleague that appearing before the FAC had put him under more pressure than any other interview he had ever had. He also told of his shock when an MP read him a long quote from the *Newsnight* report by Susan Watts and asked if he was the source.

Kelly described his appearance as 'very, very hard' to his daughter and criticised one MP who had questioned him: 'He said it very quietly, with some feeling, and that was that this man was an utter bastard,' Rachel Kelly told the inquiry. This is a reference to Andrew Mackinlay MP, who called Kelly 'chaff' and said he had been set up as a fall guy.

Rachel Kelly said her father was 'incredulous' that he was being suspected as Gilligan's principal source because he could recognise only a part of the report as anything he had told the reporter. 'He could not understand how Gilligan could make such forceful claims from the conversation that they had had,' she said. Kelly's performance had worked and the FAC concluded he was not the source.

Rachel said that her father had told her the toll of the preceding weeks had left him 'mentally shattered'.

The next day Kelly testified to the Intelligence and Security Committee in private and afterwards, according to Wells, he seemed buoyant: 'He seemed very pleased at how it had gone. He was actually in good spirits [and] we started talking actual dates for his going back to Iraq.' He told colleagues he hoped his ordeal was over.

That evening, the first at home for a week, Kelly arranged with his daughter to go for a walk the next day to see a newborn foal they had been visiting. It was the last time Rachel saw her father.

Kelly and his wife woke later than usual on Friday 17 July only to find none of the pressures in his life had relented. That morning, his friend Wing Commander Clark rang Kelly and was told of the domestic upset. Clark said: 'He said he was holding up all right, but it had come to a head and his wife had taken it really very badly. Whether that was in association with the additional pressure of having to get back on the day before under her own steam, I do not know, but he says that his wife had been very upset on the morning of the 17th.'

There was also the matter of media contacts that had arisen out of his FAC appearance. Andrew Mackinlay MP had tabled a parliamentary question for a list of Kelly's press contacts that he had not given at the hearing. Bernard Jenkin, the Tory defence spokesman, had tabled a parliamentary question asking if Kelly had been disciplined.

Wing Commander Clark had been asked to help the scientist compose his responses. Kelly had already emailed him a list at 9.22am, but said on the phone he was having difficulty remembering every reporter he had had contact with.

Kelly worked in his study, telling his wife he was doing his 'homework' for the MoD. He sent the name of Susan Watts as Susan Wells. His managers noticed the mistake and corrected it. The Secretary of State's office rang Wing Commander Clark to point out Dr Kelly had missed one contact in his list. The scientist agreed that the name should be included.

Kelly responded to a string of emails that had arrived while he was on the run. To one American reporter he sent an ominous email talking of 'dark actors playing games', but the tone of most was forward-looking, with him telling well-wishers and friends that he hoped to soon be back in Iraq. He sent the last email at 11.18am.

By 12.30pm Kelly was so consumed by events that he could barely speak. Mrs Kelly told the inquiry of finding her husband in the lounge: 'He just sat and he looked really very tired. By this time I had started with a huge headache and begun to feel sick. In fact I was physically sick several times at this stage because he looked so desperate.'

He had some sandwiches for lunch, and a glass of water. 'I was feeling pretty wretched, so was he. He looked distracted and dejected. I just thought he had a broken heart. He had shrunk into himself. He looked as though he had shrunk, but I had no idea at that stage of what he might do later, absolutely no idea at all. He could not put two sentences together. He could not talk at all.'

After lunch, at around 1.45pm, Mrs Kelly lay down to help with the pain of her arthritis. 'I said to him, "What are you going to do?" He said, "I will probably go for my walk,"' Mrs Kelly remembered.

The last words Mrs Kelly remembers from her husband of 36 years were ones of concern: 'Shortly after I had laid down he came to ask me if I was okay. I said, "Yes, I will be fine." And then he went to change into his jeans. He would be around the house in a tracksuit or tracksuit bottoms during the day. So he went to change and put on his shoes.'

More phone calls delayed the walk and Mrs Kelly came down from her rest to find her husband talking quietly on the phone. A few minutes before 3pm, Clark told the inquiry, he had his last conversation with Kelly, during which the position of Watts in the list was discussed.

Close to 3.20pm Clark rang Kelly again, to be told by his wife that he was out.

The last known person to see Kelly alive was his neighbour Ruth Absalom. They met a mile from their homes and he seemed his normal self: 'We just stopped, said hello, had a chat about nothing in particular. He said, "Hello, Ruth" and I said, "Oh hello David, how are things?" He said, "Not too bad."'

With outstanding answers needed, Clark called Kelly's mobile at 15-minute intervals for nearly two hours, but it remained switched off. He said that was unusual for the scientist who prided himself on how easy he was to contact.

James Harrison, who took over the task of trying to reach Kelly at 4.45pm, tried again at 5.50pm when, he said, 'my recollection is it rang and was not answered'. By 6pm Wells was ringing him and found the mobile ringing out. He was surprised it was not answered because his name would have come up on the mobile's display as being the caller. If Kelly was still alive, he was ignoring the call from his boss.

If the weapons expert had switched his mobile on again he would have found numerous messages asking for yet more details about his media contacts.

Sometime late in the morning of 17 July Kelly decided to kill himself, said Professor Keith Hawton, an expert in suicides, who was asked by Lord Hutton to testify.

As he ploughed through the replies about his media contacts and answered the demand for information from his bosses, the feelings of personal disgrace the row had triggered within Kelly codified in his mind.

Professor Hawton said: 'During that morning there was an escalation in his distress.'

Kelly, according to the expert, made a decision on how to end the furore surrounding him: to take his own life.

Hawton said: 'It is my opinion that it is likely that he formed the opinion either during the morning, probably later in the morning or during the early part of the afternoon, before he went on that walk.'

Asked what contributed to Kelly's death, Professor Hawton said the major factor was the 'severe loss of self esteem, resulting from his feeling that people had lost trust in him and from his dismay at being exposed to the media.'

Hawton said Kelly would have viewed his exposure in the media 'as being publicly disgraced'.

The expert added: 'He is likely to have begun to think that, first of all, the prospects for continuing in his previous work role were diminishing very markedly.'

A year from retirement Kelly had begun to fear he would lose his job altogether, which the professor said 'would have filled him with a profound sense of hopelessness; his life's work . . . undermined.'

Hawton described Kelly as being unable to share his problems and feelings with others and increasingly locked into himself: 'So in a sense he was getting further and further from being able to share the problems with other people; that is extremely important.'

It is another contradiction about Dr Kelly. A man so emotionally closed was so spiritually curious. His wife had once found him reading the Koran.

But his privateness meant few knew he had converted to the Baha'i faith, which he joined after a trip to the US in 1999.

Few also knew that his mother, Margaret, committed suicide, killing herself after suffering a stroke.

According to Hawton, an MoD vetting file showed the weapons expert had said in an interview in 1985 that his mother had suffered from depression before her death.

GP records from 1964, when Kelly was a student in Leeds, showed that after his mother Margaret's death he had suffered insomnia and may have been prescribed tranquillisers. Kelly had been brought up in Pontypridd, Wales, and was reared mainly by his grandmother after his father left the family. His mother worked long hours, restricting time to care for her child. She died aged 47, just short of Kelly's twentieth birthday.

Professor Hawton said that Dr Kelly had been aware of his mother's suicide and had told his wife about it.

After a life of meticulous service in tracking down weapons of mass destruction, Kelly was equally meticulous in ending his life. He walked to an isolated beauty spot near his Oxfordshire home, and then clambered 150 metres through near-impenetrable woodland thick with brambles to a secluded glade. By 6pm, when he failed to return from his walk, Rachel was phoned by her mother to be told the news.

She arrived at her mother's home and by 6.30pm was scouring the nearby countryside, checking routes that her father may have taken. 'Then I came back to the car and it occurred to me for the first time then that Dad might not be coming home,' she said.

She thought of checking barns but did not, fearful of what she might find inside. Her sister Sian also joined the family's search that would prove fruitless.

By 11.40pm Mrs Kelly rang the police to report her husband missing. On the morning of 18 July, he was discovered slumped against a tree near Harrowdown Hill in Longworth.

Nearby on the ground was a three-inch pruning knife, his flat cap, wristwatch and a small bottle of water that he used to help him take an overdose. Those who found him said the scientist had blood covering his left wrist.

PC Andrew Franklin said: 'He was lying on his back with his right hand to his side and his left hand was sort of inverted with the palm facing down, facing up on his back. The wristwatch was lying away from the body, next to a knife. The wristwatch was just to the left of the left arm, with the knife next to it, and also there was an open bottle of water at the scene.'

The inquiry heard Kelly swallowed 29 of the powerful painkillers, well beyond the recommended dose. Such was his state when he gulped them down that some of the plastic from the packing was found in his stomach. Also on the scene was PC Martyn Sawyer, who said there were no signs of a struggle: 'When I first saw Dr Kelly I was very aware of the serious nature of the search and I was looking for signs of perhaps a struggle, but all the vegetation that was surrounding Dr Kelly's body was standing upright and there were no signs of any form of struggle at all.'

Dr Kelly was pronounced dead at 10.07am.

A mile away at the Kelly home, the family were still hopeful, said Sergeant Geoff Webb, who talked to them for clues as to where the scientist might be: 'They were very hopeful that no harm had come to Dr Kelly. They genuinely believed that perhaps he had become ill somewhere.'

The family view of the cause of the devastating effects of these last 18 days on Dr Kelly were summed up by their barrister Jeremy Gompertz QC in his closing speech: 'The government and the nation have lost their greatest expert in biological weapons of mass destruction, yet he was characterised by his employers to suit their needs of the hour as a middle-ranking official and used as a pawn in their political battle with the BBC. His public exposure must have brought about a total loss of self esteem, a feeling that people had lost trust in him. No wonder Dr Kelly felt betrayed after giving his life to the service of his country. No wonder he was broken-hearted and, as his wife put it, had shrunk into himself. In his despair he seems to have taken his own life.'

The evidence from a post mortem suggests Kelly died between 4.15pm on Thursday and 1.15am on Friday.

After news of the death, Sergeant Webb searched the Kelly home. In a Sainsbury's notebook, he found a list of journalists' names, and elsewhere in the study reporters' business cards. On a low coffee table was a copy of Kelly's letter to his bosses of 30 June titled 'Andrew Gilligan and his single anonymous source'. In his briefcase police found the letter of reprimand from his bosses. It was unopened.

For Kelly it was over; for everybody else, it had only just begun.

The inquiry begins

David Hencke and Tom Happold

Posing awkwardly for the cameras following his appointment, James Brian Edward Hutton looked little like a believer in open government or the democratic potential of the internet. Wild-eyed radicals do not become Lord Chief Justice of Northern Ireland; septuagenarian law lords tend not to embrace the opportunities of online disclosure.

The conduct of his inquiry was truly radical, revealing not only how ministers and mandarins dealt with a troublesome civil servant but also how they went about making the case for war. Technology was at the heart of this. Whitehall's reliance on email allowed the inquiry to follow the decision-making process step by step. And Lord Hutton's willingness, and his inquiry's secretary Lee Hughes's determination, to upload 'every word of evidence' and 'every document' onto the internet allowed the public to participate in that journey. The inquiry's website was to become the most popular political site in Britain.

Lord Hutton had neither the right to subpoena witnesses nor demand evidence. He was also commanded to investigate only the 'circumstances surrounding the death of Dr Kelly' not the wider events leading to war. Presenting his opening statement Lord Hutton outlined its format – like Sir William Macpherson, who chaired the inquiry into the death of Stephen Lawrence, he said he would allow interested parties, including the Kelly family, to appoint counsel, who would be permitted to cross-examine certain witnesses.

He also explained that the inquiry would take evidence in two stages, an arrangement similar to that of Sir Richard Scott's investigation into the arms-to-Iraq scandal. Lord Hutton's decision to bar television cameras from the inquiry provided further cause for pessimism. His view was straightforward, and unsurprising for someone charged with investigating the suspected suicide of a man humiliated by a televised grilling by overexcited politicians. He believed that the presence of cameras would cause unnecessary 'distress' for the witnesses.

'Urgently' was the first word of Lord Hutton's terms of reference. He would meet the challenge by using information technology that encouraged and aided greater openness, even without the presence of cameras.

He did so with the help of an able team, the nucleus of which was James Dingemans QC and Hughes. Dingemans was Lord Hutton's personal choice; he had spotted him when he appeared before him in the Privy Council. Hughes, the head of the Department of Constitutional Affairs section responsible for tribunals and inquiries and a passionate exponent of freedom of information, was appointed by the department's permanent secretary, Sir Hayden Philips.

It was at their first meeting that Lord Hutton and Hughes came to a key decision on the question of openness and transparency. Under both the current code of practice on access to government information, introduced by John Major's government, and the new Freedom of Information Act, Lord Hutton need not have released anything. Both men chose to ignore any restrictions they could have imposed under the code or the act. Essentially the Hutton Inquiry showed how the Freedom of Information Act could work in practice. Virtually all documents and emails, including those headed confidential and restricted, were regarded as public information. Only documents marked secret and top secret were not published in full, but redacted versions were released where possible. The website also followed a practice regularly used by the Swedish government – to disclose the existence of documents even if the documents are not released. Thus every single piece of information passed to the inquiry has been logged, which means future historians will have access when the files are passed to the Public Records Office for posterity.

The onus was put on the Cabinet Office and others submitting evidence to say what should not be published. If nothing was said, the material appeared on the site. There were only two serious gaffes. The names of two spies were inadvertently put on the internet, only to be withdrawn within hours without the press realising what had happened, and Andrew Gilligan's home telephone number also made a brief appearance but was quickly spotted and removed.

Court 73 at the Royal Courts of Justice was quickly transformed for Lord Hutton: out went the legal textbooks, in came 44 desktop and plasma screens. To help him, the various lawyers and the media follow proceedings, a 'livenote' computer system flashed the stenographer's transcription of spoken evidence across the screens within seconds of its being heard. Facilities for video and audio conferencing were also installed, allowing witnesses, such as the head of MI6, Sir Richard Dearlove, to give evidence without having to be appear in the court room.

Lord Hutton surveyed the proceedings from a dais at the front, looking down upon the three rows of lawyers and three rows of journalists, the public being granted only a single row of seating. The only people the judge found difficult to see were the witnesses themselves, who were seated at a 90-degree angle in the corner of the court. In a bizarre league of its own was the journalists' tent, erected after the first week in the court's quadrangle. It resembled a marquee at a home county wedding, complete with chandelier.

For most members of the public the face of the inquiry would be its website. Lord Hutton's announcement that it would carry the transcript of the day's hearing and written evidence hardly hinted at the acres of testimony that would appear. The site was built in two days and the sheer size of the information being posted presented the eight-strong Department of Constitutional Affairs' web team with a formidable challenge.

The inquiry's first serious test of openness came within days. The censors were not the security services but one of Whitehall's more obscure departments – the ceremonial secretariat in the Cabinet Office. Lord Hutton wanted a copy of the honours citation given to Kelly when he was awarded the Companion of the Most Distinguished Order of St Michael and St George. The reason was to establish officially how highly the scientist was regarded in Whitehall. Gay Catto, head of the ceremonial secretariat, simply refused to release it, citing a precedent, backed by the present access code, that honours citations are never published.

An extraordinary Whitehall dispute followed that stopped just short of a telephone call to Tony Blair to demand the release of the information. Eventually Sir Andrew Turnbull, the Cabinet secretary, had to prevail on Catto to allow Lord Hutton at least to see the citation.

It was duly delivered with strict instructions that it must never appear on the inquiry website. Lord Hutton worked out a clever trick. He gave the document to Dingemans, who promptly read it out when questioning a witness. The result is that Kelly's honours citation is the first and so far only full citation that has ever been made public.

Whether this bruising row sent out a signal that deterred others in Whitehall is not known. But there was remarkable cooperation from the rest of the civil service for the rest of the inquiry, including redacted release of minutes of meetings in Downing Street and the Joint Intelligence Committee.

The two biggest disputes did not involve Whitehall at all. The first involved the failure of the BBC to release emails sent by Andrew Gilligan to members of the Commons Foreign Affairs committee. Lord Hutton was only alerted to their existence when David Chidgey, Liberal Democrat MP for Eastleigh and a member of the committee, sent the email from Gilligan to Hughes. The disclosure of this minute led to a flood of emails being sent to the inquiry by the BBC, and also contributed to the recall of Gilligan.

The second was the appearance of Alastair Campbell's diaries. The committee realised the significance of the diaries after they were referred to in a Cabinet Office document. Campbell was asked to release selected extracts and neither resisted nor thought it an opportunity to boost his diary's capital value. He was expecting the documents to be used in evidence but had not quite realised that they would be published on the website. Nor had he realised the extent of the revelations that would be published. Lord Hutton is said to have found them rather good.

The release of documents by the Hutton Inquiry is likely to have an impact that goes much wider than the hearings. In the words of one minister 'the roof has not fallen in ' after such an unprecedented release of information. The case for an even more radical and open Freedom of Information Act is now being argued in Whitehall. The Hutton Inquiry showed that even No. 10 can release emails and redacted minutes of meetings without the government coming to halt. What is there to stop the release of other exchanges of internal Whitehall information when the government announces future policy decisions?

Lord Hutton's attitude to the release of information has been groundbreaking. What happens next will indicate if the government is committed to a genuinely open society. If it is the latter Lord Hutton's work will have been in vain. If it is the former, there will be a radical shift in the way Britain is governed.

The evidence day by day

What follows is a guide to every day's evidence, in date and time order – everything you need to know about the twenty-four days of evidence heard in Court 73 by Lord Hutton. It is comprehensive, rather than complete: not every witness is detailed here, just those we thought were the key or relevant ones. Witnesses that have been left off were called on points of procedure or to simply confirm another's testimony.

For each witness, we have summarised the main points of what they said, and lifted the key quotes from the thousands of words of transcript that were published each day of the inquiry. We have also included as much of the key documentary evidence as possible with direct quotes from the emails, memos, letters and reports where they add to a witness testimony. These come at the end of each day's report.

The introductions to each day, in italics, are written by Richard Norton-Taylor. He sat through most of the inquiry and stepped back to draw the key lessons from each set of witnesses.

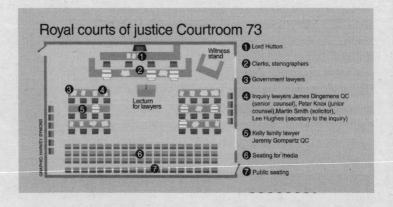

Royal courts of justice Courtroom 73

1. Lord Hutton
2. Clerks, stenographers
3. Government lawyers
4. Inquiry lawyers James Dingemens QC (senior counsel), Peter Knox (junior counsel), Martin Smith (solicitor), Lee Hughes (secretary to the inquiry)
5. Kelly family lawyer Jeremy Gompertz QC
6. Seating for media
7. Public seating

Day 1
11 August 2003

The first day of the inquiry revealed that unease about the government's dossier on Iraq's weapons of mass destruction ran much deeper than Downing Street admitted and was shared within the intelligence community. It also revealed that David Kelly's involvement in the dossier – and his status – was more significant than the government admitted. Dr Kelly felt he was missing out on pay rises because he was in a 'black hole', working for the MoD and the FO as well as the UN. 'The poor chap hasn't had a pay rise for three years,' recorded his personnel boss in 1999.

Terence Taylor
President and executive director for the International Institute of Strategic Studies (US)

- The close friend and former colleague of Kelly – who gave evidence via satellite link from Australia – said the scientist was focusing on returning to Iraq to continue his work when they last spoke four days before his death.
- Said they had not discussed the Iraq dossier row during the phone call from America. Instead, they talked about Kelly's plans to join the Iraq Survey Group, and a visit Taylor was planning to Kelly's home in July.
- He first met Kelly in the mid-1980s and they worked together investigating Russia's biological weapons programme, and in Iraq as UN weapons inspectors.

On Kelly's work in Iraq

'He was very determined and resolute in carrying through the inspections and supported us all, sharing his insights and so forth in a very effective way. This resulted, of course, in 1995 in the UN Special Commission (Unscom) making a breakthrough and forcing the Iraqi side to admit they did indeed have a biological warfare programme, a very extensive one as it turned out. A large amount of this was due to Dr Kelly's superb work.'

Richard Hatfield

Personnel director MoD (also appeared on days 18, 19 and 22)

- Kelly was authorised to brief the media on Iraq's weapons of mass destruction and had given attributable and unattributable briefings to a string of news organisations around the world over a 12-year period. His media skills and discretion were praised.
- Hatfield said Kelly had broken government rules on what civil servants should tell reporters when he met Andrew Gilligan, although it was 'effectively part of his job description' to lecture and brief journalists.
- Kelly was not a senior civil servant and had no responsibility for management.
- Documents produced during Hatfield's cross-examinations showed Kelly complaining about his treatment, status and pay. He was on secondment to one department from another.

Asked if Kelly had access to 'all levels of information'

'There are what is known in the trade as "compartments", which mean people are given access to particular lines of information because they need to know that and they are not given access to other lines of information.'

On the discretion Kelly was allowed in talking to the media
'If he was acting as he has described there, there is absolutely no difficulty about it at all. That would be, for somebody in his position, within the grounds of his discretion.'

On revealing Kelly's name
'We would be just as likely to be criticised if we suppressed the name. Indeed, I am afraid I cannot resist making this comment: I find some difficulty in squaring the press's desire to know the name of Dr Kelly with the press's criticism of us for providing it to them.'

Patrick Lamb

Deputy head of the Counter Proliferation Department, FCO (also appeared on days 4, 14 and 22)

- Kelly was hailed as such an expert on Iraq that senior officials would trust information he gave them over that contained in documents.
- He was used as a sounding board on chapter three of the dossier regarding life in Iraq under Saddam Hussein and also contributed to chapter two, giving information on Iraq's weapons programme from 1971 to 1998, when the inspectors stopped their work in Iraq. Kelly also wrote a box in the dossier on Iraq's biological weapons programme.
- Kelly did not get clearance for every conversation he had with a reporter, instead using his discretion.

Asked how involved Kelly was with the dossier
'At all times we would show the text to David and we would very much rely on his expertise and knowledge, as the source and person who could verify the accuracy of what we were producing.'

cont'd p.96

A sense of history – so take off your jacket

Sketch
Oliver Burkeman

The British court system has always been a natural home for great rhetoricians – judges and barristers with the inspiring capability, when the moment requires it, of investing their words with a palpable sense of history being made. Lord Hutton is not one of them.

'I hope the air-conditioning is going to work rather more effectively,' he said as he took his seat yesterday morning. 'If anybody would like to take off a jacket, please feel entirely free to do so.'

But no one did. Compared with the throbbing heat outside, Court 73 of the Royal Courts of Justice was pleasantly cool.

This might also be said precisely to describe the questioning style of the inquiry's lead counsel, James Dingemans QC, the pinstriped manifestation of non-confrontational calm.

Where TV lawyers bark 'No further questions, your honour!', Mr Dingemans asks his witness if there is anything they would like to add.

You half-expect him to slip into job interviewer mode: 'And are there any questions you'd like to ask us?'

His first witness was Terence Taylor, who used to be a UN weapons inspector alongside David Kelly. He appeared live on a videolink from Australia.

'I understand that it is evening in Australia,' Lord Hutton said, sounding a little surprised at the thought. 'So I bid you good evening.'

A transcript of the inquiry appears in real time, on a forest of monitors crowding the courtroom, but something very strange is going on with the stenographers.

'Mr Terence Thomas Taylor,' said the witness, when asked for his full name. 'Mr Inference Thomas Taylor,' read the screens.

A week and a half ago, Mr Taylor's testimony – that Dr Kelly was a 'superb' expert on weapons of mass destruction, the go-to guy for all the other go-to guys – might not have mattered all that much now, though it came as a defiant answer to the Walter Mitty question.

But it left the scientist's suicide as mysterious as ever: on the phone four days before his death, Mr Taylor said, Dr Kelly had been upbeat, looking forward to going back to Iraq.

Mr Dingemans pushed gently for any memory of distress.

Well, said Mr Taylor, perhaps he was 'mildly irritated' at the US consultants who had joined the weapons search.

But only mildly. It wasn't even the beginning of the shadow of an explanation.

Next came Richard Hatfield, the MoD's personnel chief, a pale man in a paler suit, who was asked to explain Dr Kelly's seniority in the civil service. Big mistake: if you think understanding the history of Iraq's programme of chemical and biological weaponry is intellectually challenging, try figuring out the difference between MoD payscale five and the Defence Evaluation and Research Agency payscale nine. Dr Kelly's work for the Proliferation and Arms Control Secretariat ('Professor Politician and Arms Control Secretariat,' read the live transcript) had left him adrift in a sea of incomprehensible salary-related bureaucracy, understandably concerned that his pay prospects had fallen into a 'black hole'.

But the documents describing his security clearance could not lie. Dr Kelly had reached the highest level, cleared for access to any top secret intelligence of British or American origin, Mr Dingemans noted.

'Yes,' said Mr Hatfield testily, 'but on a need to know basis.'

It wasn't clear what this distinction meant, if anything. Mr Dingemans, evidently, did not feel that he needed to know.

From then on, as the day's other witnesses took the stand, the evidence of Dr Kelly's role in the preparation of the September dossier – and the doubts of other senior experts over its claims – began to flow rapidly.

Mr Dingemans prefaced his interrogations with a courtesy that occasionally bordered on the patronising. 'If I say "the 45-minute claim", would you know what I was talking about?' he asked both Martin Howard, the MoD's amiable deputy intelligence chief, and Patrick Lamb, the Foreign Office weapons expert.

Mr Lamb, whose testimony of his happy working relationship with Dr Kelly was easily the most moving of the day, nodded to say that he did.

His expression, the merest flicker of a sad smile, seemed to suggest the answer to another question, one that all yesterday's witnesses would have answered unanimously, too: 'Do you wish that you didn't?' ∎

On Kelly's expertise
'If I had to make a choice between a textural choice and Dr Kelly, I would often back Dr Kelly ahead of the textural source.'

Asked if they had discussed chapter 3 of the dossier with Kelly
'When he came into the department we would, as a matter of course, show him and tell him where we were up to . . . We were keen . . . to use him as a sounding board and a source, if need be, of information and confirmation of any facts.

How Kelly felt about the dossier
'He was very supportive of the dossier and very supportive of the analysis put forward in the dossier.'

On the death of Kelly
'We worked extremely well in a very relaxed manner, a very happy manner in many respects. It was not a labour of love, it was something we thought was extremely important, continue to believe to be extremely important. I am only very saddened that that happy atmosphere has the shadow of Dr Kelly's death hanging over it.'

Martin Howard
Deputy chief of defence intelligence, MoD (also appeared on days 4 and 17)

- Disquiet on the dossier led two intelligence officials to protest to their bosses about the use of language and not the substance.
- Document passed by the government to the inquiry showed three areas of concern labelled 'recent production of CBW [chemical and biological weapons]', '45 minutes', and 'Saddam and the importance of CBW'.

- An internal assessment of Kelly said his advice had 'helped formulate' UK policy on Iraqi WMD.
- Intelligence about Iraq being able to use WMD within 45 minutes was received on 30 August 2002, and probably did not appear in the various drafts of the dossier until 15 September. He confirmed the information came from a single source, an Iraqi military officer, who was 'reliable'.

On intelligence doubts over the use of the 45-minute claim
'They were not differences of view about whether intelligence should be included or not, it was more about how the intelligence was described or how it should be interpreted. It was, for example, the difference between saying "intelligence suggests", "intelligence shows", "intelligence indicates". These meanings have quite a lot of – you know, to intelligence analysts they are quite important distinctions.'

Julian Miller

Chief of the assessment staff in Cabinet Office [provides classified assessments for the Joint Intelligence Committee]

- The September dossier on Iraq's weapons of mass destruction had been in preparation since February or March 2002, and those involved were aware from the outset that it might be published.
- It was not until 3 September 2002 that Tony Blair officially announced that the dossier was to be made public, and at that stage a decision was taken 'to slightly expand the basis to be more explicit about the role of intelligence'.
- The 45-minute claim was not included until 10 or 11 September, just a fortnight before the dossier was published on 24 September.

The evidence

- Miller insisted that Alastair Campbell was not responsible for the last-minute insertion of the 45-minute claim.

Asked if there was a transformation in the dossier that came about the week before publication, because of Campbell

'No, it would not have been true in either sense, in that I do not think there was a transformation the week before publication. And certainly changes such as the inclusion of the reference to 45 minutes were nothing to do with No. 10.' ■

Key Documents

David Kelly's citation for the Companion of St Michael and St George, 1996 (read out)

He devised the scientific basis for the enhanced biological warfare defence programme and led strong research groups in many key areas. Following the Gulf war he led the first biological warfare inspection in Iraq and has spent most of his time since either in Iraq or at various sites in the former Soviet Union helping to shed light on past biological-warfare-related activities and assisting the UK-US-RUS trilateral confidence-building process. He has pursued this work tirelessly and with good humour despite the significant hardship, hostility and personal risk encountered during extended periods of service in both countries. In 1991 he was appointed adviser to the UN Special Commission. His efforts in his specialist field have had consequences of international significance.

Email from defence intelligence official re the dossier, 10 September 2002

I have just spoken to David Kelly (ex Unscom BW and cleared) about the growth media amount . . . It states that UN inspectors could not account for up to 20 tonnes of growth media . . . The existing wording is not wrong — but it has a lost [lots] of spin on it!

Letter dated 16 July 1999 from Dr Andrew Shuttleworth, technical manager threat reduction, to Heather Skelton, personnel manager at DERA Porton Down

. . . Please could I ask for your help in resolving this issue as the poor chap hasn't had a pay rise for three years.

Letter from Kelly to then line manager Richard Scott on his annual review, 26 April 2001

I enclose my annual review form for your consideration and compilation. As you are aware I seem to have eluded the system for a while and I remain uncertain as to when I last completed such a form (if ever) . . . As you are aware I have been concerned that my responsibilities in my international work have not been recognised in terms of status and financial reward.

. . . I am sure that these issues can be resolved, and it is important that they are, since it affects such things as pensions!

'Objectives' section of Kelly's staff assessment, April 2002 to March 2003

David has provided excellent authoritative and timely advice to the FCO on all aspects of Iraqi WMD, he is recognised internationally as an expert.

Note of concerns expressed by DIS Staff re dossier 17 July 2003

The concerns fall into three main groups.

Recent Production of CBW Agent The DIS personnel concerned suggested that language in the dossier was too strong on the continued production of chemical and biological agents. These concerns related to the foreword, executive summary and main text.

The language in the dossier was stronger on this issue than it had been in the 9 September JIC assessment. This reflected the arrival of the further, corroborative intelligence on 11 (and 23) September. Because of its sensitivity, this had not been seen by the personnel concerned (as they acknowledged).

45 minutes Concerns related to the level of certainty in the foreword and executive summary. By this stage in the drafting process, following consultation with the DIS, the main text said 'intelligence indicates that the Iraqi military are able to deploy chemical or biological weapons within 45 minutes of an order to do so'. This reflected the language in the 9 September JIC paper. The executive summary expressed the point differently, as a judgement. The personnel concerned did not share this judgement. But it was agreed by the JIC.

Saddam and the importance of CBW The DIS personnel did not agree that intelligence 'shows' Saddam attached great importance to possessing WMD. They judged it only 'indicated' this. Several reports contributed to the stronger judgement, however. Again it was agreed by the JIC.

Letter: deputy chief of defence intelligence, 8 July 2003

Having scanned the Foreign Affairs Committee report of its 'Inquiry into the Decision to Go to War with Iraq' I have some concerns. I am not clear whether I have any obligations with regard to these matters, nor the extent of any conflict which may exist between my responsibilities to the department and the government, and my responsibilities to Parliament. I write to seek your advice on this issue.

Your records will show that as ADI NBC ST, and probably the most senior and experienced intelligence community official working on 'WMD', I was so concerned about the manner in which intelligence assessments for which I had some responsibility were being presented in the dossier of 24 September 2002 that I was moved to write formally to your predecessor, Tony Cragg, recording and explaining my reservations.

The Foreign Affairs Committee appears to consider it important that the Foreign Secretary told them 'that there had been no formal complaint from members of the security and intelligence services about the content of the (September 2002) dossier'. I believe his evidence was, in fact, that he was not aware of any such complaint, and there is no reason to suppose he should have become aware of mine. None the less, it is now a matter of record, and I feel very uneasy that my minute could be uncovered at some future date, and that I might be judged culpable for not having drawn attention to it.

I would be grateful if you could consider this and advise me accordingly. ■

Day 2
12 August 2003

Two BBC reporters – Andrew Gilligan and Susan Watts – told the inquiry that David Kelly named Alastair Campbell, Tony Blair's communications director, as the official who 'sexed up' the government's dossier on Iraqi weapons.

Kelly, under pressure from the MoD and perhaps concerned about his career and reputation, did not tell his Whitehall employers the full truth.

Andrew Gilligan

Defence and diplomatic correspondent of the *Today* programme, BBC Radio 4 (also appeared on days 18 and 19)

- On 22 May 2003 Gilligan and Kelly met at a central London hotel and talked for 45 minutes, consuming a bottle of Coca-Cola and a bottle of Appletise. Gilligan made notes on an electronic personal organiser.
- First official confirmation that the BBC harboured doubts about Gilligan's controversial report.
- Kevin Marsh, editor of the *Today* programme, wrote a memo warning that his report had been 'marred' by 'loose use of language and lack of judgement', and proposing a change to his working practices. The BBC governors also raised concerns, noting that 'careful language had not been applied' by Gilligan throughout his reporting.
- Gilligan admitted for the first time that his reporting was flawed.

On his first meeting with Kelly, 2001

'He was really quite open and helpful and, you know, often with officials they are rather cautious . . . In a funny way he was a sort of teacher almost.'

On the questions he asked Kelly

'We started by talking about other things and then we got on to the dossier; and I said, "What happened to it? When we last met, you were saying it was not very exciting." He said, "Yes, that is right, until the last week it was just as I told you. It was transformed in the week before publication." I said, "To make it sexier?" And he said, "Yes, to make it sexier." Then I said, "What do you mean? Can you give me some examples?" And he said the classic – he did not use the word example, he said the classic was the . . . the statement that WMD could be ready in 45 minutes, and most things in the dossier were single source . . . These are notes . . . They do not note everything that was said. They are not a verbatim transcript of the conversation. They are only highlights. Some words are abbreviated, some sentences are abbreviated. There are quite large portions of the conversation which I have not noted at all.'

On the wording of his earlier unscripted 6.07am broadcast on the *Today* programme

'With the benefit of hindsight, looking at it now with a fine toothcomb, I think it was not wrong, what I said, but it was not perfect either, and in hindsight I should have scripted that too.'

On concerns raised by *Today* editor Kevin Marsh over his reporting, a month after the story came out

'I do not think that an entirely fair analysis. It was written, as I say, a month after the broadcast. That is the only time in all the correspondence I see where Kevin expresses any kind of concern about the reporting of that story. And he never expressed it to me. It was written at a time of maximum pressure ... I mean, I have an email from him to me on 30 May which is the day after the story [see documents below].'

Asked if he was sure he was not mistaken over Kelly raising the issue of Campbell
'Absolutely. It is one of the things I remember most clearly.'

On his attempts to contact Dr Kelly after the story had come out
'In the later stages I very badly wanted to speak to him; but I knew ... that the risk might be that I would compromise him by trying to phone him. In fact, I did try to phone him once from a phone box and again I just got the answerphone and I did not leave a message again.

... I tried to contact him twice. Once before the main sort of fuss about my story blew up and then once after.

... I decided not to try to contact him on his mobile because I was concerned ... and this might be paranoid but it might be sensible, that either my calls or his were being monitored and any attempt by me to call his number might have led people to him.'

Susan Watts
BBC *Newsnight* science editor (also appeared on day 3)

- Had discussed the claim that Iraq could deploy weapons of mass destruction in 45 minutes with Kelly on 7 May 2002.
- Was told by Kelly that Campbell was responsible for 'sexing up' the Iraq intelligence dossier but dismissed the comment as a 'gossipy aside'.
- Confirmed that Kelly had 'extraordinary access' to government information – he had lunched with the Defence Secretary Geoff

Hoon. But she added that she had no other information to back up the notion that the comments about Campbell were anything other than throwaway gossip.

Asked if Dr Kelly mentioned the 45 minutes issue to her
'My shorthand notes show that regarding the 45 minutes issue Dr Kelly said to me that it was, and I quote, "a mistake to put in Alastair Campbell seeing something in there, single source but not corroborated, sounded good." ... Certainly not a revelation at all, I would characterise it as a gossipy aside comment.'

Asked why she did not make use of it
'I did not consider it particularly controversial. I felt it to be a glib statement. I was somewhat surprised that he would use a name and he appeared to be speculating in a way that he did not generally.' ∎

Key Documents

Excerpt from *Plague Wars* by Tom Mangold
If David Kelly were a tax inspector, he would recoup Britain's entire national debt. With his soft voice and his semantic precision, he is an inspector's inspector. He's led teams in the Soviet Union, then Russia, and is the oldest hand on the Unscom inspectorate; he is also the most respected – and, in Iraq, the most feared. He wears Clarks shoes, saggy comfortable pullovers, and silver-rimmed glasses. He is a Welshman from the Rhondda Valley, where you either drift into a life of local unemployment or rise to great heights elsewhere. He is married with three daughters, has been to Iraq 35 times, and knows where most of the biological bodies ought to be buried. Despite real strains on his marriage, he has made this assignment his life-work in the autumn of a long and honourable career.

Excerpt from Andrew Gilligan's note re the dossiers, read from the shorthand recorded on his electronic organiser and translated by him in court

Transformed week before publication to make it sexier. The classic was the 45 minutes. Most things in dossier were double source but that was single source. One source said it took 4 [5] minutes to set up a missile assembly, that was misinterpreted.

Most people in intelligence weren't happy with it because it didn't reflect the considered view they were putting forward.

Campbell: real information but unreliable, included against our wishes. Not in original draft – dull, he asked if anything else could go in.

Uranium from Africa – not nuclear expert but was very suspect, documents certainly forged or forgeries.

10 to 15 years ago there was a lot of information. With the concealment and deception operation there was far less information.

It [the programme] was small because you could not conceal a large programme and because it was actually quite hard to import things. The sanctions were effective. They did limit the programme. No usable weapons.

Excerpt from the *Mail on Sunday* article by Andrew Gilligan, 1 June 2003

'Nothing changed,' he said. 'Until the week before, it was just like I told you. It was transformed the week before publication, to make it sexier.'

. . . 'The classic,' he said 'was the statement that WMD were ready for use in 45 minutes. One source said it took 45 minutes to launch a missile and that was misinterpreted to mean that WMD could be deployed in 45 minutes. There was no evidence that they had loaded conventional missiles with WMD, or could do so anything like that quickly.' I asked him how this transformation happened. The answer was a single word. 'Campbell.'

Email from *Today* editor Kevin Marsh to Gilligan, 30 May 2003

Statement of the obvious I guess but it's really good to have you back here in the UK. Great week, great stories, well handled and well told. Course it's meant *Today* has had a great week too, and that has lifted everyone. We still have to have that conversation [annual appraisal] but since you are entirely nocturnal while I'm a normal human being we don't seem to meet too often. Maybe you could creek [sic] the coffin lid open next week during daylight hours. Anyway, it's great to have you back on your beat. Talk soon.

E-mail from Kevin Marsh to Stephen Mitchell, 27 June 2003

Some thoughts . . . clearly I have to talk to AG early next week: I hope that by then my worst fears — based on what I'm hearing from the spooks this afternoon — aren't realised. Assuming not, the guts of what I would say are: This story was a good piece of investigative journalism, marred by flawed reporting — our biggest millstone has been his loose use of language and lack of judgement in some of his phraseology.

It was marred also by the quantity of writing for other outlets that varied what was said or was loose with the terms of the story.

That it is in many ways a result of the loose and in some ways distant relationship he has been allowed to have with *Today*. ■

Day 3
13 August 2003

Evidence emerged revealing the full extent of Dr Kelly's concerns about the government's dossier. He described claims made by the government as 'spin', adding that it was 'desperate for information'. Divisions within the BBC, notably between Andrew Gilligan and Susan Watts, came into the open.

Susan Watts
BBC *Newsnight* science editor (also appeared on day 2)

- Watts criticised her BBC managers for attempting to 'mould' her work to corroborate Gilligan's controversial report.
- Kelly's tape recorded comments about Alastair Campbell were played to the inquiry.
- Watts accused Richard Sambrook, the BBC's head of news, of placing intense pressure on her to identify her source.

On the interpretation of her previous day's evidence
'I feel that there were significant differences between what Dr Kelly said to me and what Andrew Gilligan has reported that Dr Kelly said to him ... He did not say to me that the dossier was transformed in the last week. He certainly did not say the 45 minutes claim was inserted either by Alastair Campbell or by anyone else in government. In fact, he denied specifically that Alastair Campbell was involved, in the conversation on 30 May, which we will come to, which will become clearer. He was very

clear to me that the claim was in the original intelligence material
... And just to be clear on this, in my reports I did not mention
Alastair Campbell, for reasons which I think will become clear. I did
not say that he or any member of the government had inserted the
claim and I did not say that my source was a member of the intelligence services.'

On pressure to corroborate her story with Gilligan's
'I felt under some considerable pressure to reveal the identity of my
source [from] the BBC.

'And I also felt that the purpose of that was to help corroborate
the Andrew Gilligan allegations and not for any proper news
purpose. I continually stressed through all of this that I felt that my
two broadcasts on *Newsnight* stood and spoke for themselves.'

Asked what the differences were between her story and Gilligan's
'... I am most concerned about the fact that there was an attempt
to mould them so that they were corroborative, which I felt was
misguided and false.'

On Kelly's name being revealed
'When he gave evidence to the Foreign Affairs Committee, I formed
a view on listening to that evidence, that if I had been called to the
Foreign Affairs Committee which was a possibility ... I would then
have felt able to reveal him as the source of my stories. And the reason
for that is because under questioning from Mr Ottaway MP he was
given some – loosely quoted the quotes from him in my reports ...
he appears to deny that those are his quotes. I felt that together with
his having acknowledged having spoken to me, although I think he
was less than frank in describing the full nature of our relationship
and conversations, that those factors together relieved me of my obli-
gation to protect his identity as a confidentiality source.'

Gavin Hewitt
Special correspondent for the BBC's *10 O'Clock News*

- Said he had heard of Kelly when researching previous reports on Iraqi WMD, and decided to call him to speak, off the record, about Gilligan's story.
- Kelly told him that 'No. 10 spin came into play' and, while he believed that Iraq did have weapons of mass destruction, they were not 'a major threat'.
- When he asked if the 45-minute claim was inserted into the dossier against the advice of the intelligence services, Kelly told him: 'I am not sure I would go that far'.
- Considered the scientist a credible source who 'did not have an axe to grind' and was familiar with the subject.

Reconstructing his conversation with Kelly
'He said, "No. 10 spin came into play." I asked him what he meant by this, and he elaborated and he said he felt the essential quality of the intelligence provided by the intelligence services was fundamentally reasonable. That is the phrase, "fundamental information reasonable", but – and this is where his reservation came in – he felt that the dossier had been presented in a very black and white way. He expressed some caution about that. I think he would have liked more caveats.'

Richard Sambrook
BBC's director of news (also appeared on day 18)

- Rejected Watts's claim that he had attempted to mould her story.
- Said he had been 'struck by the similarities' between the Gilligan and Watts reports.

- He first asked Watts for the identity of her source. After Watts refused to tell him, Sambrook asked the editor of *Newsnight*, George Entwistle – a request later withdrawn.
- Said the BBC had owed Kelly a duty of confidentiality even after his evidence before a committee of MPs.

Asked if the BBC management were 'fed up' with the complaints made against them

'I would like to say that although Kevin [Marsh] has a colourful turn of phrase in internal emails to his colleagues, I do not think some of that tone characterises our approach or view of these complaints from Downing Street. We always take complaints from Downing Street extremely seriously. It was true we had a very high volume of them during the war, as indeed we generally tend to have at moments of tension, such as war or elections and so on. We do take them seriously but we did believe that we, from experience, had to look very closely at what was being complained about and in what terms because it is not always straightforward or clear cut.'

Asked about approaching Watts for Kelly's name

'Yes, it seems to me at that time what I was trying to do, having seen Ms Watts's reports on *Newsnight* I was struck by the similarity to the allegations made in Andrew Gilligan's report and it seemed to me highly likely they had come from the same person and, if so, it seemed to me the only responsible thing to do was to try to find out, if that was the case, what more might have been said in order either to corroborate or simply to establish what this source believed, given that Andrew Gilligan's report was coming under such vehement criticism.' ∎

Key Documents

Letter from Alastair Campbell to Richard Sambrook, BBC head of news, 1 April 2003

Andrew Gilligan claimed on Radio 5 that 'people here are saying the Republican Guard hasn't really been damaged at all and they could be right'. (R5 12.20). Can you tell me who told him the Republican Guard hasn't been damaged – the Iraqi Ministry of Information?

On what evidence does he base this claim – in particular the assertion that 'they could be right'?

Was this report monitored? Does Mr Gilligan have a minder?

Would you agree Andrew Gilligan's report yesterday broke several of the BBC's own guidelines. . .?

Reply from Richard Sambrook, 2 April 2003

Andrew was relaying what Iraqis had told him – and that is the way he puts it. Further, Andrew's judgement was self-evidently not definitive . . . On your point about monitoring and minding – I am sure that you have watched and listened enough to know that for nearly a fortnight – since the Iraqis changed their way of dealing with foreign journalists – we have been alerting our audiences that reporters cannot move around the city exactly as they please – and that pieces are monitored . . . You will not be surprised in the light of my remarks above that I do not accept that we have breached the guidelines in the way you state.

Letter from Alastair Campbell to Richard Sambrook, 2 April 2003

On Radio 4 this morning, Andrew Gilligan said:

'I've seen Saddam give two televised speeches and then a couple of other silent appearances if you like just talking to ministers and the two televised speeches I saw looked completely different. Indeed you might even say it was a different Saddam. Maybe it was. The backdrop was different, the appearance of the president was different, the way he spoke, one he was wearing

111

glasses the second he wasn't, one he was reading from a handwritten text the second he had a prepared speech. Lots of things were different so I'm not quite sure where these intelligence assessments come from it might just be more rubbish from Central Command.'

Do you believe the sentence was justified?

Letter from Richard Sambrook to Alastair Campbell, 4 April 2003

Thank you for your letter and the transcript of Andrew Gilligan on News 24. I agree his final phrase is unacceptable. In mitigation I would only say it was live at the end of an interview, the rest of which seems appropriate . . . this particular phrase was unacceptable, which I regret, and will take up with Andrew Gilligan.

Letter from Alastair Campbell, to Richard Sambrook, 5 June 2003

I am writing to complain about Andrew Gilligan's irresponsible reporting of what he claims to be information from 'intelligence sources'. As was clear from his report on the *Today* programme this morning he continues to display an extraordinary ignorance about intelligence issues. He said, for example, that the Joint Intelligence Committee (JIC) is a 'No. 10 committee on which intelligence agencies are represented'. He should know, because this is public knowledge, that the JIC is a Cabinet Office committee.

Email from Kevin Marsh, *Today* programme editor, to his boss Stephen Mitchell, 9 June, about Campbell's complaints

I started to look at this point by point but it's all drivel and, frankly, it'd be easy to get as confused as Campbell is. The man's flapping in the wind.

In another email, Marsh writes

I am more convinced than I was before that he is on the run or gone bonkers or both. ∎

Day 4
14 August 2002

Fresh evidence was revealed about how Tony Blair and Geoff Hoon, the Defence Secretary, personally intervened in the affair, backing a strategy that led to Dr Kelly having to give evidence to a televised hearing of the Commons Foreign Affairs Committee. The inquiry heard how Hoon overruled Sir Kevin Tebbit, the top civil servant at the MoD, who said Kelly should not be subjected to such an ordeal. Whitehall should 'show some regard for the man himself, he has come forward voluntarily, is not used to being thrust into the public eye, and is not on trial'. John Scarlett, chairman of the Joint Intelligence Committee (JIC), had no such sympathy. 'Kelly needs a proper security-style interview,' he advised.

Dr Bryan Wells

Kelly's line manager, director of counter proliferation and arms control at the Ministry of Defence. UK commissioner to Unmovic (also appeared on day 22)

- Suspicions in government at Kelly's contacts with the press first arose after an *Observer* article on 15 June 2003. Kelly denied that he was the source. By 19 June, Martin Howard, deputy chief of defence intelligence, had heard that Kelly had talked to Andrew Gilligan, and wanted the weapons expert interviewed.
- On 30 June Kelly wrote to Wells admitting meeting Gilligan, but denied being his source. On 4 July Kelly was interviewed by Richard Hatfield, the MoD head of personnel. The meeting

ended with Hatfield saying there would be no disciplinary action, but there would be if he repeated the offence.

- Kelly was called to a second interview on 7 July. Howard joined the interview. The same day Scarlett demanded a 'proper security-style interview [of Kelly] in which all these inconsistencies are thrashed out'. Wells and Howard coached Kelly on 14 July about possible questions he would face at the FAC and ISC. At the end of the 'coaching' session, Wells handed Kelly a reprimand letter.

- At 6pm on 17 July, Wells called the scientist's mobile. He got no reply. The next day, Kelly was found dead.

On Kelly's expertise
'David acted as my fount of knowledge on Unmovic . . . David was an official in the Ministry of Defence who had that sort of knowledge; so he was very important in briefing up the chain on that.'

Asked about the *Observer* article of 15 June 2003
'To the best of my recollection, the *Observer* article quoted a UK source who had seen the facilities – now, that is a very few number of people – and it said that that source believed that the mobile facilities were not for biological weapons but for hydrogen production. I recall David expressing that view to me.'

Asked how Kelly responded when the 'version of the riot act' was being read out to him at the interviewon 4 July 2002
'Mr Hatfield's office is close to Holborn and I walked with Dr Kelly back to my office in the Metropole building, that takes about 25 minutes. I then asked him into my office, after 10 minutes or so; and I said that he must obviously reflect and take on board what Mr Hatfield had said, we must await the letter that Mr Hatfield said he

would write and that I would help him take through further any actions that were necessary at that point.'

Asked whether he would describe a further meeting that took place on 7 July 2002 with Kelly as a 'security-style interview'

'No, I would not. The meeting was actually very friendly in tone. We wanted to be sure of certain aspects of David's account of his meeting with Mr Gilligan; and we wanted to help him explain, to elicit the details of his story.'

On his last attempts to contact Kelly, 17 July 2002

'I was phoned shortly before 6 o'clock to say that the second set of amendments were still in the process of being cleared by Dr Kelly; and he was not responding to his mobile. We had learned from Mrs Kelly that David had gone for a walk, so at around about 6 o'clock I rang David's mobile myself, and I did that because David had got into the habit in recent times of checking the number of the incoming mobile phone to check who it was. He would have instantly recognised my mobile phone. I did not receive an answer, but I left the mobile on. I believe it did [ring].'

Patrick Lamb

Deputy head of the counter-proliferation department, Foreign and Commonwealth Office (also appeared on days 1, 14 and 22)

- Concerns raised over a *Sunday Times* article of 13 April 2003 quoting Kelly on the capture of Iraqi General al-Saadi as saying he knew 'where all the bodies were buried'.
- Lamb said Kelly told him he had spoken to Gilligan before the controversial *Today* broadcast.

On Dr Kelly telling him that he had spoken to Gilligan and Watts
'My recollection is that on one meeting to my office, around late May, he mentioned [it] . . . I can remember David standing at the end of my office and he was talking to me . . . he said to me that he had spoken to Andrew Gilligan and Susan Watts . . . I consciously remember thinking that I had not been approached by him or asked by him to agree to any meeting with either Mr Gilligan or Ms Watts . . . I think it must be before the *Today* programme story broke . . . He simply said, "I have spoken to Gilligan and Watts".'

When he informed the MoD of Kelly's meetings with Watts and Gilligan
'At [an] informal reception on 17 June there was a meeting involving myself some, senior colleagues . . . and, in particular, Mr Howard. And in the context of that discussion, as we were discussing, as I recall, primarily the trailer issue, I said that I believed that David Kelly had spoken to Mr Gilligan and Ms Watts, that he had told me some time earlier that he had spoken to Gilligan and Watts, and I conveyed that information to Mr Howard on that occasion.'

Martin Howard

Deputy chief of defence intelligence, Ministry of Defence (also appeared on days 1 and 17)

- Blair said that Kelly should face a second grilling by MoD officials because he was not satisfied with the scientist's initial response to questions about whether he was Gilligan's source.
- Scarlett called for Kelly to face a 'proper security-style interview'.
- Howard had seen high-level correspondence saying the PM wanted 'more detail' about the differences between what Gilligan had told the FAC about his source, and what Kelly had told officials.

- Geoff Hoon, the Defence Secretary, overruled his most senior civil servant to insist that Kelly should appear before the Commons Foreign Affairs Committee
- Kelly told Howard he would deny to the MPs being Gilligan's source for the 45-minute claims. Howard told the scientist that he must answer questions 'according to your conscience'.

Asked about his knowledge of the circumstances of second personnel interview with Kelly

Martin Howard: I understand there were quite a lot of high-level discussions over the telephone between Sir Kevin and Sir David and possibly others. I recall seeing the response from Sir David Omand to Sir Kevin Tebbit which recorded the Prime Minister's views that before we decided on what are the next steps that should be taken, it would be sensible to try to go into a bit more detail, into the differences between what Dr Kelly had said and what Andrew Gilligan had claimed.'

James Dingemans: 'Your broad understanding lower down, although not that lower down the chain, sorry, was that people at a higher level had become involved and there was then going to be a second interview?'

MH: 'Yes, I think that sums it up; yes.'

On his coaching meeting with Kelly to prepare him for the FAC and ISC

'The third "tricky" area was if he was asked whether or not he was Gilligan's source. I said to him: well, you must answer that how you see fit according to your conscience. He asked me specifically, you know: "Can I say that I do not think I am Gilligan's source?" I said: "Well, you must say what you think right and what you think the facts are."'

John Williams

Director of communications, Foreign and Commonwealth Office

- During the hunt for Gilligan's source, media suspicion had earlier fallen on Lamb, Kelly's friend and head of counter proliferation at the Foreign Office.

On why he was called by the press

'Don [Macintyre, the *Independent*] and Ewan [MacAskill, the *Guardian*] both rang, to my recollection, believing it was a Foreign Office official, and I said, "Look it is not a Foreign Office official", because I did not see why Foreign Office officials, for instance like Patrick Lamb, who might have been speculated about ...' ■

Key Documents

Letter from David Kelly to Bryan Wells, 30 June 2003

I met with [the BBC reporter Andrew Gilligan] on 22 May for 45 minutes to privately discuss his Iraq experiences and definitely not to discuss the dossier (I would not have met with him had it been the case) . . . The issue of 45 minutes [the claim that Iraq could deploy chemical weapons within 45 minutes of an order that was included in the government's dossier last September] arose in terms of the threat (aerial and land launch) and I stated that I did not know what it refers to (which I do not).

He asked why it should be in the dossier and I replied probably for impact. He raised the issue of Alastair Campbell and since I was not involved in the process (not stated by me) I was unable to comment.

This issue was not discussed at any length and was essentially an aside. I made no allegations or accusations about any issue related to the dossier or the government's case for war . . . I did not discuss the 'immediacy' of the threat.

The discussion was not about the dossier. Had it been so then I would have indicated that from my extensive and authoritative knowledge of Iraq's WMD programme . . . the dossier was a fair reflection of open source information. I most certainly have never attempted to undermine government policy in any way especially since I was personally sympathetic to the war.

Letter from personnel director Richard Hatfield to Kelly, 9 July 2003

I interviewed you with your line manager, Dr Bryan Wells on Friday 4 July, about your letter to him of 30 June . . . I explained that your letter had serious implications since, on the basis of your own account, you appeared to have broken departmental regulations in having unauthorised and unreported conversations with journalists. Your conversation with Andrew Gilligan also appeared to be relevant to the controversy surrounding allegations made by Gilligan about the government's September 2002 dossier WMD.

. . . At the end, I concluded that you had indeed breached departmental instructions on numerous occasions by having conversations with journalists which had been neither authorised by nor reported to the MoD press office. I accepted your assurance that in general these were essentially background, technical briefings and that on many – but not all – occasions you had consulted the FCO press office informally. In the case of Gilligan, you had two arranged meetings (in February and May 2003) subsequent to your initial contact in the margins of an IISS seminar last September.

. . . As I made clear, these are serious breaches of standard departmental procedure and you were unable to give me any satisfactory explanation for your behaviour. Your contact with Gilligan was particularly ill-judged. Your discussion with him in May has also had awkward consequences for both yourself and the department which could easily have been avoided. I accept your assurance that these consequences were unforeseen and unintended and, in particular that as you state in your letter you did not make any allegations or accusations about the preparation of the September 2002 dossier. I also concluded on the basis of your account that you had not divulged any classified or otherwise privileged information. On that basis, I have concluded that although your behaviour fell well short of the standard that I would expect from a civil servant of your standing and experience, it would not be appropriate to initiate formal disciplinary proceedings . . . any further breach of departmental guidelines in dealing with the media would almost certainly result in disciplinary action, with potentially serious consequences.

You should be absolutely clear that while you are working in the MoD you are required to seek explicit authority from your line manager and the MoD press office before agreeing to talk to journalists, even if there may be occasions when there may be an advantage, additionally, in consulting the FCO. I would also urge you to be very cautious in any comments you might make at or in the margins of public seminars and the like. There is always the danger that such remarks may be taken out of context.

I should also remind you that the possibility of disciplinary action could be reopened if any facts were to come to light which appeared to call into question the account and assurances that you gave to me.

Letter from John Scarlett to Sir David Omand, the government's security co-ordinator, 7 July 2003

Gilligan must have got the 45-minute single intelligence report [revealing that the 45-minute claim was based on a single uncorroborated source] from somewhere, presumably Kelly. Conclusion: Kelly needs a proper security-style interview in which all these inconsistencies are thrashed out.

Letter from Martin Howard, deputy chief of defence intelligence, to John Scarlett, chairman of the Joint Intelligence Committee, 8 July 2003. The letter was copied to Alastair Campbell at Downing Street. At the top of the letter, in handwriting, were the words: 'the Prime Minister may find this of interest'

[Kelly] claims that he has never attempted to undermine government policy as he was personally sympathetic to the war because he recognised from a decade's work the menace of Iraq's ability to further develop a non-conventional weapons programme. He feels no unease over the dossier because it is completely coincident with his personal views on Iraq's unconventional weapons capability.

Undated memo from the MoD press office on what to tell the media when asked to justify the claim that Iraq could deploy chemical weapons within 45 minutes when the claim was based on a single source

Because it came from a reliable and established source, quoting a well-placed senior officer. The same standard was used for the public and classified assessments. Against the background of other reporting at the time, the reporting was assessed as credible.

From Kevin Tebbit, MoD permanent secretary, to Geoff Hoon, 10 July 2003

There have been requests to you for Dr Kelly to appear before both the FAC and the ISC (on the same day, 15 July).

We had already offered him to the ISC and I recommend that you agree to that request . . . As regards the FAC, however, I recommend that you resist, on grounds that the FAC inquiry is completed . . . and that a separate session to question Kelly would attach disproportionate importance to him in relation to the subject of their inquiry as a whole. The ISC, on the other hand, are only just beginning their work and are better placed to ensure that Kelly's views are placed in the proper context (he is, after all, not the government's principal adviser on the subject, nor even a senior one).

. . . A further reason for avoiding two hearings, back to back, is to show some regard for the man himself. He has come forward voluntarily, is not used to being thrust into the public eye, and is not on trial . . . This line may not be sustainable in strict institutional terms: the FAC reports to parliament, whereas the ISC, although drawn from Parliament, report formally to the Prime Minister. And I do not believe that the ISC have taken testimony in public before. But I think it worth a try at least.

Letter from Geoff Hoon's private secretary Peter Watkins to Jack Straw's private secretary Geoffrey Adams, 11 July 2003. Letter cc'd to Jonathan Powell, Alastair Campbell, Sir David Omand and John Scarlett

The Defence Secretary has given the request from the FAC careful consideration. There are reasons for resisting this request . . . It is fairer on the man himself not to expect him to appear before two parliamentary committees within the space of three hours.

On the other hand . . . presentationally, it would be difficult to defend a position in which the government had objected to Dr Kelly appearing before a committee of the House which takes evidence in public in favour of an appointed committee which meets in private.

. . . The Defence Secretary has, therefore, concluded that on balance we should agree to the FAC's request. Given that Dr Kelly is a relatively junior official who played only a limited role in the preparation of the dossier, we should invite Donald Anderson to agree that the committee will confine its questioning to matters directly relevant to Andrew Gilligan's evidence. I understand that No. 10 would be content with this approach.

Email from a civil servant, Colin Smith, to Tim Dowse, head of the Foreign Office non-proliferation department, on 14 July, a day before Kelly appeared in front of MPs in the Foreign Affairs Select Committee

David Kelly [is to be briefed] this afternoon for his appearances tomorrow before the FAC . . . [we] will strongly recommend that Kelly is not drawn on his assessment of the dossier (but stick to what he told Gilligan). Kelly is apparently feeling the pressure, and does not appear to be handling it well. ■

Day 5
18 August 2003

It was a day of potentially highly damaging evidence which went right to the heart of the government's case for war. The inquiry heard that Jonathan Powell, Tony Blair's chief of staff, sent an email to other close advisers of the Prime Minister just days before the Iraqi weapons dossier was published. He warned it would be wrong for Blair to claim Iraq's weapons programme showed Saddam Hussein presented an 'imminent threat' to the west, or even his 'Arab neighbours'.

The inquiry was also told that one of Blair's official spokesmen described the government's battle with the BBC as a 'game of chicken'.

Pam Teare
Ministry of Defence director of news (also appeared on day 19)

- Defended the way that Kelly's name was put into the public arena. Downing Street and the MoD provided clues to journalists, and the MoD offered to confirm the identity if they came up with the right name. Peter Knox, junior counsel for the inquiry, described the process as a 'charade'.
- The *Financial Times* got the correct name at around 5.30pm on 9 July 2003, followed by the *Guardian* 'fairly soon afterwards'.
- Said that Geoff Hoon had been denied the opportunity to appear on the *Today* programme to put his side of the story.

Asked if the process was 'a bit of a charade'
'The idea of Dr Kelly's name being made public had not been discussed with him. The time that you would have had to consider it,

between when he was consulted about the final version of this statement and when it went out, would have been insufficient for him to consider it properly and to make what other arrangements he needed. One of the purposes for saying to people that we would be prepared to confirm the right name was going back to what I have originally said, which was that we were seeking to avoid the people who were not involved being named in the media, and the only way we could seek to do that was to make it clear to journalists we would correct wrong names so they did not get into the public domain . . .'

Jonathan Powell
Downing Street chief of staff

- Admitted in an email that the draft document on Iraq's weapons of mass destruction failed to demonstrate a threat from Saddam Hussein.
- Government documents released show that Downing Street authorised a substantial rewrite of the dossier 'as per TB's discussion' – a reference to Tony Blair.
- Tied Blair – much more than had been realised until now – into the discussion about how to handle David Kelly.

Asked about a meeting on 7 July 2003 to discuss the government's response to the imminent publication of the Commons Foreign Affairs Committee meeting

'On 7 July we had – well, the meeting would be – it was a sort of running meeting, that the Prime Minister popped into a working breakfast that morning. He then came down to his office about 9 o'clock and asked to see David Omand and Kevin Tebbit and John Scarlett. They were not immediately available and a separate meeting was going on in Alastair Campbell's office to discuss the government's response to the FAC report including the Foreign Secretary and a number of officials.'

Asked if any minutes of meetings were kept
'No minutes were kept of this meeting or subsequent meetings we are probably going to discuss, no . . . It may seem odd to people from outside, so I looked through the diary for the two weeks of the period we are talking about and the usual pattern is about three written records for 17 meetings a day is sort of the average you get to because there is no purpose served by minutes unless they are either recording people visiting from outside, the president of Nigeria, or something like that, or if they are action points that need to be taken forward, something on school funding for example.'

Asked if any thought was given on 8 July 2003 to protecting Kelly's identity
'From the very beginning it was the view of most of us, in fact probably all of us . . . that in the end this was going to become public. This was the sort of thing we thought would become public if enough people knew about it. In fact in many ways we were surprised it had not already become public, both the fact that a person had come forward and who that particular individual was. So really the premise we were working from was not that this would indefinitely remain secret but that it probably would become public at some stage.'

Sir David Manning
British ambassador to the US and formerly foreign policy adviser to Blair and head of the overseas and defence secretariat in the Cabinet Office

● Acknowledged feelings running high in Downing Street when Kelly came forward.

- Said it was inevitable Kelly's name would become public.

Asked for his views on the way Kelly's name became public
'I believed from the time he came forward it was almost inevitable, given the processes in which we work, that his name would become known.'

Asked about the atmosphere in Downing Street just before Kelly came forward
'It was seen as a pretty direct attack on the integrity of the Prime Minister and officials at No. 10.'

Asked how senior civil servants perceived the allegations
'I think there were certainly moments of personal anger. I do not want to pretend they were not personally affronted by some of these attacks. But I think there was a sense this was an attack or a charge or an allegation of a different kind. It struck the very heart of whether or not you believe that the Prime Minister is going to tell the chairman of the Joint Intelligence Committee that his conclusions of his committee are inconvenient and they must be changed . . . And I think that was a charge that went beyond the usual sparring that goes on and was seen as a very fundamental attack on the processes of government and trust therein.' ■

Key Documents

MoD statement, released 8 July 2003, 5.45pm
An individual working in the MoD has come forward to volunteer that he met Andrew Gilligan of the BBC on 22 May. It was an unauthorised meeting. It took place one week before Mr Gilligan broadcast allegations against the government about the WMD dossier on the *Today* programme.

The person who has come forward has volunteered that he has known Mr Gilligan for some months. He says that he met Mr Gilligan in a central London hotel at Mr Gilligan's request. During the conversation Mr Gilligan raised the Iraqi WMD programme, including the '45-minute' issue. The official says that Mr Gilligan also raised the issue of Alastair Campbell.

The individual is an expert on WMD who has advised ministers on WMD and whose contribution to the dossier of September 2002 was to contribute towards drafts of historical accounts on UN inspections. He is not 'one of the senior officials in charge of drawing up the dossier'. He is not a member of the intelligence services or the Defence Intelligence Staff.

He says that when Mr Gilligan asked about the role of Alastair Campbell with regard to the 45-minute issue, he made no comment and explained that he was not involved in the process of drawing up the intelligence parts of the dossier.

He says he made no other comment about Mr Campbell. When Mr Gilligan asked him why the 45-minute point was in the dossier, he says he commented that it was 'probably for impact'. He says he did not see the 45-minute intelligence report on which it was based.

He has said that, as an expert in the field, he believes Saddam Hussein possessed WMD.

We do not know whether this official is the single source quoted by Mr Gilligan. Mr Gilligan told the FAC he had only one source for his story, and that the other three sources he mentioned to the FAC did not talk to him about the September dossier, or did so after the broadcast.

The MOD, with the individual's agreement, intend to give his name to the chairman of the Intelligence and Security Committee, in confidence, should they wish to interview him as part of their inquiry.

Briefing Q and A to MoD press officers on how to answer queries on Kelly's identity after he had come forward as a possible BBC source but before his name was made public. Date unknown
Who is the official? The official works in the MoD.
What is his name and post? We wouldn't normally volunteer a name. IF THE

CORRECT NAME IS GIVEN, we can confirm it and say that he is senior adviser to the proliferation secretariat.

Is he a senior figure? He is a middle-ranking official.

Do you believe he is the single source? It is not for us to say – only the BBC can confirm that.

Email from Alastair Campbell to Jonathan Powell, 5 September 2002

Re dossier, substantial rewrite, with JS And Julian M in charge, which JS will take to US next Friday, and be in shape Monday thereafter. Structure as per TB's discussion. Agreement that there has to be real intelligence material in their presentation as such.

Email from Powell to Campbell, 5 September 2002

What is the timing on preparation of it and publication? Will TB have something he can read on the plane to the US?

Email from Powell to John Scarlett, 17 September 2002

The dossier is good and convincing for those who are prepared to be convinced.

I have only three points, none of which affect the way the document is drafted or presented.

First the document does nothing to demonstrate a threat, let alone an imminent threat from Saddam. In other words it shows he has the means but it does not demonstrate he has the motive to attack his neighbours let alone the west. We will need to make it clear in launching the document that we do not claim that we have evidence that he is an imminent threat. The case we are making is that he has continued to develop WMD since 1998, and is in breach of UN resolutions. The international community has to enforce those resolutions if the UN is to be taken seriously.

Second we will be asked about the connections with al-Qaida . . .

Third, if I was Saddam I would take a party of western journalists to the Ibn Sina factory or one of the others pictured in the document to demonstrate there is nothing there. How do we close off that avenue to him in advance?

Email from Powell to Campbell and Scarlett, 19 September 2002

Found my copy. I think it is good.

I agree with Alastair you should drop the conclusion.

Alastair – what will be the headline in the *Standard* on day of publication? What do we want it to be?

I think the statement on p19 that 'Saddam is prepared to use chemical and biological weapons if he believes his regime is under threat' is a bit of a problem. It backs up the Don Macintyre argument that there is no CBW threat and we will only create one if we attack him. I think you should redraft the para. My memory of the intelligence is that he has set up plans to use CBW on western forces and that these weapons are integrated into his military planning.

It needs checking for typos, eg Iraqi in middle of page 27.

Email from Tom Kelly to Jonathan Powell and Clare Sumner, 10 July 2003

This is now a game of chicken with the Beeb – they only way they will shift is if they see the screw tightening. ■

Day 6
19 August 2003

The first star witness from Downing Street minimised his role in the drafting of the government's Iraqi weapons dossier, insisting it was under the 'ownership' of John Scarlett, chairman of the Joint Intelligence Committee, but also a man with whom he developed a close relationship. His evidence also revealed the close links between Tony Blair's chief spin doctor and the security and intelligence agencies.

Alastair Campbell
Prime Minister's director of communications and strategy (also appeared on day 20)

- Denied inserting the claim Saddam could activate WMDs within 45 minutes of an order to do so into the Iraq dossier, and said this was in the first draft which he received from the Joint Intelligence Committee (JIC).
- Stressed the dossier was entirely the work of John Scarlett, whose 'ownership' of the document was crucial to its credibility and whom he encouraged to use 'dry' language that was not colourful.
- Distanced himself from the Defence Secretary, Geoff Hoon, describing the naming strategy – which he insisted he had no part in – as wrong, and admitted that, with hindsight, the government could have handled Kelly better.
- The inquiry heard extracts from Campbell's diary, in which he referred to the 'ghastly Gilligan story'.

Asked why the publication of the dossier had been delayed

'There were two reasons really. The first was that it was not a terribly good document overall, as something that you would want to put into the public domain. The other reason was that the fear that doing it at the time it was being suggested was actually going to ramp up the issue at a time when, in fact, the Prime Minister and the government were trying to calm it. By September the Prime Minister took the view that this exclusively Iraq dossier should be put into the public domain.'

Asked who was involved in the writing of the dossier

'The decision was taken, either at that meeting or certainly by the 9th, that John Scarlett . . . he used the word "ownership", that John Scarlett felt he ought to have ownership of the dossier . . . I emphasised that the credibility of this document depended fundamentally upon it being the work of the Joint Intelligence Committee; and that was the touchstone of our approach right from that moment.'

Asked about a meeting with Scarlett on the presentation of the dossier

'I said, "The drier the better, cut the rhetoric." I think there were areas where the language was too colourful. And I also said the more intelligence-based it was, the better. We needed to have a clear explanation of where the material information in this dossier took things forward from what was in the IISS report and then gave some suggestions later re the different structure.'

Asked if he had any influence on the inclusion of the 45-minute claim

'None whatever. The words that you read out earlier were the words that were in the draft of the dossier that I saw on the evening of

cont'd p.134

131

British Richelieu takes his place in history

Sketch
David Aaronovitch

'How did he get here?' hissed a young journalist, suddenly spotting Alastair John Campbell sitting on a chair at the side of court 73. 'He just materialised.'

Perhaps one of the 12 empty MFI beech veneer bookcases that line the room had indeed silently revolved allowing the master of manipulation to slip in unseen. Or perhaps he'd just walked the few yards from the door when the young journalist wasn't looking. Here he was, the second power in the land, the PM's *eminence grise*, the British Richelieu, waiting his turn to be grilled in public.

Nothing quite like it had ever been seen in these isles before. In the gallery, a mixture of hacks, Tory frontbenchers with nothing better to do and incredulous members of the public congratulated themselves on being there and helping to make history.

Before the judge arrived Alastair John moved to his place in the witness box, with its personal computer screen and microphone with a lit-up red tip. Sitting at 90 degrees to the rest of us, AC was in full profile, and you could see what a contrast he was to his arch-enemy, Gilligan of the BBC. Where Gilligan was all uninviting curves, Campbell was made up entirely of angles.

The widow's peak of his hair, the vertical of his forehead, the long downward sweep of the nose, the set of the jaw, the long, equal lines running from nostril to chin, the cheekbones, the position of the hands and elbows, all as though some great didactic power was using him to illustrate advanced geometry.

But the Hutton inquiry isn't the kind of thing that *eminences grises* and powers behind thrones are used to. For a start, their private messages aren't usually displayed on large screens, or anywhere else.

How would Richelieu have fared, faced with something like, 'To: Milady, From: CR, cc: Jonathan Parvelle, Subject: Discrediting Queen. Agree re diamond tags idea. Suggest cut off two for surprise presentation HM. Authorise 200 pistoles re expenses (accommodation, assassins, ambushes etc.)'?

The inquiry's own top lawyer, Mr Dingemans – his pinstriped back turned to us and maintaining a heroic standing position behind his little lectern for hours – had the Campbell diary and asked questions based on its entries. Mr Campbell had the diary and answered them. We alone did not have the diaries, so we couldn't see whether he also recorded what he'd had for lunch, when he practised the bagpipes and what he really thought of George Bush.

What we did discover, as Campbell answered questions, in his own chalk-lined voice (emphatically not the ridiculous 'I will kill you now, Mr Bond' one given to him by the BBC PM programme yesterday), was just how much stuff there was going around.

He was continually being pestered by messages from flunkeys acting 'beyond their pay grades', volunteering unwanted suggestions about dossiers and WMDs, and usually stating the bleeding obvious.

'I receive an awful lot of emails,' said Campbell, 'that I don't read.' You could see why. He'd get a message from Tim Dim, copied to Brian Brown. 'Who is Tim Dim?' Mr Dingemans asked at one point. 'He was at the Cabinet Office but he's gone to defence,' answered Campbell. 'And who's Brian Brown?' 'He was at the Cabinet Office, but he's gone to defence,' came the reply. No wonder it's a bit chaotic.

And phone calls. They arrived for him when he was on holiday, when he was in the bath, in Kuwait, in New York at a funeral ('sorry, I must just get this'), at Wimbledon with his son. And all of them, for months, were about Andrew Gilligan, the Moriarty of the BBC.

But how had the man of power become so obsessed with this one journalist that we had all eventually ended up here, enjoying ourselves so enormously (whatever the sombre occasion for our presence)? Well, he revealed, he'd tried everything in his repertoire with the BBC, from soft bullying, through medium bullying to hard bullying. And none of it had worked.

It was frustrating and infuriating, he said, 'that an allegation can be made by the foremost broadcasting organisation in the country, and there's absolutely nothing we can do about it'.

Had the gallery been made up of less cynical people, there would have been tears. And that was the point really. Because it was difficult to know, as it has been all through this business, who the powerful people really were – the man in the box speaking, or the folk with the notebooks deciding which words to report and what the story was going to be.

And hard to tell whether this new Hutton way of doing business, out in the open, might not ultimately diminish the power of both. ∎

Guardian, 20 August 2003

133

September 10th; and I had no input, output, influence upon them, whatsoever at any stage in the process.'

On his discussions with Hoon on what to do about the source for the Gilligan stories

'I had always felt about this story that Mr Gilligan probably did have a source, but that he exaggerated the source and he exaggerated what the source said. I think what Mr Hoon was saying was his initial instinct, was this person has to be dealt with severely, but then he actually thought: well, he has come forward, he has come forward in the spirit of openness and honesty and he is claiming he has been misrepresented if he is the source.

. . . He [Hoon] actually said his initial instinct was, as I say, to be severe in this regard but there was a case for trying get some kind of plea bargain . . . In other words, the person had been honest and open in coming forward, had acknowledged some of the, if you like, offences that were being described, but was adamant he had not been responsible for others.'

Asked about the MoD's naming strategy

'I was being instructed by the Prime Minister just to stay a little bit distant from this, because I was so centrally involved in relation to the events concerning the Foreign Affairs Committee. I feel . . . we did not push this in the way that we should . . . what I feel I maybe should have expressed more forcefully at that time is: look, if you are in this kind of situation you do have to have some element of control over the process here. You cannot just let this sort of dribble out in a way that you are not clear how it is then going to unfold . . . far better it would have been for that to be announced properly, cleanly, straightforwardly and then you can actually put in place all the proper support that somebody who is not used to this kind of pressure can then maybe better deal with.'

Asked by Lord Hutton if the government could not have 'battened down the hatches' to protect the identity of Kelly

'The impression I got was of a very strong, resolute character, clearly of deep conviction and who had been in many difficult, stressful circumstances, and I just do not think it crossed anybody's mind that it might take the turn that it did.'

Asked about the death of Kelly

'Like everybody, I have found it very distressing that Dr Kelly, who was clearly somebody of distinction, had died in this way and obviously I have . . . thought very, very deeply about the background to all this. So I think all I would say is that I just find it very, very sad.'

On his diary

'I write a diary not every day but several times a week. It is not intended for publication. It is a series of observations about what I do and what I witness.' ∎

Key Documents

Alastair Campbell's diary (read out by Campbell)

[3 September 2002, the toughest questions faced by the government]
Why was this such an important issue to the British government now? Why Iraq? Why only Iraq, as it were, that was being singled out? The answer which I think the Prime Minister gave was that it was a unique threat.

[5 September 2002, on the contents of the dossier]
It had to be revelatory; we needed to show it was new and informative and part of a bigger case.

The evidence

[24 September 2002, on the publication of the dossier]
Gilligan and Marshall [who works for Sky News] and the so-called experts banged on about nothing new but a combination of TB statement and the gradual serious build-up to the dossier had brought us into a better position.

[29 May 2003, on the Gilligan story]
Talking to the press about a ghastly Gilligan story claiming that the intelligence services were not happy with the dossier . . . this may be a repeat of some of the stories that were published at the time, the stories of discontent within the agencies.

[1 June 2003, reaction to press coverage]
It was grim. It was grim for me and it was grim for TB and there is this huge stuff about trust.

[2 June 2003, after the PM's visit to Iraq]
The main problem was that there had been no WMD discoveries beyond the two labs and no matter how much we said about other priorities, the public were being told as a matter of fact that we had done wrong.

[27 June 2003, after appearing on *Channel 4 News*]
I felt my response was angry and probably too angry, but I did feel at that point the sense of frustration when I knew the story was wrong. I had a very strong sense that most people at the BBC were admitting privately they knew the story was wrong but I could not get any form of public redress at all. ∎

Day 7
20 August 2003

Alastair Campbell wanted to leak details about David Kelly to a favoured newspaper two days before his identity was publicly revealed, the inquiry heard. Downing Street press officers and special advisers discussed how to harden up the Iraqi weapons dossier to convince the public and MPs that Saddam Hussein presented a serious threat.

Sir Kevin Tebbit

Permanent secretary at the Ministry of Defence (also appeared on day 24)

- The top civil servant at the Ministry of Defence, Sir Kevin testified to the Hutton Inquiry about the keen interest the Prime Minister took after Kelly came forward, and why the scientist had to testify in public about his meeting with a BBC reporter.
- On 30 June Kelly admitted meeting Gilligan and on 3 July Sir Kevin discussed the development with the Defence Secretary, Geoff Hoon. A *Times* article on 5 July had hardened his view that Kelly was the source.
- The seriousness with which ministers viewed the charges could not be underestimated.
- Sir Kevin said it was seen as 'inevitable' that Kelly's name would be learnt by the media, and even before any statement was made by the MoD his identity was the subject of office gossip.

On Hoon's early feelings on the matter

'Mr Hoon was very concerned about the finalisation of the Foreign Affairs Committee report into – based really on Andrew Gilligan's allegations; and he was very concerned that information should be brought to light to correct, as it were, the public record, and that we should not be seen to be covering it up, since it was highly relevant to the inquiry that the Foreign Affairs Committee was conducting. My view was this was absolutely right and proper but we did first need to establish whether there was a disciplinary issue here.'

On his reaction to the *Times* article on 5 July 2003

'I decided that it was necessary to update my assessment over the weekend to suggest more strongly that this probably was, indeed, the source.'

Asked if he knew of the Prime Minister's views

'I was told by David Omand that the Prime Minister was following this very, very closely indeed, that he was not minded to ask for any precipitate action but he did want to consider this carefully before taking further steps; but the implication was that he wanted to do something about it.'

On pressure put on Kelly

'I believed it important that whatever Dr Kelly did was of his own volition and of his own free will, and that he was not being put under duress to say or do anything that he did not believe.'

On Kelly being known as the source

'After all of this had happened, a member of my staff came to say farewell to me, a commodore who was the director of operational audit, and said to me, "Oh we knew all about this. I was at a cocktail party on the Tattershall Castle and it was talked about then." I said, "Really. What was the date?" He said it was 4 July . . . Mr Hatfield told me that his discussions with Dr Kelly were always on the basis that it was almost certain that this would come up, that it was virtually inevitable. He did not record it in those terms but those were his words to me. And Dr Kelly seemed to accept that.'

On the state of Kelly
'I was not aware that he was not appearing to handle pressure well. That did not correspond to anything else I was hearing.'

On his attitude towards Kelly
'I confess there I was still having a certain feeling for the man; I did not want to put him through more than I had to.'

Asked if he agreed with the line taken by Hoon that Kelly should appear before both committees
'I acquiesced. It is perfectly reasonable that it is for ministers to decide who appears before committees, not for officials, I mean, and that was the Secretary of State's prerogative and I accepted it.'

On his feelings about the affair
'I have thought long and hard about this issue. As you can imagine, as permanent secretary I have felt a deep sense of responsibility, not of culpability but of responsibility in this area, since he was a member of my staff and my staff were talking to him. So his death came as a terrible shock. I have thought long and hard about the approach that was taken, whether it was reasonable to ensure that Dr Kelly came forward to tell his story. I still believe that to have been the right course of action.'

Godric Smith

One of the Prime Minister's two official spokesmen (also appeared on day 21)

- The Downing Street press office discussed how to harden up the contents of the draft dossier.
- Godric Smith took part in a teleconference between Campbell and Hoon on 7 July 2003 at which naming Kelly was discussed.
- Campbell suggested leaking Kelly's name to selected media.

On the Downing Street press office's involvement in compiling the dossier

'My view was clearly this was an issue where people would have very strongly held views, I think that went without saying, but that given we were setting out to the public the intelligence which underpinned the Prime Minister's belief, that was what was guiding us.'

Asked about the teleconference on 7 July

'. . . Alastair floated the idea that the news that an individual had come forward who could be the possible source be given that evening to one paper . . . [Afterwards] I reflected on what I had heard and thought that it was a bad idea. I said as much to Tom and asked whether he agreed; and he did, so I said that the best thing was to get Alastair on the phone so we could tell him. [Campbell agreed with him].'

Tom Kelly

One of the Prime Minister's two official spokesmen (also appeared on day 21)

- Controversial description of David Kelly as a Walter Mitty fantasist was an attempt to explain issues 'from the government's perspective' – a shift from his previous position that the remark was 'one of several questions facing all parties, not as a definitive statement of my view, or that of the government'.

● Questioned about his email reference to Downing Street's battle with the BBC as a 'game of chicken with the Beeb'.

On his contribution to the dossier debate in the Downing Street press office

'I was being asked to comment, if you like, as a sounding board rather than as someone who is going to make a substantive contribution to the dossier. I also needed to, if you like, get sight of some of the drafts, so as to be prepared to answer questions on the document.'

Asked to explain his email talking of a 'game of chicken with the Beeb'

'The language . . . is not one that perhaps I would normally use but I was talking to a close colleague with whom I talk on a very regular basis, and one whom, in particular, I had talked a lot to about this issue. I had, throughout this whole dispute, been of the view that we should try and look out for any way at all of de-escalating the dispute consistent with getting the original charge corrected . . .'

Asked why he told an *Independent* journalist that Kelly was a Walter Mitty fantasist

'I wanted simply the journalist to be aware of the possible questions and issues from the government's perspective. I was not expecting what I said to be reported in any way . . . Whatever my motives, it was a mistake that led to that intrusion and I have to take responsibility for that mistake.' ■

Key Documents

Nearly contemporaneous notes of a meeting in the Prime Minister's study, 7 and 8 July 2003, written by Sir David Omand and dated 21/07/2003

There was also a review of the weekend decision not to inform the FAC before the publication of their report that Dr Kelly had come forward to say that he had met Mr Gilligan . . . There was some questioning from the PM about what we knew about Dr Kelly, and whether we could find out more about his views. Kevin Tebbit agreed to report back. Kevin Tebbit warned that Dr Kelly was an expert on Iraqi WMD and if he was summoned to give evidence some of it might be uncomfortable on specifics such as the likelihood of there being weapons systems being ready for use within 45 minutes. But he believed from what he had said to Richard Hatfield that Dr Kelly had no doubts that there were Iraqi WMD programmes . . . He reiterated that Dr Kelly had come forward of his own volition, and that as far as MoD was concerned there was no question of any offence having been committed under the Official Secrets Act . . . Dr Kelly's continued cooperation was therefore essential.

Email from Downing Street press officer Daniel Pruce to Alastair Campbell, 11 September 2002, 10.04am, with the subject Draft Dossier (J Scarlett Version of 10 Sept). Under the heading 'Feel'

Our aim should also be to convey the impression that things have not been static in Iraq but that over the past decade he has been aggressively and relentlessly pursuing WMD while brutally repressing his own people.

Reply email from Campbell's adviser Philip Bassett, 10.34am the same day

Very long way to go, I think. Think we're in a lot of trouble with this as it stands now.

Reply email from Godric Smith to Campbell and Daniel Pruce, 11 September 2002, 12.35pm

I think there is material here we can work with but it is a bit of a muddle and needs a lot more clarity in the guts of it in terms of what is new/old.

Reply email from Bassett to Smith, Campbell and Pruce, 3.27pm, the same day

Agree with Godric & also think it needs to be written more in officialese, lots of it is too journalistic as it now stands, with some of it (eg opening chapter as a biog of Saddam!) reading like *STimes* at its worst . . . crucially, though, it's intelligence-lite.

Reply email from Tom Kelly to Campbell, cc'd to Pruce, Smith and Bassett, 11.59am

This does have some new elements to play with, but there is one central weakness – we do not differentiate enough between capacity and intent. We know that he is a bad man and has done bad things in the past. We know he is trying to get WMD – and this shows those attempts are intensifying. But can we show why we think he intends to use them aggressively, rather than in self-defence? We need that to counter the argument that Saddam is bad, but not mad.

Email from Tom Kelly to Jonathan Powell

This is now a game of chicken with the Beeb — the only way they will shift is they see the screw tightening.

From a statement by Tom Kelly, apologising for referring to David Kelly as a Walter Mitty fantasist

I deeply regret, therefore, that what I thought was a private conversation with a journalist last week has led to further public controversy. ■

Day 8
21 August 2003

Journalists described in detail how the Ministry of Defence and Downing Street press officers helped them to identify David Kelly. Earlier, Donald Anderson MP, chairman of the Foreign Affairs Committee (FAC), struggled to defend his committee's questioning of Kelly and the restrictions imposed by Defence Secretary Geoff Hoon.

Donald Anderson MP
Foreign Affairs Committee chairman

- Chaired the Foreign Affairs Committee which interviewed Kelly, Andrew Gilligan and Alastair Campbell on 15 July 2003.
- Gilligan had sent an email to two MPs on the Commons Foreign Affairs Committee suggesting questions to ask Dr Kelly.
- Anderson said he learnt that Kelly was subjected to an 'extensive [MoD] briefing' before his grilling by MPs which went 'well beyond the parameters' set out to him by Hoon.

On Kelly's appearance at the FAC
'When he did not want to answer directly, he clearly was on top of the subject and did so. The only problem we had was he was speaking extremely softly and we had a – it was a very sultry, hot afternoon, and the fans were on and I had to ask the clerk to turn the fans off I recall at one point. I do recall, my lord, that I personally could not hear some of what Dr Kelly was saying, and I had the

problem as: look I do not want to intervene too often but let me say, from time to time, please speak up.'

On Kelly's preparation for the FAC hearing
'I honestly, my lord, did not think about that at the time although I have subsequently learnt that there was an extensive briefing provided for Dr Kelly by the Ministry of Defence and a briefing which went well beyond the parameters which the Secretary of State had provided for me in his letter.'

Asked if it was appropriate that someone who has previously appeared before the FAC should be suggesting questions to one of its members
'I know of no precedent for someone who is a witness and therefore it is very unusual – well, it is unprecedented in my view.'

Nicholas Rufford
Sunday Times reporter (also appeared on day 22)

- Had known Kelly for some time, speaking to him up to 40 times.
- On the day after the MoD statement that an official had come forward was released, Rufford drove to see Kelly.

On Kelly's state when he drove to see him
'In appearance he looked thinner than I remember. He looked pale and he looked tired.'

What happened when he asked Kelly if he was the source for the Gilligan story
'First of all, I said, "Did you meet Andrew Gilligan?" He said that he had. I said had he met him at the Charing Cross Hotel. He said he had.

And I said, "Has the account of the conversation been accurately reported?" His response to that was, "I talked to him about factual stuff, the rest is bullshit . . ." It was very strong language for Dr Kelly to use.'

His treatment by the MoD

'He then split his comments. He said, for the record he said they had been pretty good about it. He said he had not been reprimanded. Then he said, off the record: I have been through the wringer. I asked him whether he knew his name was going to come out and he said: I am a bit shocked. I was told it would all be confidential . . . He said to me: it has been a pretty difficult time for me, as you can imagine.'

James Blitz

Political editor of the *Financial Times*

- Helped to identify Kelly by a briefing at Downing Street.
- Was told that the official was an expert in chemical and biological weapons – and that he worked for the MoD but was paid by another department.

On his putting the name to the MoD press chief, Pam Teare

'I told Ms Teare I had gathered from Mr Adams [another *FT* journalist] that she had confirmed to him that the individual was Dr David Kelly. She told me this was correct. I established with her what his job title was and this appeared in the article which I had given the inquiry and which appeared that night. During that conversation I told Ms Teare I was planning to write in the *FT* the next day that Dr David Kelly was the individual who had been mentioned in the MoD statement. I told Ms Teare I wished to speak to Dr Kelly directly about this matter to see if he wished to make any comment. I asked Ms Teare if she could put me in touch with him. Ms Teare told me the MoD had a policy to confirm the name to any journalist who offered it. Ms Teare also told me that a decision had been taken by the MoD that in the event the name was confirmed to a newspaper, that newspaper would be told that he would not be available for interview.'

Richard Norton-Taylor
Security affairs editor of the *Guardian*

- Detail from the MoD press office that the source was a former UN weapons inspector narrowed the field of candidates to 10 people.
- Clues led Norton-Taylor to enter 'Britain' and 'Unscom' into an internet search engine, which produced Kelly's name, which was then put to the MoD press office.
- Tells of widespread unease in the intelligence community over dossier.

On the intelligence community's attitude towards the dossier
'There was widespread unease throughout the intelligence community, which was not happy about the dossier in the first place. That was early spring probably in 2002 . . . People were saying there was nothing new to say, they felt under pressure probably they would have to come up with something "new" – The nature of intelligence is made of judgements and assessments and interpretation, rather than hard evidence and . . . as the year went on they knew that the government was pressing for and by September had decided to have a published dossier. But in the end, I think they learnt to live with it. They said their political masters wanted this and rather through gritted teeth I think they accepted that.'

Asked about the clues given by the MoD on 9 July 2003
'I was told this person had been a former – I was asking about their background, what kind of work he had done and so on, that he was a former Unscom weapons inspector . . . A crucial thing I would say I was told.'

How he discovered the name
'A colleague mentioned someone who he remembered as an Unscom person . . . So I then just quickly passed on that name to the MoD and they said no. But at the same time I went to the internet and searched through Google and I pressed a couple of words in. I typed in the search engine something like "Britain" plus "Unscom" plus maybe one other word. About the first or second item on that list that came up on Google was a lecture David Kelly had given, I think in America, and it said that he was a former British Unscom inspector. So that was one name I had very early on . . . It was by chance actually.'

Peter Beaumont
Foreign affairs editor of the *Observer*

- Told of intelligence service concerns following publication of the dossier.
- Wrote an article published in the *Observer* on 15 June 2003 that quoted a biological weapons expert working for the government who said that the mobile facilities then found in Iraq were not for biological weapons but for hydrogen production.

Asked about his conversation with Kelly before the *Observer* article of 15 June 2003
'He had a vague idea what I was calling about but he wanted to know, and I pointed to the article we had written the week before and he

said, "I am sorry, I could not possibly have seen that." So I told him the substance of what it was . . . When I pressed him on . . . what he meant, he said, "Well, the facilities are as the Iraqis describe them.""

Thomas Baldwin
Reporter for *The Times*

- Wrote an article published on 4 June 2003 quoting cabinet minister John Reid suggesting that rogue elements in the intelligence services were trying to undermine the government.
- Attended a meeting with BBC executive Richard Sambrook in which he said Gilligan's freelance writing would be curtailed.
- Refused to identify sources for his stories.

On the issue running out of steam before Kelly was named
'I think by the time the name was actually disclosed interest was waning. I think you have heard already that there was some frustration within government that – certain parts of the government anyway, that the name could not come out earlier; and a lot of journalism is about timing; and this . . . sense was that the heat was going out of this issue.'

Michael Evans
Defence editor of *The Times*

- Put 20 names to the MoD culled from an official book of civil servants.

Asked where Kelly was on the list
'Dr Kelly was not on that particular list . . . He is name number 21 . . . Clearly Dr Kelly was the last name.'

David Broucher

Member of the diplomatic service and currently a permanent representative
to the Conference on Disarmament in Geneva

- Kelly told the diplomat six months earlier that he would
  'probably be found dead in the woods' if the American and
  British invasion of Iraq went ahead.
- Kelly confirmed to him there had been a 'robust' debate between
  Downing Street and the intelligence services about the
  September dossier on weapons of mass destruction.
- He also expressed scepticism about British claims that Iraq's
  weapons capability could be deployed quickly.
- Kelly had been in direct contact with senior Iraqi scientists and
  officials he knew, promising them the war could be avoided, and
  feared he had 'betrayed' these contacts and that the invasion had
  left him in a 'morally ambiguous' position.

Asked how Kelly had felt about the situation in Iraq, February 2003

'My impression was that he felt that he was in some personal difficulty or embarrassment over this, because he believed that the
invasion might go ahead anyway and that somehow this put him in
a morally ambiguous position . . . I drew the inference that he might
be concerned that he would be thought to have lied to some of his
contacts in Iraq.'

On Kelly's views of the dossier

'He said to me that there had been a lot of pressure to make the
dossier as robust as possible; that every judgement in it had been
closely fought over; and that it was the best that the JIC could do. I
believe that it may have been in this connection that he then went
on to explain the point about the readiness of Iraq's biological

weapons, the fact they could not use them quickly, and that this was relevant to the point about 45 minutes.'

On the last conversation they had

'As Kelly was leaving I said to him, "What will happen if Iraq is invaded?" And his reply was . . . "I will probably be found dead in the woods."' ■

Key Documents

Letter from Geoff Hoon to Donald Anderson, chair of the FAC, 11 July 2003

Although the FAC has now completed its own inquiry, I can understand why you also wish to see Dr Kelly. I am prepared to agree to this on the clear understanding that Dr Kelly will be questioned only on those matters which are directly relevant to the evidence that you were given by Andrew Gilligan, and not on the wider issue of Iraqi WMD and the preparation of the dossier. Dr Kelly was not involved in the process of drawing up the intelligence parts of the dossier.

As I noted above, Dr Kelly will have appeared earlier the same day before the ISC. I hope that you will bear this in mind and not detain him for longer than about the same period of time indicated by the ISC [45 minutes]. As he is not used to this degree of public exposure, Dr Kelly has asked if he could be accompanied by a colleague. MoD officials will discuss this further with the clerk.

Email from Gilligan to Greg Simpson, researcher for David Chidgey MP, member of the FAC, 14 July 2003

. . . He also told my colleague Susan Watts, science editor of Newsnight (who described him as 'a senior official intimately involved with the process of pulling together the dossier').

The evidence

'In the run-up to the dossier, the government was obsessed with finding intelligence to justify an immediate Iraqi threat. While we were agreed on the potential Iraq threat in the future, there was less agreement about the threat the Iraqis posed at that moment.

'That was the real concern – not so much what they had now, but what they would have in the future. But that unfortunately was not expressed strongly in the dossier, because that takes the case away for war to a certain extent . . .

'(The 45-minute point) was a statement that was made and it got out of all proportion. They were desperate for information. They were pushing hard for information that could be released. That was one that popped up and it was seized on, and it's unfortunate that it was. That is why there is the argument between the intelligence services and No. 10, because they picked up on it and once they'd picked up on it you can't pull it back from them . . . So many people were saying "Well, we're not sure about that" . . . because the word-smithing is actually quite important.'

Is Kelly our source?

We are not ruling anyone in or out as the source. I had many conversations with people inside and outside the intelligence community about the issue of Iraqi WMD and the dossier. We suspect the MoD of playing games to try to eliminate names.

However, if, as the MoD has said, Dr Kelly's involvement in the dossier was only tangential, he cannot be our source. Two of my source's claims which have proved to be true – that the 45-minute point derived from a single informant, and that it came in late – have been shown to be true. Some facts could only have been known to someone closely involved in compiling the dossier until a late stage.

Note of a Downing Street briefing on the afternoon of 9 July 2003, held by Tom Kelly

Asked if the person who had come forward was a man, the Prime Minister's official spokesman said that journalists had a 50% chance of being right. Asked whether he had been suspended from his job, he declined to get into personnel matters. Put to him that the person did not work for the MoD, the PMOS said the person was a technical expert who had worked for a variety of government departments including the MoD with whom he was currently working, salary paid by another department.

Email from David Broucher to Patrick Lamb at the Foreign Office, 5 August 2003

In a conversation in Geneva which I think took place in late February, he [Dr Kelly] explained to me that he thought that the weapons inspectors could have a good idea what the Iraqis had built and destroyed, because they [Iraqis] were inveterate keepers of written records, something they had, he thought, learnt from us. There was a paper file on everything down to the smallest item.

Dr Kelly said that his Iraqi contacts had pointed out to him that revealing too much about their state of readiness might well heighten the risk that they would be attacked. To gain their trust he had been obliged to assure them that if they complied with the weapons inspectors' demands they would not be. The implication was that if an invasion now went ahead, that would make him a liar and he would have betrayed his contacts, some of whom might be killed as a direct result of his actions. I asked what would happen then, and he replied, in a throwaway line, that he would probably be found dead in the woods. I did not think much of this at the time, taking it to be a hint that the Iraqis might try to take revenge against him, something that did not seem at all fanciful then. I now see that he may have been thinking on rather different lines. ■

Day 9
26 August 2003

John Scarlett and Sir David Omand — two of the Prime Minister's closest security and intelligence advisers — delivered the strongest criticism so far of BBC allegations that Downing Street 'sexed up' the weapons dossier inserting claims it knew were wrong.

In stark contrast, Andrew Mackinlay earlier gave a robust defence of his questioning of Dr Kelly at the Commons Foreign Affairs Committee and of the rights of parliament.

Andrew Mackinlay MP
Labour member of the Foreign Affairs Committee

- Labour MP who asked Kelly a series of tough questions during a televised hearing of the Commons Foreign Affairs Committee, had received hate mail. Defended his questioning of Kelly when he appeared before the committee on 15 July 2003.
- Told the inquiry of his anger that Geoff Hoon would only allow the weapons expert to testify on what he had told Andrew Gilligan.
- Accused ministers of obstructing scrutiny of their actions and said he did not believe Kelly had come forward of his own volition.
- Described as 'highly inappropriate' an email sent by Gilligan to the Liberal Democrat MP David Chidgey on questions to ask Kelly.

On Hoon seeking to limit what the committee could ask Kelly
'I consider it a monumental cheek of the Secretary of State to try and tell us what we should and could inquire into and the duration.

I was prepared to live with it because I was prepared to do battle, if and when it was necessary.'

On Gilligan sending his fellow committee member David Chidgey MP an email suggesting questions to put to Kelly

'I think this highly inappropriate . . . [If I was sent one] I would consider it an affront that I was going to be fed this by somebody who was so, so central to all the debate and discussion, absolutely outrageous.'

On Kelly's appearance before the FAC

'He was softly spoken, I thought very controlled, except for – I mention this in my witness statement – two people who accompanied him and sat immediately behind him. To me that was quite significant . . .

'I noticed these two people who I would say escorted him in, sat immediately behind him . . . I immediately I think started to imagine he had been sort of like briefed, programmed, prepared, that these were the minders.'

On referring to Kelly as 'chaff'

'A lot of people do not understand the word "chaff" . . . chaff to a weapons expert is what is thrown out by our destroyers and from our fighter aircraft to deflect incoming [missiles] . . . In the context of this it did not seem to be inappropriate. He was a defence expert. I told you I thought he was set up. I told you he was the fall guy. I think that is self-explanatory why I think that is so. That was the reason for that word. No offence was meant.'

On Kelly coming forward voluntarily

'I do not buy this business of him coming forward voluntarily. I think by this time the heat was on.'

The evidence

On his own role in the Kelly case
'The repeated showing of that narrow clip has resulted in an awful lot of hate mail and so on . . . I think also that clip does not educate or inform, it misleads, because it does not give the backdrop of this, but it created a very bad climate and I have had lots of things . . . Just to complete the picture, my local newspaper had daubed on its walls, "Kelly's blood on Mackinlay's hands".'

John Scarlett
Chairman of the Joint Intelligence Committee (also appeared on day 21)

- British intelligence chiefs, under pressure from Downing Street, made a desperate plea to their agencies to search for something fresh to put into the government's dossier.
- Insisted that Downing Street had not interfered in the intelligence judgements in the dossier, but admitted Alastair Campbell, the director of communications at No. 10, had asked if the language could be 'tightened'.
- Said that the 45-minute claim referred to battlefield munitions, not missiles.
- Denied that senior members of the intelligence community were unhappy with the contents and judgements of the unfinished document, but he admitted that there were some who were uneasy that a precedent was being set in which intelligence assessments were being made public for the first time and that this might harm operational security.

About the origin of the 45-minute claim
'This was a report from a single source. It was an established and reliable line of reporting; and it was quoting a senior Iraqi military officer in a position to know this information.'

**Asked who was in overall charge of the dossier and Alastair
Campbell's use of the word 'ownership' to describe Scarlett's
involvment**

'Ownership, that I was absolutely to be in charge.'

Asked if he was in final charge or if it was someone else

'It was almost completely clear by this stage, by the time this note
went out, that I was that person. But there was still some slight
ambiguity about who would be responsible for the parts of the
dossier which were not going to be intelligence-based. This relates
to human rights and weapons inspections, in particular, where the
FCO had been seen to be the lead department.

'. . . In practice, and I am sure it was Alastair Campbell's understanding at the time that I went away as the person in charge of the
whole exercise.'

**Asked if an email with a 'last! call for any items of intelligence
that agencies think can and should be included' (see 'Key
Documents' below) meant pressure was being brought to
bear about the dossier's contents**

'No, it is not a fair analysis. This is simply part of the work in
progress. In effect these questions are questions seeking more detail
to support statements or areas of discussion which are in the draft
. . . It was entirely consistent with what I wanted to do, and the fact
that it was wanted for the document to be as strong as possible was
also what I wanted – strong in the sense of it being comprehensive,
as detailed as possible, as the intelligence allowed, and as informative as possible.'

On Campbell proposing changes to the dossier

'Yes, I was accepting. And I see absolutely nothing difficult in that
at all. It was entirely up to me as to how to respond. I was

completely in control of this process. I felt it at the time and feel it subsequently.'

Asked if intelligence staff felt the draft dossier had been too strong on the 45-minute claim

'The proposal from DIS related to the way in which it was worded in the executive summary, as a judgement. They had no objection to this item being included in the text of the dossier and they did not object to it being included in the executive summary, but they queried whether it was right to include it as a judgement and they suggested that it should be qualified in the executive summary with the words, I think it was "intelligence suggests that", rather than it being placed as a judgement.'

Asked about his email calling for a 'security-style' interview with Kelly

'What I meant was that the interview that had taken place so far seemed to me to leave important questions uncovered, these needed to be pursued, and so a further interview was necessary. That interview would need to be thorough and forensic, and designed to reach as satisfactory an answer as possible, one way or the other, to these outstanding questions. I thought and meant no more than that.'

On Kelly and the nature of the 45-minute claim

'Andrew Gilligan, when quoting his source, said that the source believed that the report was relating to warheads for missiles. Which, in fact, it was not; it related to munitions, which we had interpreted to mean battlefield mortar shells or small calibre weaponry, quite different from missiles. So it is possible that Dr Kelly, who, as I still understand it, never did see or probably did not see the original report, was in a state of genuine confusion about what the report actually said.'

Sir David Omand
Security and intelligence coordinator at the Cabinet Office

- Provided further evidence of Blair's intense interest in the Kelly affair.
- Told the inquiry of discussions about whether details of Kelly should be released.
- The inquiry heard evidence that Kelly had not given his 'specific consent' to being named publicly.
- The government initially dismissed Kelly as a relatively junior civil servant. But it has since emerged that he helped write parts of the dossier and was a member of a key Ministry of Defence intelligence committee which reviewed it only days before it was published.
- Giving Kelly's name to the Foreign Affairs Committee, which was notoriously leaky, was, in fact, 'tantamount to making it public'.

Asked if there was a 'looking into cupboards' to see if there was anything that had been overlooked that might be put in the dossier
'I think you have to remember the Joint Intelligence Committee itself was anxious to produce as strong a document as possible, consistent with the protection of intelligence sources and methods.'

On the high-level discussion of the Kelly case
'The explanation lies in the front pages of the newspapers, that this was an issue which had dominated political debate in the country for a considerable time and showed no signs of diminishing. It was a matter of intense interest and concern to the Prime Minister, in view of the nature of the allegations which were being made. It was a matter of concern to me, because it was directly challenging the integrity of a process for which I was responsible.' ■

Key Documents

Excerpts from Kelly's appearance before the FAC, 15 July 2003

Kelly: I have met very few journalists.

Andrew Mackinlay: I heard 'few', but who are the ones in your mind's eye at this moment? What are their names?

Kelly: That will be provided to you by the Ministry of Defence.

Andrew Mackinlay: No, I am asking you now. This is the high court of Parliament and I want you to tell the committee who you met . . . I reckon you are chaff; you have been thrown up to divert our probing. Have you ever felt like a fall guy? You have been set up, have you not?

Email from one of Scarlett's assessment staff sent on 11 September 2002 at 12.42pm. Subject: Iraq dossier – Questions from No. 10

We have now received comments back from No. 10 on the first draft . . . they have further questions and areas they would like expanded.

. . . Can we say how many chemical and biological weapons Iraq currently has by type? If we can't give weapon numbers can we give any idea on the quantity of agent available?

. . . I appreciate everyone, us included, has been around at least some of these buoys before . . . But No. 10, through the chairman, want the document to be as strong as possible within the bounds of available intelligence. This is therefore a last! call for any items of intelligence that agencies think can and should be included.

Responses needed by 12.00 tomorrow.

Memo from Campbell to Scarlett, 17 September 2002

. . . In light of the last 24 hours, I think we should make more of the point about current concealment plans. Also in the executive summary, it would be stronger if we said that despite sanctions and the policy of containment, he has made real progress, even if this echoes the Prime Minister.

Letter from John Scarlett to Sir David Omand, 7 July 2003

Gilligan must have got the 45-minute single intelligence report [revealing that the 45-minute claim was based on a single uncorroborated source] from somewhere, presumably Kelly. Conclusion: Kelly needs a proper security-style interview in which all these inconsistencies are thrashed out.

Note made by Scarlett of 7 July 2003 meeting in Prime Minister's office

Brief discussion of whether Dr Kelly should be the source. Prime Minister states that it must be handled according to proper MoD and Civil Service procedures.

[Later meeting] Brief discussion of MoD source. If he appeared before a committee, would he be likely to support or otherwise the government position? JSC [John Scarlett] to seek advice from MoD. Was he/was he not the source? No further decision possible without knowing more about his contact with Gilligan.

Memo from Sir David Omand, 21 July 2003, headed 'Meetings in the Prime Minister's study, 7 and 8 July 2003'

There was some questioning from the PM about what we knew about Dr Kelly, and whether we could find out more about his views. ■

Day 10
27 August 2003

Geoff Hoon was the first minister to give evidence. He distanced himself from decisions on Dr Kelly taken by his own officials while also pointing the finger at Downing Street in what was widely described in the media as a 'not me guv' approach. Two of Kelly's close colleagues in the MoD described how pressure was being put on the scientist to provide more and more information about his contacts with journalists during the day he took his final walk.

Geoff Hoon
Secretary of State for Defence (also appeared on day 20)

- The Defence Secretary denied he had been part of a 'conspiracy' to publicly name David Kelly.
- The decision to issue a press statement disclosing that an unnamed official had come forward as Andrew Gilligan's potential source had been taken by officials in Downing Street and the Cabinet Office.
- He knew of the media strategy to confirm Dr Kelly's identity if put by reporters, but had not seen the question and answer briefing, compiled by his head of news, Pam Teare, that gave strong hints to Dr Kelly's identity. Nor was he aware Downing Street was briefing political journalists with clues.
- He said the Prime Minister's chief of staff Jonathan Powell told him to write to Gavyn Davies, the chairman of the BBC board of governors, naming Dr Kelly.

- Believed Kelly had been fairly treated, and was not convinced he was Gilligan's source until after his death.

His responsibilities as the cabinet minister in charge of the Ministry of Defence

'When I first arrived in the Ministry of Defence I think it was the then Chief of Defence Staff described the leadership of the Ministry of Defence as a three-legged stool. He had responsibility for military matters; the permanent secretary had responsibility for personnel matters, civil service; and I was responsible for political leadership of the department.'

On his own role in the drafting of the dossier

'I saw two drafts of the dossier in the week beginning 16 September 2002, a relatively late stage in the process of the drafting, and I did not offer any comments or suggest any changes to it.'

On suggestions he had lunch with Kelly

'It is my practice from time to time to eat in the Old War Office Building canteen. That was particularly the case in the course of the conflict because I was there for long periods of the time and throughout weekends. When I am there, I routinely talk to members of the armed forces but also obviously to officials. On this particular occasion I had lunch with a private secretary from my private office. At the end of lunch we were approached by an official, I did not know who it was. We talked about Iraq. We discussed the government policy, which the official said he strongly supported; and it was not a formal occasion in any sense at all. It was the kind of conversation that I had routinely with people in the Ministry of Defence. I did not know that it was Dr Kelly at the time. I only realised that it was Dr Kelly when, after his death, I visited his

cont'd p.166

163

Need a decision? Ask the boys in the postroom

Sketch
Simon Hoggart

Geoff Hoon slid into his seat at the Hutton inquiry. He looked relaxed, a lawyer being questioned by a lawyer, in front of a dozen or so lawyers, under the aegis of a jolly important lawyer. This was not a dolphin trying to ride a bike. He was comfortable, in his own world, among his own people.

And he started well. There was a poignant moment when he described enjoying a tasty meal in the Ministry of Defence canteen: we got the impression that the Secretary of State likes nothing better than scoffing an all-day breakfast with the lads from procurement.

Once an official he didn't know, but who, he learnt later from David Kelly's daughter, was Dr Kelly himself, had approached his table and told him he 'strongly supported' the government's Iraq policy.

Nice one! It was the first time in the inquiry that Dr Kelly had

spoken from the grave, and it turned out he was backing Geoff! Our boy was playing a blinder.

Then it started to go wrong. He became more uncomfy. He began to wriggle. His sentences became longer and convoluted. They straggled like drunks past a bus stop, each new clause and phrase offering fresh hope that the sentence might finish, but the hope dashed as the end remained as elusive as ever.

He was asked if he or Alastair Campbell had wanted Richard Hatfield, the MoD personnel wallah, to offer Dr Kelly a 'plea bargain'.

'In a sense, my lord, without it being in any way a formalised agreement, and I would want to emphasise that this was not, in any way, acted on by Richard Hatfield, or anyone else, that that might have been seen to be of the kind Alastair Campbell in the course of his summarising our conversation ...'

As the sentence wove leglessly about, the judge halted its progress by emitting a fine, growling, swooping and diving legal 'Yurrrrrrrs', its magnificent cadence echoing round the court like the bell of a great cathedral.

I am told that at chamber dinners, judges compete to see how many syllables they can squeeze into the word 'yes'. If the appreciative laughter which greeted this superlative utterance is any guide, Lord Hutton is a shoo-in winner this Christmas.

Then we got to the main point of the matter, which was that Geoff knew nothing. Or very little. The picture he painted of himself was as Young Mr Grace in the sitcom *Are You Being Served?* He might be the figure-head of the MoD, this vast semi-military operation, but that was all he was.

Over in Downing Street the hotshot new McKinsey-trained management team were making big decisions without telling him. In the store itself, junior staff were rushing round interviewing people, finding things out, taking steps, sending memos – and all without bothering to tell him.

It got embarrassing. 'I was not aware that those doubts were being expressed elsewhere ... I was not present at that meeting ... well, I was aware that there had been a number of discussions ...'

Then he was asked: 'Were you aware that this material was being distributed at lobby meetings?'

'I wasn't aware at the time,' he said.

Had he known that his own special adviser was overlooking the outing of Dr Kelly to the press? 'I wasn't aware at the time, but I subsequently became aware ...'

In other words, the boys in the postroom knew more than he. The canteen ladies were better briefed.

So Geoff knew nothing. If they fire him when Hutton reports, he might learn more. At least he won't be Secretary of State, up there in his lonely office, out of touch with everyone, Jim Hacker plaintively begging Sir Humphrey to come upstairs and tell him something – anything. ∎

Guardian, 28 August 2003

wife and daughters and one of the daughters reminded me of this meeting and this occasion.'

On the role of Sir Kevin Tebbit, pointing out that it was up to Sir Kevin, along with Richard Hatfield, the ministry's personnel director, to decide whether or not Kelly should be disciplined and how he should be treated

'As far as any personnel issues were concerned, the responsibility was clearly that of the permanent secretary.'

On his decision to put Kelly before both the ISC and the FAC, against the advice of Sir Kevin Tebbit

'I was certainly aware that the Prime Minister took essentially the same view that I did, that it would be extraordinarily difficult to explain to parliament and to the Foreign Affairs Committee why we were refusing permission for an official who clearly had something relevant to say about their previous deliberations, why we would refuse permission for him to appear before that select committee.'

Asked how he knew what Tony Blair's views were

'I had not spoken to him directly. I think that came in a view from Jonathan Powell.'

Where the idea had come from to send a letter to the BBC chairman of governors, Gavyn Davies, on 9 July 2003, in which Hoon named Kelly for the first time to someone outside the inner Whitehall circle

'There was certainly some discussion, because I think the suggestion for naming Dr Kelly at this stage to Gavyn Davies, I think it actually came from Jonathan Powell.'

When asked what Campbell had meant when he told the inquiry that Hoon had mentioned a 'plea bargain' in dealing with Kelly

'There was no mention of any kind of a deal or plea bargain. It was simply perhaps Alastair's summary of the material that I had set out to him and the material I had set out was entirely retrospective. It was not in any way suggesting how the matter would be taken forward.'

Asked about the key question and answer document where MoD press officers agreed to identify Kelly if his name was put to them

'I did not see this Q and A and played no part in its preparation, so it is a little difficult for me to comment about any underlying purpose. But if you are suggesting that there was some deliberate effort here to identify Dr Kelly, I say that is absolutely wrong and there was certainly no effort by me or my office to do that.'

On the letter sent by his private secretary Peter Watkins to the Foreign Office setting out Hoon's apparent view that Kelly should appear before the Commons Foreign Affairs Committee

'It was certainly a summary of the decision I took. My private secretary is at pains to point out that the word "presentation-ally", which has attracted a great deal of interest, was not used by me.'

On the Prime Minister's security co-ordinator Sir David Omand's idea to contact the parliamentary Intelligence and Security Committee about Kelly as a means of applying pressure on the BBC to reveal Gilligan's source

'I was not party to these discussions.'

John Clark

Wing commander in the Royal Air Force (also appeared day 22)

- Wing Commander Clark, a colleague and friend who accompanied him to his interviews by MPs on two successive days, said Kelly was under stress.
- Kelly had left his home and gone to Cornwall to avoid the media. He returned to London to testify to MPs, but that left his arthritic wife to get back home on her own.
- Kelly found his interviews before the Foreign Affairs Committee and the Intelligence and Security Committee the most pressured he had experienced.
- On the day of Kelly's death, MoD staff were trying to get answers to questions tabled by FAC member Andrew Mackinley MP on the extent of Kelly's dealings with journalists. Wing Commander Clark rang his mobile 20 minutes after he set off on his final walk, and kept trying every 15 minutes.

On Dr Kelly's contacts with the media

'He made no secret of that fact. He was quite proud that he had many press contacts, from diverse backgrounds.'

Asked how Kelly had felt before the FAC and ISC hearings

'I asked him how he felt. He was tired. He was clearly not looking forward to the hearings. I did say: did you think when you wrote the letter to Dr Wells that we would end up in this position in the full glare of the press and he said under no circumstances had he felt, when he submitted his letter to Dr Wells, that he would have ended up in that position.'

On a question put by Liberal Democrat MP David Chidgey on the FAC, who read to the scientist a quote he was alleged to

**have made to Ms Watts. The quote was when compiling the
September 2002 dossier the government was 'obsessed' with
finding intelligence that Iraq was an immediate threat. He
also said the 45-minute claim had 'got out of all proportion'.
That quote was exactly the same as one that Gilligan had
emailed to the MP, telling him that Kelly had been the source
of Ms Watts's story**

'He was totally thrown by the question or the quotation that was
given to him from Susan Watts. He spoke about that when he
came back to the office. He did say that threw him. He had not
expected or anticipated that that would have come to the fore at
that forum.'

What Kelly had said to colleagues after the hearings

'He said that the pressure associated with the hearings was worse
than that associated with the interview he had had in association
with his PhD. I think up until then that had been the most stressful
interview he had perhaps had.'

**When told of the domestic turmoil in the Kelly household
when Kelly had returned from Cornwall to London**

'He basically said he was holding up all right but it had all come to
a head and his wife had taken it really very badly. Whether that was
in association with the additional pressure of having to get back the
day before under her own steam, I do not know, but he did say that
his wife had been very upset on the morning of the 17th.'

On his last attempts to get hold of Kelly

'I was surprised that I could not get two-way with him because he was
always very proud of his ability to be contacted. He took his mobile
phone everywhere . . . So on this occasion when I rang him I asked his
wife in the first instance when she said he went for a walk, did he have

his mobile, and she did not know. I rang and it was switched off and I was very surprised that it had been switched off . . .

'I hoped that he would perhaps switch on his mobile so I probably tried about every 15 minutes for the remainder of the time.'

James Harrison

Deputy director for Counter Proliferation and Arms Control, Ministry of Defence (also appeared on day 22)

- Took over the task of trying to reach Kelly at 4.45pm, tried again at 5.50pm and failed to get through.
- Said that the phone had rung, and not been answered – which suggests that Kelly had switched his mobile on again and would have found messages asking for more details about his media contacts.

On his last attempt to get hold of Kelly
'My clear recollection was that I had rung his mobile number and that the phone had rung but not been answered.'

Ann Taylor MP

Chair of the Intelligence and Security Committee

- Senior Labour MP said the dossier had failed to provide enough evidence to justify action against Saddam Hussein and had outlined her reservations in an email to Downing Street six days before the dossier was published.
- Underlined her irritation with No. 10 when she accused it of attempting to use her committee to announce that an unnamed

scientist – later identified as Kelly – had confirmed that he had met Andrew Gilligan, the BBC reporter. She said her colleagues had turned down a request to make the announcement about the scientist in a letter to the committee.

On why her colleagues had turned down a request from the MoD to announce that an unnamed scientist had come forward

'If the government or Ministry of Defence or any other part of the government wanted to make a public statement about somebody coming forward as a possible source, then they should do that, not do it by way of a letter to the committee . . . we did not want to be party to something which was probably being bounced on us . . . it did not seem appropriate . . . that the fact of a possible source coming forward should be made public by way of that open letter.' ■

Key Documents

Letter from Hoon to Davies, 9 July 2003

This is not about the divulging of sources.

So that you can establish whether the name of the person who has come forward is the same as the name given to BBC management by Andrew Gilligan, I am now prepared to tell you that his name is David Kelly, adviser to the Proliferation and Arms Control Secretariat in the MoD.

I trust that the BBC internal inquiry into Mr Gilligan's dealings with the MoD press office will be broadened to include this matter.

Letter from Peter Watkins, Hoon's private secretary, to Jack Straw's office, 11 July 2003

Presentationally, it would be difficult to defend a position in which the government had objected to Dr Kelly appearing before a committee which takes

The evidence

evidence in public in favour of an appointed committee which meets in private. Although the ISC has considered taking evidence in public before and might decide to do so on this occasion, this could set an unwelcome precedent . . .

Note taken by James Harrison of his attempts to get hold of Kelly
Rang Mrs K about 17.50 or so. Having tried mobile – rang, no answer to see if back. Gone for a walk by the river. Bad headache. Had intended to go about 2 o'clock, but delayed (by phone calls?) Sometimes goes on long route . . . Rang PS/S of S [private secretary to Secretary of State, Peter Watkins] 18.30 to report delay. Defer till am. Rang Mrs K about 18.40. To say leaving – don't ring back. We'll speak in the morning. Mrs K sounded okay.

Email from Matthew Rycroft to Jonathan Powell, John Scarlett, Alastair Campbell and others outlining Ann Taylor's views on the dossier, 19 September 2002
. . . The hardest questions in the debate, not fully answered by the dossier, remain why now and why Saddam. The PM should take these on in his statement to undercut critics. ■

Day 11
28 August 2003

The Prime Minister insisted that the government's dossier was under the 'ownership' of John Scarlett, chairman of the Joint Intelligence Committee. He said he backed a plan by his close advisers, notably Sir David Omand, his security co-ordinator, for Dr Kelly to give evidence to the parliamentary Intelligence and Security Committee – a process which was to hasten the scientist's public outing. Tony Blair argued that Kelly's name would anyway come out sooner or later and that he did not want the government to be accused of a cover-up.

Gavyn Davies, chairman of the BBC, acknowledged that some of the BBC's journalists made mistakes. But he also accused the government of playing games, and Downing Street of exaggerating allegations made by the BBC and of escalating the dispute.

Tony Blair MP
Prime Minister

- Insisted the original BBC report that prompted the row went to the heart of the integrity of the government and the intelligence services. Blair portrayed it as a resigning issue.
- He revealed that he decided to publish the dossier after a phone call with President George Bush late in August 2002.
- Said the dossier should be read in conjunction with his Commons statement on the day it was published in which he softened the Iraqi threat, saying he did not know when Saddam might use his weapons but he had to be stopped.

173

- Placed himself at the heart of the naming strategy, testifying that he had passed on details to the BBC chairman, Gavyn Davies, in private on 7 July 2003 that 'someone' had come forward to admit that he had met Andrew Gilligan. The admission undermined earlier attempts by Downing Street to portray the Ministry of Defence as the 'lead department' in the naming strategy.

Edited extracts of Blair's testimony, grouped by issue

The drafting of the Iraq dossier

Lord Hutton: Good morning ladies and gentlemen. Good morning, Prime Minister.

Tony Blair: Good morning, my lord.

James Dingemans: I do not think we need an introduction. May I start with the dossiers? We have heard that a dossier was being produced in February 2002 which related to four countries, one of which was Iraq. Could you explain the background to that?

TB: After September 11 there was a renewed sense of urgency on the question of rogue states and weapons of mass destruction and the link with terrorism, and there was some thought given to trying to bring all that together, identifying the countries that were a particular source of concern to us, one of which was Iraq. [It was not published in case it 'inflamed' the international situation. Instead a new dossier, featuring only Iraq, was ordered on 3 September.]

JD: Had you been aware of the proposed role that Mr Campbell was going to take in assisting with the presentation?

TB: Well, I was in no doubt that he would assist with the presentation. I . . . knew that it had to be a document that was owned by the Joint Intelligence Committee and the chairman, John Scarlett. That was obviously important because we could not produce this as evidence that came from anything other than an objective source.

JD: Were you aware that this [editing] process was going on?

TB: Yes, of course, and it was important that it made the best case that we could make, subject, obviously, to it being owned by the Joint Intelligence Committee and that the items of intelligence should be those that the agencies thought could and should be included. So, if you like, it was a process in which they were in charge of this, correctly, because it was so important to make sure that no one could question the intelligence that was in it as coming from the genuine intelligence agencies. But obviously, I mean I had to present this to Parliament. I was going to make a statement. Parliament was going to be recalled. We were concerned to make sure that we could produce, within the bounds of what was right and proper, the best case.

JD: Can you help us on how the foreword was produced?

TB: The normal practice here is I would have told Alastair Campbell what are the items I think that are important, specific points that should be in it, on the basis of the drafts produced, and the foreword was expressed obviously to be my foreword.

JD: I imagine there were various discussions about the dossier, is that right?

TB: There were discussions going on about the dossier. I mean, as I say, it was more the facts in the dossier and the statement that were the key items. There could well have been discussions as drafts of the foreword were circulating around.

JD: Also on 17 September Mr Powell sends an email . . . to Alastair Campbell and David Manning. And he says he has three comments: 'I think it is worth explicitly stating what the Prime Minister keeps saying, this is the advice to him from the JIC.' Then: 'We need to do more to back up the assertions . . .' And: 'In the penultimate para you need to make it clear Saddam could not attack us at the moment. The thesis is he would be a threat to the UK in the future if we do not check him.'

TB: Yes.

JD: Did those comments get reflected in the dossier?

TB: I think so, yes, but I think the most important thing was I was very careful in my statement to make it clear what we were and were not saying. The purpose of the dossier was to respond to the call to disclose the intelligence that wc knew but at that stage the strategy was not to use the dossier as the immediate reason for going to conflict, but as the reason why we had to return to the issue of Saddam and weapons of mass destruction, preferably, as I said later, through the United Nations.

JD: Were you aware of these type of responses from Mr Scarlett [when he refused to strengthen the word 'might']?

TB: No, I was not aware of the absolute detail of it but on the other hand, I mean, having read it, it seems to me a perfectly right way of proceeding. In other words, there are certain things that we are asking if they can improve on this or improve on that and they say: well, we can or we cannot. I think the important thing I would say is that once the decision had been taken that, as it were, John Scarlett and the JIC should actually own this document, it should be their document, then I think everything that was done was subject to that.

JD: Were you aware at the time about any unhappiness amongst members of the intelligence services with the process by which the dossier was being produced?

TB: Absolutely not, no . . . The whole business was unusual, but it was in response to an unusual set of circumstances. We were saying this issue had to be returned to by the international community and dealt with. Why were we saying this? Because of the intelligence. Not unnaturally, people said: Well, give us the intelligence insofar as you can.

JD: One other criticism that has been made, again after the event . . . is in the report from the Foreign Affairs Committee. What they say is this: 'We conclude that the language used in the September dossier was in places more assertive than that traditionally used in intelligence documents . . .' Do you agree with that comment?

TB: I think that we described the intelligence in a way that was perfectly justified and I would simply make this point. Although obviously people look back now on the September dossier in a quite different way, if I make these two points: the first is that the dossier, at the time, was not received as being particularly incautious in tone. On the contrary, a lot of people said that it was done in a fairly prosaic way. So the commentary at the time was not actually that it seemed to be, you know, advancing the case in an adventurous way, if I can put it like that, at all. The commentary was rather to the opposite effect.

Secondly, the 45-minute claim, as I think I say in my witness statement, just a point to make, I mentioned it in the foreword, I mention it in my statement. I think after then I do not think I mention it again in Parliament. And I think there is a sense in which it is important to recognise that the September dossier was not making the case for war, it was making the case for the issue to be dealt with and our preferred alternative was indeed to deal with it through the United Nations route.

The battle with the BBC

JD: Was there a feeling in Downing Street that the government was not being properly represented by the BBC at this stage?

TB: There was a feeling, but I do not doubt we are not the first government to be in such a situation, that there were parts of the BBC that were not covering it in as objective a way as we thought, but that happens – I think it happened throughout the business in Afghanistan too. I should imagine we are not the first government and will not be the last government to have such concerns.

JD: Were you aware of Mr Campbell's letters of complaint and the apparent absence of success, so far as getting any major corrections were concerned?

TB: Yes, I was aware he had made complaints about certain of the stories. It was not from all parts of the BBC, incidentally, at all. But there were complaints about certain stories.

JD: Can I turn, now, to the 29 May *Today* broadcast. Where were you at the time?

TB: I was in Basra with the British troops when I was told about the claim, I think shortly after it was made.

JD: And what was your reaction to that?

TB: Well, it was an extraordinary allegation to make and an extremely serious one.

JD: What were you told of the allegation, Prime Minister? How was it reported to you?

TB: It was reported to me – I cannot actually recall whether I got an actual written transcript of what was said, but I think I even may have, but the things that absolutely stood out and were extraordinary, in my view, were (1) that this 45-minute claim had been inserted into the dossier at the behest of No. 10 Downing Street, (2) that it was done by us I think the words were 'probably knowing it was wrong', and (3) that we had done it contrary to the wishes of the intelligence services. I think that then the report went on to say: and that this information had been supplied by someone who was in charge of the process of drawing up the dossier.

JD: Was that the main charge to which you were responding at the time?

TB: Yes, I mean, this was an absolutely fundamental charge. It is one thing to say: we disagree with the government, you should not have gone to war . . . This was an allegation that we had behaved in a way that were it true – as I say in my statement, tested in this way, had the allegation been true, it would have merited my resignation. It was not a small allegation, it was absolutely fundamental. What really I think from that moment on made the thing extremely difficult was there was then a *Mail on Sunday* article by Mr Gilligan that named Alastair Campbell as the person who had done this effectively. There was some huge great headline.

JD: You considered putting this to the intelligence and security committee, in a way of dealing with the issue?

TB: It was clear, because there were a lot of calls for inquiries, there was going to have to be some sort of inquiry into it. I thought that the Intelligence and Security Committee were the right people to deal with this . . . I agreed I would publish their report, so there was no question of suppressing their judgement on it. They meet in private. Contrary to what some people say, I appoint the people but after consultation with the opposition leaders in respect of their people serving on it.

JD: This is the broadcast that was made, the early morning broadcast. [Excerpts were read out]

TB: Yes. Well, you know, look, any person listening to that would think that we had done something improper, The whole thing since then has been, not did the government make the wrong decision, but did the government dupe us, did the government in a sense defraud people over it? That has been the central charge. My view . . . has been that the only thing that was going to remove that was . . . a clear and unequivocal statement that the original story was wrong. There is no doubt that [the BBC] shifted to saying: look, we are not attacking your integrity, we just say this is what was told to us, and so on. But the real problem was that the original allegation had been made, it had then been, as I say, backed up and really had booster rockets put on it by the *Mail on Sunday* article . . . The fact is that the entire original allegation was an attack on our integrity . . . an attack that went to the heart of not just the office of prime minister but also the way our intelligence services operated. It went in a sense to the credibility, I felt, of the country, never mind the Prime Minister.

JD: Mr Campbell also made what the BBC perceived to be wider attacks on their journalism. He described the story as a lie and he described the BBC in less than flattering terms. Was this an escalation of the dispute between No. 10 and the BBC that you were aware of?

TB: No, I do not think it was – I mean, it was important, frankly, for reasons that I say in my witness statement, that we made it clear we were not attacking the BBC's independence.

JD: I think a possible indication from Mr Sambrook's statement is that there is a difference between the BBC directly making an allegation that someone or the government has acted improperly and the BBC reporting someone else's view that a person or the government has acted improperly. Do you have any comment?

TB: I think if you are to make that distinction then in your reporting of it on 29 May you make it a very clear thing. I think if one takes the newspaper article on the Sunday, I think you would be hard put to say: somebody said this thing but we stand back from it. It was not coming across like that . . .

On the morning of 7 July, I had an entirely private conversation with Gavyn Davies, chairman of the BBC, at my request, to see if there was some way we could find a way through this and it was a perfectly amicable discussion but we were not able to come to an agreement. He explained that he felt he . . . could not actually retract the original story, that would compromise the BBC's independence . . . I think all the way through we were anxious to get things back on a normal footing and indeed the lunch on 12 June was a part of a desire to do that. After all, the BBC is the main broadcasting outlet. It is not really very sensible for the government to be in a situation where we have a continuing dispute with the BBC.

The outing of Dr Kelly

JD: When was the first time you heard that a possible source for Mr Gilligan's story had come forward?

TB: I was away on a visit in the North West on 3 July and I was telephoned by Jonathan Powell, my chief of staff.

JD: Were you given a name, at that time?

TB: No, I do not recall being given a name at that time. I cannot recall when I first heard the name. I mean, it may have been in these telephone conversations. It may not have been . . .

JD: Did you get [a] letter that evening [4 July] ?

TB: Yes. I got that letter that was faxed to me, I think, by David Omand and that then, you know, gave a certain amount of evidence obviously as to what Dr Kelly had said in the interview that he had had with the Ministry of Defence.

JD: Your own judgement was?

TB: My own judgement was obviously with an issue with so much political focus on it as this, when someone was being interviewed and reinterviewed and presumably people were talking about it within the system, then you have an article in *The Times*, I think I would have thought there was a fair possibility it would leak in any event.

JD: Who did you have your discussions with over that weekend?

TB: Yes. I mean, my recollection is that on the Saturday Alastair called me . . . he raised the issue of the source because he had been told that by the Defence Secretary and his worry, he thought the information was plainly relevant and were we not going to be criticised for withholding it. I said to him what was my firm view throughout, that we had to proceed in a way that Sir Kevin and David Omand were entirely content with . . .

JD: Did you know that at this stage there was no question of the Official Secrets Act being invoked?

TB: I cannot recall exactly when, but I think during the course of that weekend, and if not certainly pretty early on the Monday, I said: what is going to happen here? And it was explained to me that this was not an Official Secrets Act point.

JD: So you had understood, at this stage, that any public involvement of Dr Kelly was to be on the basis of his cooperation?

TB: Yes. Look, right at the very outset, part of this difficulty was he had come forward. The question was: what do we now do with that information, in particular in relation to the FAC and I cannot recall exactly when I was told this, but I think it was said he realised he might end up having to give evidence.

JD: What was your view about the situation with Dr Kelly now, in terms of disclosing that someone had come forward?

TB: I thought that it was likely on the basis of what we had been told that he was the source, and in any event, in a sense, as important as anything else, he had been interviewed and reinterviewed, and certainly, as it was relayed to me, it looked more likely than not that he was the source.

cont'd p.186

Forever a dull moment in the very busy life of honest Tony

Sketch
Simon Hoggart

Tony Blair got away with it. Like the hero of some fiendish computer game, he survived the rolling boulders and the gobbling monsters, to make it to the next stage. But the game is not over yet.

He arrived promptly at the inquiry, sat down and gave Lord Hutton a little smile, perhaps to put him at his ease, though since Lord Hutton didn't notice the smile it probably didn't work.

(He kept calling him 'my lord', which was faintly creepy, since there's only one person who creates lords in this country – Mr Blair.)

The atmosphere in court 73 was oddly muted. We might have been witnesses to a great historic event, but for most of the dozen or so lawyers and the press it was just another day at the office – the same faces, the joshing, the same forest of computer screens, the same Caffe Nero run, the same endless box files.

Even Lord Hutton and the inquiry's fleshily handsome brief, James Dingemans, looked firmly unimpressed. When you're a top judge or QC, being unimpressed is cool.

What did the rest of us expect? That he would break down? 'I killed Dr Kelly as surely as if it had been my hand on the knife!' But Tony Blair doesn't do sobbing, or rueful contrition. What he does well is calm, factual, reasonable. This week we heard that Dr Kelly had been greatly stressed by the oral exam for his PhD. Tony Blair would have turned up with a ring binder, a Caffe Nero and a welcoming smile for the examiners.

He began well. Where had he first heard of the allegations on the *Today* programme? 'I was in Basra, with British troops.' (Thanking our brave lads for their sacrifice, while the wretched Gilligan was peddling his lies around the metropolitan sewers, we were supposed to think.)

The gist of his defence was, and I paraphrase, 'Look, I'm a pretty straight sort of guy. If I'd lied, I'd resign, but I didn't. I'm also very busy, so I had plenty on my mind. I agreed to release Dr Kelly's name because I thought it would have been wrong to keep it from MPs. That's because I'm a pretty straight sort of guy. As I may have mentioned.'

He didn't seem nervous, except when questions reached the period after Dr Kelly had admitted talking to the BBC. At this point – how did he decide to name Dr Kelly? – his language began to go haywire, in that it flew all over the place, tangled up and then sprang apart again, liable to poke out its user's eye:

'The quandary was this. We didn't want the Foreign Affairs Committee to look into this, at the last minute, forward comes someone who might be the source of the allegation – did you inform the FAC immediately, which is one possibility and which I have no doubt afterwards people would have said to us we should have done? Did you try to get greater clarity of whether this was indeed the source or not? So how did you handle this? And the reason why I thought it was very very important to involve the senior officials is that he made the whole allegation ...'

At this point he started to wave his hands in strange shapes and patterns. Us old-time Blair watchers know that this indicates a 'why won't you believe me?' kind of agitation, as if somehow the gestures will make the point where words alone can not succeed.

He seemed happiest when he led us through all the work he, as Prime Minister, has to do on our behalf. On Monday July 7, one of the most important dates in the Kelly story, he had 'breakfast with information technology consultants, a series of meetings on school funding, a big speech at the Queen Elizabeth conference centre on the criminal justice system, a meeting with the head of the Olympic committee, a government reception in the evening, I had to prepare for the liaison committee on Tuesday and prime minister's questions on Wednesday ...'

Enough already! I wanted to shout. Those aren't real tasks, they're make-work. Much of it doesn't matter at all! And it must be so dull you'd want to rip off your own ears rather than listen to another word, especially another word of one of your own speeches!

We went through a memo Alastair Campbell had written, asking for changes to the September dossier. He had been picking holes in it. '"Might" reads very weakly. "Could" is weak – "capable of being used" is better. Doesn't need "probable"'.

It seemed familiar, and I sensed we were back in Mr Campbell's past, as a *Daily Mirror* trainee in the West Country, working on the *Tavistock Times*. 'Oi, you, Campbell ,' says the chief sub-editor, 'this agency stuff is crap. You've got four to five minutes to knock it into shape. What's this "probable" crap? Blimey, come on, put a bit of life into it. It's crap, this is.'

I don't think the dossier was sexed up. Instead, it was put into tabloidese, which must have shocked the spooks, who write in measured, balanced prose, designed to protect their own backsides. But there is a ferocious chief sub somewhere, perhaps retired, possibly dead, whose voice was ringing in Alastair's ears as he read that original dossier. 'Oi, that's crap, Campbell ...'

I hope he's giving a satisfied grunt right now. ■

Guardian. 29 August 2003

JD: Why was there a need to make public the fact that a source had come forward?

TB: I think, first of all, we were at any point concerned, as I said a moment or two ago, I think we were quite surprised on the Monday it had not already come out, but we thought that it was likely to come out at any particular point. And, secondly, because once you had copied it to the FAC – I thought there was a remote possibility the FAC might decide not to interview him, but I rather thought that they would.

JD: We know that a press statement is issued by the Ministry of Defence. Were you aware of any assistance with the drafting of this press statement being given by officials within No. 10?

TB: I think certainly it came to Jonathan and I may have scanned my eye over it myself, but I cannot absolutely recall that.

JD: Was there any discussion about pressure Dr Kelly might be exposed to when you were having the meetings on 8 July?

TB: Obviously, one of the things that was part of the conversation that we were having was what Dr Kelly did, what sort of person was he, what experience did he have. I mean, all I can say is that there is nothing in the discussion that we had that would have alerted us to him being anything other than someone, you know, of a certain robustness . . .

JD: Was, at this stage, a view being taken that having put the press statement out for the reasons you have given, Dr Kelly's arrival now might be used by the government for their own advantages?

TB: In one sense, Dr Kelly had come forward and said: I did not say the things Mr Gilligan says I said. On the other hand, you can never be sure of these situations and actually what happened when the FAC did interview him was precisely that the situation was not conclusive at all.

Gavyn Davies
Chairman of the BBC (also appeared on day 22)

- Told the inquiry that when the row appeared to be petering out, Campbell stoked it up again when he appeared before the FAC on 28 June 2003.
- Faced close questioning on the distinction drawn by the BBC between reporting the claims made by a source, and endorsing those claims.
- Expressed his 'enormous regret' to the inquiry if an email sent by the reporter to an MP on the FAC, in which he suggested questions for Kelly, had increased the pressure on the weapons expert.
- Rejected the claim of Susan Watts, who accused the BBC of pressuring her to disclose her source, and of attempting to mould her stories to justify Gilligan's.

On Alastair Campbell's appearance before the FAC on 28 June 2003
'I felt this was an extraordinary moment. I felt it was an almost unprecedented attack on the BBC to be mounted by the head of communications at 10 Downing Street. Mr Campbell accused the BBC of lying directly. He accused Mr Gilligan of lying directly. He alleged that the BBC had accused the Prime Minister of lying, something which I never believed the BBC had done. And he accused the BBC of having followed an anti-war agenda before,

during and after the Iraqi conflict. I must say, I took this as an attack on the impartiality of the BBC and the integrity of the BBC, done with great vigour.'

Asked about the difference between Gilligan and Watts's stories
'I think the interpretation that individual BBC journalists put on their reports is entirely for them; and it is a great strength of the organisation that journalists and editors can come to their own views. I think she is entirely entitled to come to her views. I do not share them in every particular; I think there are greater similarities between the broadcasts than perhaps Ms Watts does.'

On his meeting with Blair where the Prime Minister said an official had come forward
'I said, "I do not know who the source is, Prime Minister, but bear in mind he talked to three or four." And I said, "Also bear in mind that Ms Watts's reports were somewhat similar to Mr Gilligan's, and therefore were taken by me as corroboration that Mr Gilligan had reported his source broadly accurately." I do not think the Prime Minister had been at all aware of Ms Watts's reports.'

On the revelation that an unnamed official had come forward
'I thought that maybe what was going on was that an official had come forward who they felt might discredit the Gilligan reports. But that was an absolute shot in the dark by me; I had no idea what was going on really.'

On being told by Hoon that Kelly was the source in a letter
'What occurred to me here was: look, I do not know whether Dr Kelly is actually Mr Gilligan's source, but if he is he has probably said some very different things to Mr Gilligan to what he has said to his employer; and my feeling, again management were the only

people in possession of the name, but my feeling was that if we had come forward and said: yes actually that is the source, if it indeed were, we would have been betraying the confidence, number one, because the source had never suggested that we should divulge his name, and number two, we would have effectively been telling his employer that he had told Mr Gilligan more than he was now owning up to his employer. And I thought that was a very bad way to treat the confidence of a source.'

On Gilligan's email to a member of the FAC
'I certainly believe that it is wrong for any journalist to divulge the source of another journalist's work. I do not know how Mr Gilligan could have done that because he did not know Susan Watts's source. So that puzzles me. I do not know how he could have. Maybe there was a misunderstanding there, I do not know. I would say that Mr Gilligan, at this stage, was under enormous pressure and perhaps felt that the FAC was trying to discredit him as a journalist and perhaps felt that he needed to take steps to counter that; but of course, I enormously regret anything that happened at this stage which may have increased the pressures on Dr Kelly.' ■

Key Documents

Statement issued by the BBC's board of governors, 7 July 2003
First, the board reiterates that the BBC's overall coverage of the war, and the political issues surrounding it, has been entirely impartial, and it emphatically rejects Mr Campbell's claim that large parts of the BBC had an agenda against the war. We call on Mr Campbell to withdraw these allegations of bias against the BBC and its journalists.

Second, the board considers that the *Today* programme properly followed the BBC's producers' guidelines in its handling of the Andrew Gilligan report

The evidence

about the September intelligence dossier, which was broadcast on 29 May
. . . We note that an entirely separate story was broadcast by an unconnected
BBC journalist on *Newsnight* on 2 June. This story reported very similar allegations to those reported by Andrew Gilligan on the *Today* programme, but the
story has not been singled out for similar criticism by government spokesmen.

. . . The board is satisfied that it was in the public interest to broadcast Mr
Gilligan's story, given the information which was available to BBC news at this
time. We believe it would not have been in the public interest to have
suppressed the stories on either the *Today* programme or *Newsnight*.

Third, the board considers that the *Today* programme should have kept a
clearer account of its dealings with the Ministry of Defence on this story and
could have also asked the No. 10 press office for a response prior to broadcasting the story. However, we note that firm government denials of the story
were broadcast on the *Today* programme within 90 minutes of the original
broadcast by Andrew Gilligan, and these were followed soon after on the same
programme by equally firm denials by a defence minister.

Fourth, the board intends to look again at the rules under which BBC
reporters and presenters are permitted to write for newspapers, once it has
received recommendations from the director of news. This examination will be
conducted during the summer.

Finally, the board wishes to place on record that the BBC has never
accused the Prime Minister of lying, or of seeking to take Britain into war under
misleading or false pretences. The BBC did not have an agenda in its war
coverage, nor does it now have any agenda which questions the integrity of
the Prime Minister.

In summary, the governors are ultimately responsible for ensuring that the
BBC upholds the highest standards of impartiality and accuracy. We are wholly
satisfied that BBC journalists and their managers sought to maintain impartiality and accuracy during this episode. ■

Day 12
1 September 2003

Janice Kelly gave a moving description of her husband's last days, accusing Whitehall of belittling him and the MoD of effectively hanging him out to dry. Her biting criticism of the MoD – the BBC was spared – was later reflected in the summing up by the family lawyer, Jeremy Gompertz QC. Her daughter, Rachel, robustly defended Dr Kelly's evidence to the Commons Foreign Affairs Committee. Kelly's sister, Sarah Pape, also gave a stout defence of her brother, insisting he was pro the war.

Janice Kelly

- Kelly's widow – who gave evidence by audio link to the inquiry room with a still picture of her on a screen – raised serious questions about the truthfulness of crucial evidence given to the Hutton inquiry by the Prime Minister's closest advisers over the Whitehall strategy that led to his exposure in the media.

- Mrs Kelly said her husband had felt 'totally let down and betrayed' when he learned that a press statement had been issued which quickly brought about his unmasking. Her husband had been given assurances by his bosses that a press statement would not be released. Kelly did not know until after the event.

- Kelly went 'ballistic' when he was told to give televised evidence to the Commons Foreign Affairs Committee.

- His stress was compounded by attempts to 'belittle' him. At one point she said he was treated 'like a fly'.

- Attacked the *Sunday Times* newspaper for offering protection from the rest of the media, in return for an exclusive article. Described how reporter Nicholas Rufford turned up at the family home on Wednesday 9 July, the day the MoD confirmed Kelly's name in connection with the Andrew Gilligan story, to warn that the press pack was about to descend. By the Sunday, the Kellys had fled to Cornwall, away from the media scrum. An article by Rufford appeared in the *Sunday Times* that day, which left Kelly 'angry and upset'.
- Kelly expressed a deep sense of hurt over a perceived slight by the Foreign Secretary, Jack Straw – when Straw gave evidence on Iraq to the Commons Foreign Affairs Committee, Kelly sat with him to provide technical advice. He had been upset on being told the Foreign Secretary was disappointed at being accompanied by someone apparently so junior.

On 8 July 2003, Kelly returned home from a short trip to RAF Honington in Suffolk. That evening, after eating dinner, he and his wife Janice sat down to watch the news. This is an edited transcript of what she told the inquiry

'He seemed a little bit reluctant to come and watch the news. The main story was a source had identified itself. Immediately David said to me: "It's me." My reaction was total dismay. My heart sank. I was terribly worried because the fact that he had said that to me, I knew then he was aware his name would be in the public domain quite soon. He confirmed that feeling of course.'

Asked 'how he seemed'
'Desperately unhappy about it, really, really unhappy about it. Totally dismayed. He mentioned he had had a reprimand at that stage from the MoD but they had not been unsupportive, were his

words. We talked a little bit generally about it and what it would mean for him in real terms. He was a bit backward in coming forward, may I say, in saying what he meant.

'I deliberately at that point said: would it mean a pension problem, would it mean you having to leave your job? He said it could be if it got worse, yes.

'Because the MoD had revealed that a source had made itself known, he, in his own mind, said that he knew from that point that the press would soon put two and two together. We have an amazing press in this country – it does not take them long to find out details of this sort and he is well known of course in his field, so that would have been another easy job for them.

'[On the following day] He was supposed to be going to London so I was quite surprised when he said he was going to work in the garden all day. Again he got on to his vegetable patch and was working in a rather lacklustre way that particular day but he did receive and make some phone calls as well.

'[Around 7.30pm] We had both been sitting out having our coffee in the garden after dinner that evening. I was watering the plants and David went to put some tools away he had been using during the day which involved him going into the yard which lay between our house and the main road outside.

'I suddenly looked up and there was David talking to somebody. I had not got my glasses on so I moved a little bit closer with the hosepipe to see who it was and I recognised it as Nick Rufford [of the *Sunday Times*]. Nick had been to our house before but only by arrangement, he never just turned up before this. No journalist just turned up before this, so I was extremely alarmed about that.

'David confirmed what I thought I had heard afterwards. I heard him say – I heard Nick say, I think, "Rupert Murdoch" and I heard David say, "Please leave now." The conversation only took place over about four or five minutes maximum.

'[David] came over to me and said that Nick had said that Murdoch had offered hotel accommodation for both of us away from the media spotlight in return for an article by David. He, David, was to be named that night and that the press were on their way in droves.

'That was the language David used, I am not sure Nick used that. He also added – he was very upset and his voice had a break in it at this stage. He got the impression from Nick that the gloves were off now, that Nick would use David's name in any article that he wrote and he was extremely upset.

'He said several times over coffee, over lunch, over afternoon tea that he felt totally let down and betrayed. It seemed to me that this was all part of what might have happened anyway because it seemed to have been a very loose arrangement with the MoD, they did not seem to take a lot of account of his time. There was a lot of wasting of his time.

'I just felt that this must have been very frustrating for him. David often said, "They are not using me properly." He felt that the MoD were not quite sure how to use his expertise at times, although I have later seen his manager's reports on his staff appraisals where he obviously did warrant his, or respect his, expertise. But that is not the impression that I got.

'He did not say in so many terms but I believed he meant the MoD [had betrayed him] because they were the ones that had effectively let his name be known in the public domain.'

Asked whether he was happy or unhappy about the MoD statement

'Well, he did not know about it until after it had happened. So he was – I think initially he had been led to believe that it would not go into the public domain. He had received assurances and that is why he was so very upset about it.'

Asked by Lord Hutton from whom had he received those assurances

'From his line manager, from all their seniors and from the people he had been interviewed by.'

Asked about Kelly's reaction to being offered a deal by the *Sunday Times*

'Extremely upset at two levels. One that he was being – you know, the press were on their way in droves, as Nick had put it, and also that his friendship with Nick – because he always used to work so hard, because he was a workaholic to all intents, most of his friendships, in fact his close friendships were all with people he worked with on a regular basis, so if he gave a regular briefing to someone, very often it would become not a close friendship but a friendship nevertheless. He felt that friendship was now at an end.'

Having heard that the press were on their way in droves

'We hovered a bit. I said I knew a house that was available to us, if we needed it, down in the south-west of England, and he did not pick up on that initially . . .

'The phone rang inside the house and he went in to answer it, came out and he said, "I think we will be needing that house after all. The MoD press office have just rung to say we ought to leave the house and quickly so that we would not be followed by the press . . ."

'We immediately went into the house and packed and within about 10 minutes we had left the house.

'We headed along the road towards the M4 and got to Weston-super-Mare and decided to pull in at a hotel there for the night.

'He was driving, very, very tense and I was trying to persuade him not to take or make any calls while we were actually driving. So before we got on to the M4, we pulled over and tried to get hold of his line manager Bryan Wells. He did make contact with someone called Kate at the MoD press office. I think he used a phrase like "cut and run".

'David would never use that phrase in normal terms. He was obviously exceedingly upset, we were both – very anxious, very stressed. His whole demeanour was very tight. I was extremely worried because he was insisting on driving.

'I asked if I could drive, he would not let me. He was very, very tired and so was I by this time.'

After one night in Weston-super-Mare they set off towards Cornwall

'[He was] not quite as tense as the night before but still very tense. I was trying to say to him how nice Cornwall was, we could visit places like the Eden Project and Lost Gardens of Heligan, and so on, which I had visited several times before, so I was trying to make conversation to relax him and try and turn this in some way into a holiday. We had not had holidays together for so long that I was trying to make this a kind of positive experience for him.

'[On arrival in Cornwall] I could not comfort him. He seemed to withdraw into himself completely. And I decided that the best I could do, and I made a policy thing here then that I would keep him properly fed, good food, attractive food and then keep him occupied as pleasantly as possible. So although he was less stressed in one sense, he was more upset by now.'

Asked how he reacted to the press coverage

'He was upset. He did not like his name being in the public domain. He did not like being – becoming the story.

'On the Friday we decided to go to the Lost Gardens of Heligan. It was only a short drive so we thought that would be apt after the long day or two before.

We spent a long morning there during which he had taken a call from several people from the MoD explaining about the Foreign Affairs Committee on the Tuesday and an intelligence committee the following Wednesday.'

Asked about his reaction to the FAC being televised

'He was ballistic. He just did not like that idea at all. He felt it – he did not say this in so many words but he felt it would be a kind of continuation of a kind of reprimand into the public domain.

'He was really upset. I had hoped the morning would be positive and pleasurable for him. He did not see the gardens at all. He was in a world of his own. He was really quite stressed, very strained, and conversation was extremely difficult.

'We went home for lunch and then went down towards the village again. I tried to keep him busy and then we just relaxed during the evening. We took some calls from the family again.'

Asked about his mood then

'Very unhappy. Very unhappy. He was worried about whether he would have to cope with briefings from the MoD on top of his thoughts and feelings that he had already got.

'[On Saturday] We set off to the Eden Project – he had never seen it – he seemed very grim, very unhappy, extremely tense, but accepting the process he was going through. He knew he would have to go forward the following week. I was trying to relax him. He was eating, he was drinking soft drinks but it was a very grim time for both of us.

'I have never, in all the Russian visits and all the difficulties he had in Iraq, where he had lots of discomforts, lots of horrors, guns pointing at him, munitions left lying around, I had never known him to be as unhappy as he was then. It was tangible. Palpable.

'Somehow we got through the day. I am not terribly sure what we did now. We certainly went back home. We wandered along the beach at some stage. That was not easy for him. It was just a nightmare. That is all I can describe it as.

'There did not seem to be anything in the way of support [from the MoD]. I was surprised nobody rang him and said: look, you know, why does not somebody come down to talk to you? And that had not happened.

'[On Sunday] I stayed in Cornwall. David wanted to set off early. I tried to delay him. He was extremely tense. The MoD had offered, by now, to put him up at a hotel in Horse Guards but we all thought, especially our daughter Rachel, he would be more comfortable with her. So he set off about 11.30. Before that he insisted on buying a *Sunday Times* to see whether Nick Rufford had in fact written anything further, and Nick had indeed written something further. The article gave the impression that Nick had had a full-blown interview with David at our home in Oxfordshire.

'That was not the case. And he said something like: thanks Nick, the MoD will think I have been talking to the press after I expressly said that I would not, and that was in no way an interview that he gave. But Nick gave the impression that it was. He was angry and upset. He almost immediately tried to get hold of Bryan Wells [at the MoD]. He could not get him straight away, but Bryan rang him later, which is why he did not leave until about 11.30.

'He told Bryan how he was feeling, that he really was upset and he did not think it was fair that this article was presenting it as a full-blown interview.

'[On Monday] He said he was very, very upset about that and I think it was on this day that he said that somebody had told him over the phone while we were down in Cornwall that Jack Straw had said he was upset at the technical support at a [foreign affairs] committee meeting, he had been accompanied by somebody so junior.

'He laughed. It was kind of a hysterical laugh in a way. He was deeply, deeply hurt. He had been working on biological weapons at a very high level and here he was being treated rather like a fly, really, I think was the phrase he used.

'He was quite modest about his work. He never boasted. In our many years together he was not a boasting man, he was a very shy, retiring guy and he just felt he could make a small difference. At an international level that really was quite enough for him. He felt that was a good place to be.'

On 15 July he appeared before the FAC

'This was our thirty-sixth wedding anniversary so I was constantly thinking of him all day. He rang that evening and said it had been a total nightmare because the times and dates had been switched and then switched again and there had been a bomb scare, I think, somewhere near the Houses of Parliament so it was difficult for the car to drive him up and he had had to run the gauntlet of the press. Certainly from the television pictures I saw later he really did look very stressed, I could see that.

'He felt that he had not done good justice to himself. He felt that they had been – I think it was Andrew Mackinlay, he misunderstood it initially and felt it was an insult, the comment about "you are chaff" and the "fall guy". He was deeply offended about that at the time. He did ask Bryan Wells later whether it was intended as an insult because he could not believe it. Bryan Wells said: certainly not, the first part was a military term. But David – that had upset him.

'His final comment about the Foreign Affairs Committee was that he just did not want to know. He just – he was in a nightmare position. He said: I did not want to know. And that was something he would say very infrequently but it just meant he wanted to put that to one side and move on.'

On 16 July he appeared before the Intelligence Select Committee. That evening he, his wife and daughter had a meal together

'He looked totally exhausted. He was able to converse a little, but it was very, very strained. I felt he was very, very tired. He was sort of used up. I asked him about the intelligence committee that day but he only said it had gone all right. And that was not a phrase he would normally use.

'He was obviously very stressed. We then made our way home. He drove. Again he insisted on driving home. He did not speak at all during that journey. He was very tense and very, very tired.

'[On Thursday 17 July] We got up at about half past eight. It is rather later than normal. We were both tired.

'He was tired, subdued, but not depressed. I have no idea. He had never seemed depressed in all of this, but he was very tired and very subdued.

'He said he had a report to write for the MoD. This is the one that somebody on the Foreign Affairs Committee referred to as his 'homework' I think. He came out for coffee. We had a quick word. That would be about 11 I think, something of that order. He was certainly on the phone quite a bit I think. I could hear the phone ringing from time to time, but he picked it up. We did not actually sit together to have coffee then and we did not really talk at that stage.

'I left the house for a few minutes to meet somebody and pick up some photographs. I came back, went into his study to try and lighten the atmosphere a bit by showing him some photographs and some other data I had got for the History Society.

'He smiled, stood up and then said he had not quite finished. But a few minutes later he went to sit in the sitting room all by himself without saying anything, which was quite unusual for him, but he went and sat in the sitting room. He just sat and he looked really very tired.

'By this time I had started with a huge headache and begun to feel sick. In fact I was physically sick several times at this stage because he looked so desperate.

'He did have some lunch. I made some sandwiches and he had a glass of water. We sat together at the table opposite each other. I tried to make conversation. I was feeling pretty wretched, so was he. He looked distracted and dejected.

'I just thought he had a broken heart. He had shrunk into himself. He looked as though he had shrunk, but I had no idea at that stage of what he might do later, absolutely no idea at all. He could not put two sentences together. He could not talk at all. I went to go and have a lie down after lunch, which is something I quite often did just to cope with my arthritis. I said to him, "What are you going to do?"

'He said, "I will probably go for my walk." It would be about half past one, quarter to two perhaps. He went into his study. Then shortly after I had laid down he came to ask me if I was okay. I said, "Yes, I will be fine." And then he went to change into his jeans. He would be around the house in a tracksuit or tracksuit bottoms during the day. So he went to change and put on his shoes. Then I assumed he had left the house. He had intended to go for this regular walk of his. He had a bad back so that was the strategy for that.

'The phone rang a little bit later on and I assumed he had left so I suddenly realised I had not got a cordless phone and I thought it might be an important call for him, perhaps from the MoD. So I went downstairs to find the telephone in the dining room. By this time the ringing had stopped and I was aware of David talking quietly on a phone. I said something like, "I thought you had gone out for a walk." He did not respond of course because he was talking on the phone.'

Asked if she knew who the caller was
'I assumed it was the MoD, I am not sure. The phone rang again at about 3.20, after which I got up and I was aware that definitely

David had left by this time. He had gone by 3.20. I was still feeling extremely ill so I went to sit in the sitting room. I could not settle, I put the TV on, which is unheard of for me at that time of the day.

'There were a few callers at the front door. I answered those and had a short chat with each of them. Then I began to get rather worried because normally if David was going for a longer walk, he would say. It was a kind of family tradition, if you were going for a longer walk you would say where you were going and what time you would be back. He had not said that. He just said, "I am going for my walk."'

Asked how long a normal walk would take
'About 15 minutes, depending if he met somebody, perhaps 20 minutes, 25 minutes.'

Asked when she started to worry
'Probably late afternoon. Rachel rang, my daughter rang to say, "Do not worry, he has probably gone out to have a good think. Do not worry about it, he will be fine."

'She had planned to come over that evening. She made a decision definitely to come over. She arrived – I am not quite sure what time she arrived, half five, six o'clock, I think. She went out. She said, "I will go and walk up and meet Dad." She walked up one of the normal footpaths he would have taken – in fact it was the footpath he would have taken.

'She came back about half an hour or so later. This must have been about 6.30 perhaps by now. I am not sure of the times. I was in a terrible state myself by this time trying not to think awful things and trying to take each moment as it came.

''Then the phone rings and it is Sian, one of our other daughters. She immediately says, "I am coming over." So she and her partner Richard set out by car from their home near Fordingbridge to drive the distance. They then spent the rest of the evening driving up and down lanes, looking at churches, bus shelters, and so on, looking for her father.

'We had delayed calling the police because we thought we might make matters worse if David had returned when we started to search. I felt he was already in a difficult enough situation. So we put off calling the police until about twenty-to-twelve at night.

'The police then turn up. Three of them come with a missing persons form to fill in. I explained the situation that David had been in and it seemed immediately to go up to chief constable level. The search begins. The Thames Valley helicopter had gone off duty by that time so they had to wait for the [RAF] Benson helicopter to come across.

'It came and the police switched on their blue light on their vehicles so it could pinpoint the position of our house, the starting point for David's walk. It must have been about one o'clock. I am not sure. Then a vehicle arrived with a large communication mast on it and parked in the road and then during the early hours another mast, 45 foot mast was put up in our garden. And a dog was put through our house.

'At twenty-to-five the following morning I was sitting on the lawn in my dressing gown while the dog went through the house. Trying to establish that he was not there.

'It was during the morning of the Friday, I think, the 18th by now, that the police came to inform us of David's death.'

Asked if they were shown a knife

'We were not shown the knife; we were shown a photocopy of I presume the knife which we recognised as a knife he had had for many years and kept in his drawer. [It was a knife he had had] from childhood I believe. I think probably from the Boy Scouts.

Asked about his use of Coproxamol

'I take Coproxamol for my arthritis. I keep a small store in a kitchen drawer and the rest in my bedside table.'

Asked if there was anything else she could tell the inquiry
'No, except that he was totally devoted to his job. It was rather muddling in the sense that he seemed to work between lots of different places, but that suited his style in a way, he liked to interact between lots of different people. But, no, there is nothing else.'

Asked about a newspaper report of a row
'We did not row. If we had a disagreement, we agreed to disagree. There was absolutely no row whatsoever. I was in no physical state anyway and neither was David. There was absolutely no row.'

Asked about a reference to him as a 'Walter Mitty' character
'I was devastated. That was totally the opposite. He was a very modest, shy, retiring guy. I once saw him at a meeting with the United Nations Association and his body language was very sort of stiff. He was always very courteous, very laid back if you like, but he kept to his brief. He did not boast at all and he was very factual and that is what he felt his job was. That is what he tried always to be, to be factual.'

Sarah Pape
Consultant plastic surgeon and Dr Kelly's sister

- Said that her brother had showed no signs of being suicidal in the days before his death.
- Kelly had talked of his 'battle' with his bosses over his pay, worrying that if it were too low it may affect his pension.
- Also tried to explain why he had denied to the Foreign Affairs Committee savaging the government in a conversation with Susan Watts, a BBC journalist.
- Kelly had persuaded his family of the case for war against Saddam.

On Kelly's mood at his daughter Ellen's wedding in February
'He was in absolutely tremendous form, as most men would be at their
daughter's wedding. He was proud of his daughter. He was relaxed, he
was cheerful. He was entertaining. He gave a wonderful speech at the
reception. He was in as good shape as I had ever seen him.'

**On her brother's meeting with diplomat David Broucher, who
gave evidence earlier in the inquiry**
'He certainly did not mention he was going to be flying almost straight
back to visit Geneva, which is what I understand David Broucher said
in his evidence, that I think on the Wednesday or Thursday they had a
meeting in Geneva. That was certainly not mentioned and I would be
rather surprised if he turned around quite so quickly.'

**Telling the inquiry that Kelly seemed no more than tired when
she spoke to him around the time of his appearance before MPs**
'Believe me, I have lain awake many nights since, going over in my
mind whether I missed anything significant. In my line of work I do
deal with people who may have suicidal thoughts and I ought to be
able to spot those, even on a telephone conversation.

But I have gone over and over in my mind the two conversations
we had and he certainly did not betray to me any impression that
he was anything other than tired.'

How her brother persuaded her family that war was justified
'I knew that he felt that the sanctions had hurt the Iraqi people very
hard but had not made that much difference to Iraq's ability to
produce weapons of mass destruction, and I was very surprised
when he was absolutely and utterly convinced that there was almost
certainly no solution, other than a regime change, which was
unlikely to happen peacefully, and regrettably would require
military action to enforce it.

He explained it in detail that I probably did not understand at the time, in a very convincing way, and made me realise that the war was not only inevitable but that it was entirely justified . . .'

Rachel Kelly

Dr Kelly's daughter

- David Kelly turned pale at the mention of the name of the Prime Minister's powerful communications chief, Alastair Campbell.
- Spoke of a walk with her father through the Oxfordshire countryside on Saturday 28 June, the weekend before Kelly was named. It was the first time she had become 'extremely concerned' about her father.
- Rachel Kelly said she was 'very close' to her father who was 'very relaxed' just weeks before he became embroiled in the storm.

**On a walk with her father in Oxfordshire on 28 June 2003.
Campbell had previously savaged the BBC on a *Channel 4
News* interview**

'On our way back I asked him if the situation in the media about Alastair Campbell was affecting him and his reaction alarmed me greatly. It was not that he jumped, but I felt that – he said "no" and he added "not really" and I felt that I had intruded and he was very quiet, very pale and he just seemed to have the world's pressures on his shoulders. He seemed under severe stress. I did not want to cause him distress so I again tried to distract him.'

**After her parents' flight to Cornwall, Kelly returned to
Oxfordshire to stay with Rachel on Sunday 13 July 2003**

'When I first looked at him there was a really strong expression on his face that really shocked me and I was actually quite distressed to see the hurt that I could see in his face . . . his eyes seemed quite sort of dilated and quite sort of liquid, quite deep. It was a really strong expression, but then the moment passed, and I was aware that he seemed very gentle, more childlike. I was very conscious that our roles seemed to be reversing, that I needed to look after him and he needed to be looked after.'

On her walk with her father that day where they discussed his impending appearances before MPs

'Dad just seemed lost in his thoughts. He just was transfixed by the water. I chatted for a bit then realised he just wanted to be quiet. He just seemed under an overwhelming amount of stress, that is the only way I can describe it, that there was something on his mind. I would guess he was contemplating the day ahead of him the next day, but he also seemed to be finding it almost painful to think about it. He was just very withdrawn, and I was just very, very concerned about him.'

Her final remarks to the inquiry

'My heartfelt wish is that as a result of your inquiry, my lord, that people will learn from the circumstances surrounding my father's death and show more compassion and kindness in future to those around them. My sisters and I loved our father very much and we are immensely proud of his achievements. His loss to us is immeasurable and we will always miss him.'

Professor Roger Avery

Administrator and scientist at Virginia Tech University in the US

- Close friend of Kelly's who had known him since lecturing at Warwick University in the early 1970s. Provided scientific assistance for him while Kelly was at Porton Down.

- Had his last conversation with Kelly on 11 July 2003, after a British journalist had contacted him.

On his last contact with Dr Kelly

'It was an extremely short phone call, probably only lasted a couple of minutes. That in itself was a little bit unusual in that we usually talked for some time when we made contact. However, he did not seem unduly distressed and did say something like "I will give you the details later . . ."

The following morning I received more calls from the press and so called him again and gave him a reporter's telephone number at that time and . . . said to him, you know: here is the telephone number should you want to call the press. He sort of chuckled and said, "No, I do not want to speak to the press."'

David Wilkins

Company director, Rachel Kelly's fiancé

- Rachel Kelly's fiancé testified about his relationship with Kelly and his manner when he arrived from Cornwall at their house in July, which he said was 'very much as somebody would [be] after a long journey'. Had not discussed the events surrounding Kelly's sudden rise to fame. ■

Day 13

2 September 2003

The police and rescue workers described how they searched for and found Dr Kelly's body.

Ruth Absalom

Neighbour of Kelly

- The last known person to see David Kelly alive, she had seen him at 3pm on Thursday 17 July, which would have been just after he set out for his walk.
- Kelly and Absalom met a mile from their homes and he seemed his normal self. Absalom said they chatted for a few minutes.

Key quote

'He said, "Hello Ruth" and I said, "Oh hello David, how are things?" He said, "Not too bad". We stood there for a few minutes then Buster, my dog, was pulling on the lead, he wanted to get going. I said, "I will have to go, David." He said, "See you again then, Ruth," and that was it, we parted.' Her conversation with Kelly was just under a mile from his home. He then headed along the road towards Kingston Bagpuize.'

Dr Malcolm Warner

The Kelly family doctor

- Testified that he had never treated Kelly for depression – and had only seen him for minor ailments, last in 1999.

The evidence

Louise Holmes
Hearing dog trainer who found the body

- Member of the search and rescue team whose border collie cross Brock found Kelly's body on 18 July 2003, at around 8am, about 200 metres into the wood.

Key quote
'I could see a body slumped against the bottom of a tree, so I turned around and shouted to Paul to ring Control and tell them that we had found something and then went closer to just see whether there was any first aid that I needed to administer . . . He was at the base of the tree with almost his head and his shoulders just slumped back against the tree . . . His legs were straight in front of him. His right arm was to the side of him. His left arm had a lot of blood on it and was bent back in a funny position.'

PC Andrew Franklin
Search team adviser, Thames Valley Police

- Officer in charge of the police search team who took charge of the scene where Kelly's body was discovered slumped against a tree near Harrowdown Hill in Longworth.
- Nearby on the ground was a three-inch pruning knife, Kelly's flat cap, wristwatch and a small bottle of water that he used to help him take an overdose. Said the scientist had blood covering his left wrist.

On his first sight of the body
'He was lying on his back with his right hand to his side and his left hand was sort of inverted with the palm facing down (indicates), facing up on his back . . .

The wristwatch was lying away from the body, next to a knife. The wristwatch was just to the left of the left arm, with the knife next to it, and also there was an open bottle of water at the scene.'

PC Martyn Sawyer

Search team leader, Thames Valley Police

- One of the first officers on the scene, he provided details of the police fingertip search around the body.
- Also searched Kelly's house, where a photograph was found of Kelly and someone bearing a resemblance to Andrew Gilligan – a theory later discounted by police.

Key quote

'This area itself was remarkable for its complete lack of human interference . . .

When I first saw Dr Kelly I was very aware of the serious nature of the search and I was looking for signs of perhaps a struggle; but all the vegetation that was surrounding Dr Kelly's body was standing upright and there were no signs of any form of struggle at all.'

Detective Sergeant Geoffrey Webb

Thames Valley Police

- Sgt Webb was sent to the Kelly home to talk to them for clues as to where the scientist might be. Gave the family the news that his body had been found.
- Searched the house after news of the death. In Kelly's briefcase, recovered from his study, he found a Ministry of Defence letter

211

reprimanding Kelly for his contact with Andrew Gilligan. It was unopened. Also recovered was a handwritten note entitled 'Gabriel's Concerns' – believed to refer to Iraq and weapons of mass destruction.

- In a Sainsbury's notebook, Sgt Webb found a list of journalists' names, and elsewhere in the study reporters' business cards. On a low coffee table was an opened letter from Kelly's line manager headed 'Andrew Gilligan and his single anonymous source'.

On the Kelly family's feelings before the body was found

'The Kelly family were very upbeat at that time. They were very hopeful that no harm had come to Kelly. In fact, they genuinely believed I think that perhaps he had become ill somewhere.'

Vanessa Elizabeth Hunt

Paramedic, Oxford Ambulance

- One of the two paramedics called to the scene, Hunt placed monitor pads on his chest to check for signs of life and agreed Kelly was dead.

Key quote

'My colleague lifted the eyelids to check for pupil reaction, also felt the gentleman's neck for a carotid pulse and I initially placed the heart monitor paddles on to the chest over the top of his shirt.

The amount of blood that was around the scene seemed relatively minimal and there was a small patch on his right knee, but no obvious arterial bleeding. There was no spraying of blood or huge blood loss or any obvious loss on the clothing.'

Barney Leith

Secretary of the National Spiritual Assembly of the Baha'is of the UK

- Leader of the religion to which David Kelly converted, Leith said that the Baha'i faith did not condone suicide. Press reports after the scientist's death had led to the posting of a statement on a Baha'i website stressing that suicide was not acceptable.
- Leith said there were five to six million followers of the Baha'i faith globally. It had emerged in the mid-19th century in Persia.
- Kelly had joined the faith in September 1999 while in the US. He was briefly the treasurer of his local Baha'i group in Oxfordshire and attended meetings at Mr Leith's home in Abingdon.
- Said a newspaper report that said Kelly had attacked the government's September 2002 dossier at a Baha'i meeting was wrong.

On the Baha'i attitude to suicide

'The act of suicide is condemned in the Baha'i writings because it is an undue curtailment of the life that should be lived to the full. However, Baha'is and the Baha'i institutions do not and never would take a condemnatory attitude to people who unfortunately commit suicide.

Quite the opposite. There would be a great deal of sympathy, as indeed there has been in the case of Dr Kelly, and Baha'is would pray for the progress of the soul of that person as they have for the soul of Dr Kelly.'

On the meeting at which Kelly was said to have attacked the dossier

'The particular press comment claimed that he had spoken at a Baha'i meeting critically about the September dossier. This was not in fact the case. I was at that meeting.'

Professor Keith Hawton

Director of the Centre for Suicide Research in the University Department of Psychiatry in Oxford (also appeared on day 22)

- Pressure from the Ministry of Defence and MPs deepened Kelly's growing despair which led him to commit suicide.
- Messages found in Kelly's computer showed that the prospect of a humiliating end to his distinguished career hung over him.
- Painted a picture of an increasingly desperate man, saying it was 'well nigh certain' Kelly committed suicide, and probably decided to do so in the morning or early afternoon of 17 July 2003.
- Asked, with the benefit of hindsight, what contributed to Kelly's death, he said the major factor was the 'severe loss of self-esteem, resulting from his feeling that people had lost trust in him and from his dismay at being exposed to the media'.
- Professor Hawton described Kelly as not being able to share his problems and feelings with others and increasingly withdrawing into himself.
- Asked if a lay person would have had any chance of knowing that Kelly could commit suicide. 'Certainly not,' Professor Hawton replied.

Key quote

'I think that taking all the evidence together, it is well nigh certain that he committed suicide.'

Asked about the factors that contributed to Kelly's death

'I think that as far as one can deduce, the major factor was the severe loss of self-esteem, resulting from his feeling that people had lost trust in him and from his dismay at being exposed to the media . . .

Being such a private man, I think this was anathema to him to be exposed, you know, publicly in this way. In a sense, I think he would have seen it as being publicly disgraced.'

Describing the important factors in Kelly's increasingly feeling more isolated, the psychiatrist pointed to a letter Kelly was sent by Richard Hatfield, the MoD's personnel director, warning of possible future disciplinary action
'In a sense he was getting further and further from being able to share the problems with other people, that is extremely important.' ■

Key Documents

Reply to an email from a friend expressing sympathy for Kelly, dated 17 July 2003, 11.18
Many thanks for your thoughts. It has been difficult. Hopefully it will all blow over by the end of the week and I can travel to Baghdad and get on with the real work.

Email to David Kelly from his office referring to parliamentary questions following on the same day
David, more PQs! but plenty of time for reply. I expect that Bryan will deal tomorrow. James. ■

Day 14
3 September 2003

Brian Jones, a former defence intelligence officer, delivered a blistering attack on the way the Iraqi weapons dossier was drawn up, accusing the government of 'overegging' the threat posed by Saddam Hussein and describing the 45-minute claim as 'nebulous'. Complaints from experts were ignored after 'the shutters came down', he said. He also expressed deep scepticism about the way the term 'weapons of mass destruction' was wrongly used to encompass all chemical and biological warfare.

The inquiry also heard further evidence relating to how Dr Kelly committed suicide.

Richard Allan
Forensic scientist and toxicologist

- Kelly had swallowed 29 prescription painkillers – Coproxamol, which belonged to his wife who suffers from arthritis – around an hour before his death.
- This was a 'considerable overdose' but probably did not kill the scientist. He gulped the tablets so fast he even swallowed some of the protective plastic coating they came in.

Michael Page
Assistant chief constable, community services, Thames Valley Police

- Said he could not think of a way that anyone else had been involved in Kelly's death. The scientist had cut his left wrist after taking the overdose of powerful painkillers.

● Police seized Kelly's computers and recovered emails from them.

● Kelly had sent an email warning of 'many dark actors playing games' hours before he went on the walk during which he committed suicide.

On the contents of Kelly's computers

'I am advised by our computer technical people that of all the memory that we have seized from Dr Kelly's various computers . . . if we were to print it out it would produce a pile of paper twice as high as Big Ben.'

Confirming there was no sign of foul play

'I am as confident as I can be that there was no third party involvement at the scene of Dr Kelly's death . . . I cannot conceive of a way in which a third party could have been involved at that location in that environment without at least leaving some trace of their presence; and I have been unable to find any trace of any presence whatsoever . . . I remain confident that he met his death at his own hand.'

Stephen MacDonald

Responsible for the day-to-day security of staff in the MoD buildings in London

● Testified that a 'burn bag' (a bag for secret documents to be disposed) had been found in a third floor office in the Metropole MoD Building including a document relating to David Kelly. MoD police were called and sealed the room.

● The Metropolitan Police examined the contents of the bag and assessed that there was nothing likely to be significant for the Hutton inquiry.

- On 1 August, an article in the *Daily Telegraph* alleged that a senior official had been caught hastily shredding documents, and a further article appeared on 3 August in the *Mail on Sunday* alleging that a mysterious blonde had been found inside the MoD removing documents.
- Spoke to a member of staff who had said that they had been responsible for the confusion that had been caused and had left the bag out. Note put on file.

Brian Jones

Former analyst in the Defence Intelligence Staff

- Now retired, at the time the dossier was published Jones was head of a scientific section in the Defence Intelligence Analysis Staff responsible for chemical and biological weapons and deeply involved in the production of the dossier.
- Accused the government of 'overegging' the threat posed by Saddam Hussein and of ignoring concerns about central claims made in the document.
- Jones chaired a meeting of senior defence intelligence officials on 19 September 2002, five days before the dossier was published. Kelly was present. The officials, including Kelly, raised a number of specific concerns about the dossier. None was accepted by Whitehall's Joint Intelligence Committee.
- He and fellow intelligence officials regarded as 'nebulous' the hotly disputed claim that Iraqi forces could deploy chemical and biological weapons within 45 minutes.
- Suggested that Iraq possessed few, if any, weapons of mass destruction in the proper meaning of the term. He said he

would struggle to place chemical weapons, and many biological weapons, in the category of 'weapons of mass destruction'.

● Said the 'shutters came down', preventing experts on chemical and biological weapons from expressing widespread disquiet about the language and assumptions in the dossier.

Pressed by Lord Hutton to explain his worries about the dossier

'My concerns were that Iraq's chemical weapons and biological weapons capabilities were not being accurately represented in all regards in relation to the available evidence. In particular . . . on the advice of my staff, I was told that there was no evidence that significant production had taken place either of chemical warfare agent or chemical weapons.'

On the source for the 45-minute claim

'We even wondered, in discussing the issue, whether he might even have been trying to influence rather than inform.'

The concerns of his top chemical warfare expert about the dossier

'They were really about a tendency in certain areas, from his point of view, to shall we say overegg certain assessments in relation particularly to the production of CW agents and weapons since 1998 . . . he was concerned that he could not point to any solid evidence of such production.'

On the 'spin merchants'

'I think there was an impression that there was an influence from outside the intelligence community.'

On whether their views would be reflected in the final dossier

'The impression I had was . . . the shutters were coming down on this particular paper, that the discussion and the argument had been concluded. And it was the impression that I had, at that time, that our reservations about the dossier were not going to be reflected in the final version.'

Mr A

Casually employed civil servant with the Counter Proliferation and Arms Control Department of the MoD

- A former United Nations weapons inspector and part of the current Iraqi survey group, hunting for evidence Iraq had WMD. He told Lord Hutton that he had raised concerns over a draft of the dossier at a 19 September meeting held by members of the Defence Intelligence Staff (DIS). Mr A said Kelly had taken him there.
- 'As a whole' he and Kelly had thought the dossier was a reasonable and accurate reflection of available intelligence, but there were serious problems with it, including the 45-minute claim.
- Prompted by an article in the *Guardian*, Mr A emailed Kelly about their mutual scepticism over an Iraqi factory at al-Qa'qa' producing phosgene – used for explosives, but also a component suitable for chemical weapons – highlighted in the government's dossier.
- The dossier said that 'parts of al-Qa'qa' chemical complex damaged in the [first] Gulf war have also been repaired and are operational. Of particular concern are elements of the phosgene production plant at al-Qa'qa' . . . While phosgene does have industrial uses it can also be used by itself as a chemical agent or as a precursor for nerve agent.' Mr A rubbished this as 'a stupid mistake'.

- On 25 September 2002 the *Guardian* reported from al-Qa'qa'. Iraq invited journalists, including reporter Ewen MacAskill, to the site within hours of the claim being published.

Why an article in the *Guardian* highlighted an issue of concern for him

'My concerns were that it really was a non-issue, and it was wrong for the government to make such a fuss about the phosgene production plant at al-Qa'qa'. I had visited there as part of a UN inspection team and many other inspection teams had visited the plant. It is true that phosgene was used as a toxication during the first world war, but some six million tons or so, I believe, are manufactured worldwide every year, and this was a small expensive way of producing phosgene dedicated to a particular process, a legitimate process within the al-Qa'qa' plant. Therefore to state it was of particular concern against a background in which the Iraqi armed forces had never weaponised phosgene nor shown any intention of doing so was, for me, the wrong emphasis. My quarrel was with the phrase "of particular concern".'

His initial view of the dossier

'There were errors of detail and there were errors of emphasis, in my view.'

On the 45-minute claim

'I think all those of us without access to that intelligence immediately asked the question: well, what does the 45 minutes refer to? Are you referring to a technical process? Are you referring to a commander control process?'

How 'the spin merchants' had been involved

'The perception was that the dossier had been round the houses several times in order to try to find a form of words which would strengthen certain political objectives.'

On his last meeting with Kelly, during their training in early July
'He seemed his normal self, chatty, friendly, gregarious.'

In Baghdad eight days after the death of Kelly
'Some 30 former colleagues of David actually gathered, which in a sense was fairly impressive, to remember the man and his achievements. And we felt that his loss is actually a sorry loss for the Iraq Survey Group and we miss his expertise and his friendship greatly.' ∎

Key Documents

Email reply from Kelly to an American journalist who said his evidence before MPs had gone well, dated 17 July 2003, 11.18am
I will wait until the end of the week before judging – many dark actors playing games.

Minute of meeting of intelligence staff sent by Brian Jones to his director, titled: 'Reference: Iraq Dossier Draft issued on 19 September 02'
2. Although we have no problem with a judgement based on intelligence that Saddam attaches great importance to possessing WMD we have not seen the intelligence that 'shows' he does not regard them only as a weapon of last resort, although our judgement is that it would be sensible to assume he might use them in a number of other scenarios. The intelligence we have seen indicates rather than 'shows' that Iraq has been planning to conceal its WMD capabilities, and it would be reasonable to assume that he would do this.
3. We have a number of questions in our minds relating to the intelligence on

the military plans for the use of chemical and biological weapons, particularly about the times mentioned and the failure to differentiate between the two types of weapon.

4. We have not seen intelligence which we believe 'shows' that Iraq has continued to produce CW agent in 1998-2002, although our judgement is that it has probably done so. Whilst we are even more convinced that Iraq has continued to produce BW agent (on the basis of mobile production intelligence) we would not go so far as to say we 'know' this to be the case.

Email from Mr A to David Kelly, 25 September 2002

Casting your mind back to Thursday's rushed little meeting, you will recall me pointing out that the phosgene plan was too small to be interesting, and regarded by Unscom as legit dual use. I was assured that rebuilding had gone on.

I also pointed out the bulk world usage of phosgene, and the small size of the unit. You will recall [blanked out] admitted they were grasping at straws.

My annotations are on draft – you'll remember [blanked out] was keen to relieve me of possession of the dossier at the end of the meeting!

So all in all – having read page 2 of the *Guardian* – I'm with the manager of al-Qa'qa: 'it is a pretty stupid mistake for the British to make'.

Another example supporting our view that you and I should have been more involved in this than the spin merchants of this administration. No doubt you will have more to tell me as a result of your antics today. Let's hope it turns into tomorrow's chip wrappers. ■

Day 15
4 September 2003

Geoff Hoon was further damaged when Richard Taylor, his special adviser, revealed that the Defence Secretary knew more about the outing strategy than he had so far admitted. The inquiry also heard evidence from one of Dr Kelly's former UN weapons inspector colleagues, Olivia Bosch, who played a key, albeit unwitting, role in the affair. She alerted Kelly to Andrew Gilligan's evidence to the Commons Foreign Affairs Committee (FAC), telling him Gilligan's source had told the BBC reporter the kind of things Kelly had told Bosch.

Olivia Bosch

Senior research fellow at the Royal Institute of International Affairs, also known as Chatham House, and former UN inspector in Iraq

- In evidence that undermined a crucial part of Gilligan's testimony, the former Unscom inspector said the reporter played a 'name game' with Kelly to discover the focus of intelligence officials' concerns.
- During one of the daily conversations held by the pair before he died, Kelly told her of being 'taken aback' by Gilligan's determination to pin the blame on someone.
- In a telephone conversation before he died, Kelly told Bosch of being surprised at the way in which the *Today* reporter tried to get him to name names.
- Bosch said Kelly was 'indignant' at the BBC's decision to link Gilligan's reports with those of Susan Watts.

● Kelly was furious at a piece by Nicholas Rufford in the *Sunday Times* after the MoD confirmed Kelly's name, which portrayed a perfunctory conversation as a full-blown interview.

On the 'name game' between Gilligan and Kelly.

'Towards mid-May he [Kelly] told me he had an unauthorised meeting with Andrew Gilligan . . . he said he was . . . taken aback by the way [he] tried to elicit information from him. I said, "Yes, but that is what journalists do." He understood that, but he said he had never experienced it in the way that Gilligan had tried to do so, by a name game was the term.

. . . He said that Gilligan wanted to play a name game as to who was responsible for inserting information into the dossier, and that . . . Gilligan said to him: I will name you some names . . . the first name he mentioned very quickly and immediately was Campbell. David told me he could neither confirm nor deny . . . but he thought he had to give an answer so he said "maybe".'

Kelly's response when Bosch read him a statement from the BBC which claimed similarities between Gilligan and Watts's reports.

'What does she have to do with this?'

On the thought that he may have indeed been a source for Watts

'He was thrown by the reference to Susan Watts. He rhetorically asked me, "Is that the kind of thing I could have said all in one long go?" . . . I got the feeling that he was having second thoughts about it.'

Kelly's reaction to the line in the *Sunday Times* article: 'In his first public comments since the row blew up . . .'

'I had never heard David so excited and so frustrated and angry . . . he was peeved and excited about the start of a second sentence in an article that Nick Rufford wrote for the *Sunday Times*.'

Leigh Potter
Neighbour of Kelly

- Barmaid in Kelly's local pub, the Wagon and Horses. Testified that Kelly came into the pub on 9 July 2003 and left a message for the landlord of the pub that he was going away and 'the press were going to pounce'.

Tom Mangold
Journalist

- The television journalist and author, who had known the weapons specialist since 1998, said Kelly had thought the government dossier's claim that Iraq could deploy weapons of mass destruction within 45 minutes was 'risible' and had laughed about it.
- He spoke to Kelly occasionally and earlier in the year had asked for his help in researching the 45-minute claim.
- Press reports had led him to identify Kelly as the unnamed official who had come forward.

His discussions with Kelly about the 45-minute claim
'Occasionally we just gossiped on the phone and on this occasion we gossiped about the 45-minutes claim because I thought it sounded risible to me, and I wondered what David felt about it . . . He thought it was risible too.

. . . it was a question of which verb was supposed to be used; and he did not feel that the weapons could be deployed or activated within 45 minutes and we spoke about the length of time it might take just to fill a munition. That alone would take 30 to 45 minutes. If you have the bacteria here and the warhead there, it still takes all that amount of time, and we spoke about the temperatures at which these things have to be kept. He just laughed about the 45-minute claim.'

On hearing that Kelly had gone missing
'I had very mixed emotions on that day. I knew the moment I got the phone call at 9 o'clock in the morning, I knew that he had to be dead because David Kelly did not go missing. If he was missing, he was dead.'

Richard Taylor
Special adviser to Secretary of State for Defence

- Said Hoon was present at a key meeting in which the policy of naming Kelly was approved.
- The meeting took place in Hoon's office on 9 July 2003. He discussed with senior advisers what the Ministry of Defence should say if a journalist came up with Kelly's name. The group decided that it was untenable to refuse to respond to journalists who had guessed Kelly's identity.
- In his account of the 9 July meeting, Taylor said it was attended by Hoon, Peter Watkins, his principal private secretary, and the MoD's director of news, Pam Teare. The group was presented with three options – whether to deny Kelly's name when it was put to the MoD press office by journalists, simply to make no comment, or to confirm the name. Agreed a plan for Hoon to name Kelly in a private letter to Gavyn Davies, the BBC chairman.

On why it was decided to name Kelly in a letter to Davies
'I offered my advice on the basis of wishing to move the argument forward with the BBC. There was an alternative view proposed at

that meeting . . . which suggested that maybe we should repeat the previous day's offer to the BBC that we would give them the name in return for them confirming or denying it. I did not believe that that was tenable for the next 24-hour period and that to move forward we should disclose the name in private in the letter.'

On discussions over the naming strategy
'If journalists rang and put the name directly to the department then, yes, they would confirm it. The discussion explored the rationale for that; and if people had said "no" in answer to the name "Dr David Kelly" that would be a lie, and that would be unacceptable for the department to respond in that way.'

Key Documents

Email from Tom Mangold to David Kelly, 9 July 2003
The Times today quotes Hoon as identifying Gilligan's source in such a way that I feel it is someone I know and admire. Could we have a chat about this. I am available for help, consultation, a drink, a dry shoulder or whatever. Bestest. Tom Mangold.

Kelly's reply later the same day
Tom. Thanks. Not a good time to be in communication.

Minutes released on this day of a high-level meeting held in John Scarlett's office on 18 September 2002. Under a heading in bold, 'Ownership of the Dossier':
Ownership lay with No. 10. ■

Day 16
15 September 2003

As the inquiry began its second phase, it heard from a surprise witness – Sir Richard Dearlove, the chief of the Secret Intelligence Service, commonly known as MI6. He gave evidence from a hidden location connected by audio link – his face was not shown. Unsurprisingly, he defended the weapons dossier. Signficantly, however, he said strong criticism by the Intelligence and Security Committee of the way the 45-minute claim was described in the dossier was 'valid' – a dig at the former MI6 officer John Scarlett.

Tony Cragg
Former deputy chief of Defence Intelligence

- Questioned about his decision to ignore the concerns of two members of the Defence Intelligence Staff, Brian Jones and Mr A, over the dossier's assessments of Iraq's WMD capacity. He said he believed these concerns had been dealt with satisfactorily and did not pass them on to Scarlett, the chairman of the JIC.
- Questioned about a memo sent on 17 September 2002 from another analyst to the joint intelligence staff putting together the dossier objecting to the claim that Iraq 'has continued to produce chemical and biological agents' as 'too strong'. Cragg said he knew the identity of the author of the memo and confirmed that it was not Jones or Mr A.

229

On whether the memo from the third analyst confirmed a trend in intelligence thinking

'In terms of patterns or trends, I think not really, in the sense that the views of Dr Jones were being informed, quite rightly, in part by the individual who wrote this, the expert who wrote this text. So it is not as if they are approaching the issue from two different angles. This is reinforcing what was already there.'

On the dossier's preparation

'In my view, from my perspective, the dossier was prepared and produced by a rigorous process of drafting.'

On DIS concerns about the dossier's wording

'I think that the Defence Intelligence sSaff, as you say, were concerned about the executive summary and its discontinuity with the main text. I put this down to the fact that the executive summary pulled together or reflected not merely recent intelligence which was being – which was contained in the main text, but also the general context of the new intelligence which had been received, such as knowledge, which we had had for many years, of the capabilities of the Iraqis in their use of chemical weapons and also our knowledge that they had commander control arrangements for the use of these weapons in place.

These other issues informed the judgement in the executive summary to which the defence intelligence staff were objecting slightly or wanting to modify the wording.'

Air Marshall Sir Joe French
Former chief of Defence Intelligence

• Acknowledged a range of views had been put forward on the

dossier and said that was the nature of the process. But he said: 'I was content with the wording that appeared in the final draft.'

On the wording of the 45-minute claim

'I have accepted what they put in the report. Again, if you are looking at 45 minutes I think it has to be understood that the intelligence that we were using in the Defence Intelligence Staff was not just an understanding of what the Iraqi forces may be capable of; we also had to put it in the context of our forces deployed to the region. We had had forces there continuously since 1991, and any potential conflict that might arise with them, we would have to make sure that we had an understanding that was passed on to our armed forces so that they could make the appropriate defensive measures themselves should they come under any sort of attack from these sorts of weapons.'

Sir Richard Dearlove

Chief of the Secret Intelligence Service

- Britain's head of MI6, Dearlove admitted the way the government claimed that Iraq could deploy chemical and biological weapons within 45 minutes was open to misinterpretation.
- Made clear he strongly objected to attempts by Downing Street to exaggerate the threat posed by Saddam Hussein's nuclear programme in the government's Iraqi weapons dossier.
- Denied there was unease within MI6 about pressure from Downing Street as the dossier was prepared before it was published.
- Said that MI6 had always assumed the 45-minute claim referred only to battlefield weapons. Many of his agency's CX reports – reports describing raw intelligence – were 'essentially single-sourced'.

cont'd p.234

Spymaster communicates with inquiry

Sketch
Simon Hoggart

In an unprecedented move, the chief of MI6 appeared in public before the Hutton inquiry yesterday.

In fact 'C', as he is known to his friends, actually did nothing so compromising of personal security as to appear. Instead he manifested himself through his voice. The link to the computer screens in court 73 seemed to have been covered by sacking just in case they inadvertently gave a clue to what he might look like.

We weren't even told where he was, though a technician said he was not in the MI6 building, but 'somewhere north of the river', which may be intelligence slang of some kind. My private fantasy was that a cupboard door in the corner of the court would fall open and a very embarrassed spook would fall out.

Wherever he was, it was rather noisy. At one point we seemed to hear a toilet flush. Then there were mysterious clangings and bangings, as if C were using a traction engine rally as cover for his briefing.

He even had to be asked to speak closer to the microphone. Perhaps he was at home, and didn't want his wife to know what his job is.

The world depicted by C, or 'Sir Richard Billing Dearlove' – which is his codename – seems a long way from the glamorous life of James Bond. There was nothing about driving his Aston Martin to Downing Street, flicking a switch to turn it into a helicopter gunship, or of fountain pens with tiny but lethal bullets.

Nor did we glimpse the hardly more realistic world of Alec Guinness as George Smiley, gazing morosely in the general direction of the Berlin Wall.

'I hear that Rczewski has gone north of the river.'

'Yes, that was a regrettable lapse in security.'

In fact, the day-to-day life of the average spook seems to consist, as it does for most civil servants, of paperwork. He attends a lot of meetings and reads a lot of reports.

We learned that intelligence reports are known as CX in the business, and he had been 'shocked' to discover that Dr David Kelly had been discussing a CX report with the press. 'It was a serious breach of discipline,' he said in the same appalled voice used by the chief of police who discovers there is gambling at Rick's Bar in Casablanca – that is, not shocked at all. We also learned that the people who get to read these CX reports are known in MI5 as 'customers', as in 'the reference to 45 minutes did not evoke any comment from customers at all'.

This may be a clue. After all, customers make demands, as in, 'have you got something a bit, er, stronger?'

'Awight, hang on, I'll have a look in the back. Can do you 35 minutes, if that's any use.'

We had a long discussion on what constitutes a reliable report, and it turns out that a single source can be enough. 'CX reports are essentially single source, and much high-quality intelligence comes from single sources.'

This is of course exactly the point Andrew Gilligan and the BBC have been trying to make, without much success. Apparently it's all right when the single source was talking to secret men with no faces.

At the end the inquiry counsel, James Dingemans, asked, as he always does, if there is any other light the witness can throw on the death of Dr Kelly. They always say no and, relieved, vamoose for a stiff drink.

I yearn for someone to shout: 'Yes! I can! It was me, me, I tell you! But you'll never catch me alive.' (Plunges out of window, last seen heading north of the river.)

By contrast, C said there was nothing he could add, and no doubt went for a cup of tea with two sugars, stirred not shaken. ■

Guardian, 16 September 2003

233

● Sir Richard said he was unaware of widespread concern among officials in the defence intelligence staff about claims made in the dossier, concerns they discussed with Kelly.

Asked by inquiry QC James Dingemans about the intelligence leading up to the 45-minute claim

'You use the word "claim"; I think I would prefer to refer to it as a piece of well-sourced intelligence.'

The source for the 45-minute claim

'It did come from an established and reliable source . . . a senior Iraqi military officer who was certainly in a position to know this information.'

Asked what he thought of MPs' criticism of the 45-minute claim

'Given the misinterpretation that was placed on the 45-minute intelligence, with the benefit of hindsight you can say that is a valid criticism. But I am confident that the intelligence was accurate and that the use made of it was entirely consistent with the original report.'

On specific criticism of the way the 45-minute claim was written from the parliamentary intelligence committee

'Given the misinterpretation of the original piece of intelligence, particularly as it was not qualified in terms of its relationship to battlefield munitions, this now looks a valid criticism.'

On complaints about the use of a single source

'CX reports as produced by my service are essentially single source; and much high-quality intelligence which is factual or proved to be factual is single source material.'

**On the response of MI6 to a memo Campbell had sent
Scarlett about Iraqi nuclear ambitions**
'I was aware, from my senior officer who was working on the
drafting, that there had been, for example, a debate over the
amount of time it might take the Iraqis to develop a nuclear
weapon; and I know that there was, let us say, a rigorous response
to questions in terms of sticking with the original intelligence in
recording those issues in the dossier.'

On Kelly speaking to journalists about the reports
'As chief of the service, I am shocked to see someone discussing one
of our CX reports, which is what he is discussing, with a journalist
without authorisation . . . it is a serious breach of discipline.'

Greg Dyke
Director general of the BBC

- Announced a wide-ranging review of the corporation's journalism at the Hutton inquiry, admitting 'lessons could be
  learned' from its reporting of the Iraq dossier row.
- Denounced as 'unacceptable' the decision by Andrew Gilligan to
  email MPs on the Foreign Affairs Committee
- Accused Campbell of mounting a 'pre-planned attack' on the
  corporation's journalism in an attempt to 'settle old scores'.
- Pointed out that the BBC employed 27,000 people, 3,400 staff in
  the news division. For every hour of the day, the BBC broadcasts
  40 hours of output. In this context, Dyke said he could not be
  expected to know every detail of every decision taken.
- When he appeared before the BBC governors to justify the
  corporation's strong defence of the story, he did not know about
  a crucial email from the editor of the *Today* programme to the

head of radio news in which Gilligan's report was characterised as a 'good piece of investigative journalism marred by flawed reporting'.

- In drafting a reply to Campbell's detailed complaint in late June, Dyke made no attempt to establish the accuracy of Gilligan's story, instead taking its veracity on trust from BBC news executives.
- The BBC's editor-in-chief announced a four-point plan to improve BBC journalism in the light of the death of Kelly. The BBC's producer guidelines, contained in a document that sets out the rules by which journalists are expected to abide, will be reviewed. The use of anonymous sources, and the way they are described on air, will also be looked at. 'Two-way' interviews – live, off-the-cuff discussions between reporters and presenters – may not in future be used to break controversial stories.

Saying the intensity of the BBC's counter-attack was in response to the nature of Campbell's strategy

'I think what informed our response at the time was the breadth of the attack. I think that was – one felt that old scores were being settled, particularly in terms of the war and the coverage of the war.'

On Gilligan's email to members of the FAC suggesting questions to ask Kelly

'It is not an acceptable email to send to members of the committee. It is not unknown for journalists to be asked to supply information to committee members across the whole board of journalism, but I think it is not acceptable that he was described. He was not in a position to know the source, at that stage, for Ms Watts and nor was he in a position to send this.'

On the lessons the BBC has to learn from the inquiry

'What the processes of the last few weeks have certainly exposed is that politics and journalism are far from exact sciences, and the forensic examination really of the events of May, June and July has revealed I think areas where in hindsight we would have – we might have behaved differently.' ■

Key Documents

Extract from a memo from unidentified intelligence analyst sent on 20 September 2002 to the joint intelligence staff

2. a. Prime Minister's foreword, 5th paragraph states:

'What I believe the assessed intelligence has established beyond doubt is that Saddam has continued to produce chemical and biological weapons . . .'

I acknowledge that in this statement the Prime Minister will be expressing his own 'belief' about what the assessed intelligence has established. What I wish to record is that based on the intelligence available to me it has NOT established beyond doubt that Saddam has continued to produce chemical [and biological] weapons.

2. b. Prime Minister's foreword, 8th paragraph states:

'And the document discloses that his military planning allows for some of the WMD to be ready within 45 minutes of an order to use them.'

A similar statement appears in the dossier. It is reported as fact whereas the intelligence comes from a single source. In my view the intelligence warrants no stronger a statement than 'intelligence suggests that military planning allows . . .'

From a speech made by Dyke to the Radio Festival, 8 July 2003

Let me say this, whatever the background of Alastair Campbell's attack on the BBC, to criticise the reputation of all BBC journalists by publicly accusing us of lying and bias is not acceptable and I thank him for stepping back from that position yesterday.

This has now dominated the headlines for two weeks and it is time for both sides to agree to disagree and move on. ■

Day 17
16 September 2003

This is the day counsel for the Kelly family and the BBC were waiting for – the chance to cross-examine government witnesses. Jeremy Gompertz, for the family, said the scientist was kept in the dark about a 'sea change' in the outing strategy which led to his naming in the media. He accused the MoD of playing 'Russian roulette' to get journalists to identify Dr Kelly. The inquiry also heard that dissent within the defence intelligence community over the dossier was kept secret from MPs.

Detective Constable Graham Coe
Thames Valley Police

● First officer on the scene when the body was found by search and rescue teams. The following day went to the Kelly home where a police search was happening.

Nicholas Hunt
Home Office pathologist

● Pathologist called to the scene by police. At 12.35pm he confirmed the death. That night he carried out the post-mortem in the mortuary at the John Radcliffe hospital in Oxford.

Key quote
'I found that Dr Kelly was an apparently adequately nourished man in whom there was no evidence of natural disease that could of

itself have caused death directly at the macroscopic or naked-eye level. He had evidence of a significant incised wound to his left wrist, in the depths of which his left ulnar artery had been completely severed. That wound was in the context of multiple incised wounds over the front of his left wrist of varying length and depth. The arterial injury had resulted in the loss of a significant volume of blood, as noted at the scene. The complex of incised wounds over the left wrist is entirely consistent with having been inflicted by a bladed weapon, most likely candidate for which would have been a knife. Furthermore, the knife present at the scene would be a suitable candidate for causing such injuries. The orientation and arrangement of the wounds over the left wrist are typical of self-inflicted injury. Also typical of this was the presence of small so-called tentative or hesitation marks. The fact that his watch appeared to have been removed while blood was already flowing suggests that it had been removed deliberately in order to facilitate access to the wrist. The removal of the watch in that way and indeed the removal of the spectacles are features pointing towards this being an act of self-harm. Other features at the scene which would tend to support this impression include the relatively passive distribution of the blood, the neat way in which the water bottle and its top were placed, the lack of obvious signs of trampling of the undergrowth or damage to the clothing. To my mind, the location of the death is also of interest in this respect because it was clearly a very pleasant and relatively private spot of the type that is sometimes chosen by people intent upon self-harm.'

Martin Howard

Deputy chief of Defence Intelligence (also appeared on days 1 and 4)

● In addition to questioning from the inquiry's lawyers, he was cross-examined by barristers David Lloyd-Jones QC for the

MoD, Jeremy Gompertz QC for the Kelly family and Andrew Caldecott QC for the BBC.

- David Kelly was kept in the dark about a 'sea change' in the outing strategy which led to his naming in the media, the Hutton inquiry heard as the Kelly family barrister delivered a blistering attack on his treatment by the Ministry of Defence.

- Gompertz described the ministry's attitude as 'cynical and irresponsible'.

- Howard persistently denied he was responsible for any unfair treatment of Kelly. The priority for the government, he suggested, was to 'correct the public record' – to show that Gilligan had embellished what Kelly had told him.

- Said that although Geoff Hoon, the Defence Secretary, was not directly involved in the strategy to name Kelly, his private office was aware of what was going on.

- Howard had advised Hoon not to disclose the existence of the complaints even when he subsequently gave evidence to the parliamentary Intelligence and Security Committee (ISC).

Key exchanges:

Jeremy Gompertz [for the Kelly family]: Can I put this suggestion to you that the combination of the information in the press statement issued . . . meant that any able journalist, with a little research, would be able to identify Dr Kelly. Do you agree?

Martin Howard: I do not think I agree entirely. I did not – was not involved in the PMOS briefing, so I have no idea how that came about. I was travelling to the Middle East at the time . . .

JG: I appreciate that you were not even in the country at the time of the press briefing, but the question I asked you was this: would you agree that the information contained in those three sources would inevitably lead any competent journalist, of whom there are more than a few about, to be able to identify Dr Kelly?

MH: I think it – those details, particularly the ones that appeared on 9 July, may well have helped. I am not sure they would inevitably have been the only way that they would have identified Dr Kelly.

JG [on how the MoD press office Q and A brief was changed to allow press officers to name Dr Kelly]: It is a sea change, is it not, from the attitude being adopted in the first draft?

MH: I do not regard it as a sea change but it is just that people, having seen the first Q and A brief, would have said: how do we respond if they actually put a name to us? That was not dealt with in the first Q and A brief.

JG: The procedure adopted, Mr Howard, I suggest, amounted to a parlour game for journalists; would you agree?

MH: No.

JG: A form, perhaps, of 20 questions, though 21 in the case of *The Times*.

MH: We are not responsible for how the media put their questions to the press office.
JG: Or was it more like a game of Russian roulette?

MH: No, it was not that either.

JG: I suggest to you that the strategy that was adopted with regard to disclosing Dr Kelly's identity was both cynical and irresponsible. What do you say?

MH: I would disagree with that completely.

JG: Was Dr Kelly ever asked whether he consented to having his identity revealed?

MH: He was not consulted over the terms of the Q and A brief, as I understand anyway.

JG: Was he ever asked whether he consented to having his identity revealed?

MH: I do not believe he was asked in those terms, but he was told that it was likely his name would come out.

JG: Do you not agree that Dr Kelly was treated shabbily in relation to this episode?

MH: No, I do not agree.

Andrew Shuttleworth
Kelly's resource manager at Porton Down

- Answered questions about Kelly's pay and grading concerns; his secondment to PACS and issues relating to Unscom; Kelly's dealings with the press.

On the battle to improve Kelly's pay
'I was being told, on the one hand, his pay could not be dealt with

because he was a member of the senior civil service and the pay was dealt with by a separate part of the system; and when I spoke to the officer who dealt with that, I was told David was not a part of the senior civil service. So there seemed to be quite a bit of confusion.'

On his media role
'He was actively encouraged to talk to the press. He had been doing it since 1991; and in 1995–96 . . . I decided to formalise that and it became one of his annual key results, a target, if you like . . . To provide briefings to the press and to government bodies, learned societies, as and when required by the . . . people employing him.'

Kate Wilson
Chief press officer, Ministry of Defence

- Defended the MoD's naming policy in the face of fierce criticism from the Kelly family's counsel. She said that the department had decided to confirm David Kelly's name to the press in the hope of ensuring the media would come to the MoD rather than contacting the weapons expert directly. Her team was 'trying to encourage journalists to come to us rather than go anywhere else'.
- Explained how the MoD changed its policy on how to brief journalists over the scientist's identity. The strategy went through three drafts: from initially saying that there was 'nothing to be gained' from giving the individual's identity, to a second version saying that, if Kelly's name came up, they would have to check with the individual before confirming it, to a final version – the one actually used – which pre-emptively told journalists that, if they gave the correct name, the MoD would confirm it.
- Wilson told Gompertz that she and Pam Teare co-wrote the first two drafts, but that Teare worked on the final draft with Martin

Howard, the deputy chief of Defence Intelligence. This version was approved by the permanent secretary, Sir Kevin Tebbit.

Key exchange

James Dingemans [for the inquiry]: But if his name was inevitably going to come out, why was it not done by the Ministry of Defence who would then have been able to answer all the follow-up questions: he will not be contacted; he will not be interviewed; he has gone away to an undisclosed location, rather than have a situation where from Mrs Kelly's evidence he felt, so it is said, betrayed that the Ministry of Defence had confirmed his name?

Kate Wilson: Well, the point was in terms of so that nobody could get in contact with him. Journalists already had his number, we knew that, so we were not in a position to stop journalists from calling him direct. All we could do was try to encourage them to come to us, which is what we did. ■

Day 18
17 September 2003

This was the day when things were beginning to look much worse for Andrew Gilligan. He admitted mistakes and was criticised by the BBC's director of news, Richard Sambrook.

Andrew Gilligan
Today programme defence correspondent (also appeared on days 2 and 19)

- Forced to retract key elements of his controversial *Today* programme report.
- In tough cross-examination lasting 2½ hours, Gilligan said he had made a 'slip of the tongue' when he said Downing Street inserted a claim in the September dossier that Iraq could launch weapons of mass destruction within 45 minutes, knowing it was wrong.
- Also conceded it was a mistake, in one of his broadcasts, to describe the weapons expert David Kelly as an 'intelligence service source'. And he admitted failing to correct the *Today* presenter John Humphrys for making the same error.
- Admitted it was a serious error of judgement to email members of the Foreign Affairs Committee (FAC), suggesting questions they might ask of Kelly and effectively outing him as the source for reports by Susan Watts.

To his barrister Heather Rogers QC on describing his source as a member of the security services in the 6.07am broadcast
'The error I made here was in expressing the understanding I had

that the views had been conveyed to the government as something which Dr Kelly had told me directly. It was not intentional, it was the kind of slip of the tongue that does happen often during live broadcasts. It is an occupational hazard, which is why it would have been better to have scripted this one.'

On sending emails to MPs on the FAC before Kelly's appearance
'It was quite wrong to send it and I can only apologise. I did not even know for sure that David Kelly was Susan Watts's source. I was under an enormous amount of pressure at the time and I simply was not thinking straight, so I really do want to apologise for that.'

Pressed by government lawyer Jonathan Sumption QC over describing Kelly as an intelligence source Radio Five Live
'It is *ex tempore*. That was the only time in all my broadcasts, and there were 19 of them on this subject, that I described him in this way. That is a mistake that I have already admitted to . . . there was no conscious purpose in doing it in this broadcast, it was simply a slip of the tongue.'

On getting a response from the government before the programme was broadcast
'In hindsight I think we should have asked the MoD for a response and – but as I say, the approach discussed and decided on by the programme team, which is me, the editor and the day editor, was not that, it was a different one.'

In answer to Jeremy Gompertz QC who had asked him about the suggestion that he had brought Alastair Campbell's name up first with Kelly
'There was no name game as she described it. Only one name was mentioned. I did not introduce a number of names or indeed any

name. Alastair Campbell's name was mentioned, it was brought up spontaneously by Dr Kelly, just as he brought it up spontaneously to Susan Watts on 7 May.'

Richard Sambrook

Head of BBC News (also appeared on day 3)

- Said Gilligan was good at gathering information but lacked 'nuance and subtlety' in the way he presented it.
- Admitted failing to correct the impression that Kelly was an 'intelligence service source' when he knew it to be wrong, even after the BBC governors used the description in their statement of support for the corporation's stance.
- As late as the end of June, Gilligan continued to insist that he had faithfully reported the views of Kelly that Downing Street knew the 45-minute claim was wrong when the dossier was published.
- Admitted the BBC needed to learn lessons from the affair, and said stories making serious allegations should be 'carefully scripted in advance'.
- Criticised Gilligan's email to members of the Foreign Affairs Committee in which he suggested questions that MPs could put to Kelly.
- Sambrook admitted the BBC was wrong to stand by the reported assertion that No. 10 had inserted the 45-minute claim into the September dossier in the knowledge it was incorrect. But he blamed Gilligan, saying the reporter continued to insist the words were an accurate reflection of what Kelly had told him.

On the email sent by Andrew Gilligan to members of the FAC
'I think it was an improper email to have sent and I do not think it would be right under any circumstances. I appreciate that Mr

Gilligan felt himself to be under a great deal of pressure and may have made a misjudgement in those circumstances, but I certainly was not aware of it and I do not believe anybody within the BBC was aware of it or could have authorised it.'

On use of the term 'member of the security services' to describe Kelly
'It very quickly got into the bloodstream of the way this issue was discussed, both by the BBC, I accept, but also outside of the BBC.'

On the Gilligan style of journalism
'There are two aspects to journalism. There is the finding out of the information and there is then how you present it. My view for some time would be that Andrew Gilligan is extremely good at finding out information but there are sometimes questions of nuance and subtlety in how he presents it which are not all that they should be.'

Richard Hatfield
Director of personnel, Ministry of Defence (also appeared on days 1, 19, 22)

See day 19 for full details of evidence. ■

Day 19
18 September 2003

Lord Hutton said the recall of witnesses for cross-examination did not necessarily mean he intended to criticise them in his final report. It seemed clear, however, that one man decided that attack was the best form of defence. The MoD's personnel director, Richard Hatfield, delivered a stinging attack on Dr Kelly, blaming the scientist for getting into trouble by talking to the press.

Richard Hatfield

Personnel director, Ministry of Defence (also appeared on days 1, 18 and 22)

- Questioned again on the decision to confirm Kelly's name to journalists and his treatment by the MoD.
- Told the inquiry Kelly's contacts with Gilligan represented a 'fundamental failing'. Said that if he had known then what he now knew about what Kelly had disclosed to the media he would have been 'forced to suspend him'.
- Referring back to evidence from Janice Kelly, Kelly's widow, that her husband had felt 'betrayed by the MoD' he said it seemed the scientist had not prepared his wife for the consequences of talking to a journalist without authorisation.

Jeremy Gompertz [for the Kelly family]: He [Kelly] did report the contact to Mr Lamb, did he not?

Richard Hatfield: He did not report the contact in giving any description of its content and I am afraid I do not accept just saying 'I have met a journalist' amounts to, in this context, reporting the contact.

JG: He did not say 'I have met a journalist', he gave the names, did he not?

RH: And he did not give any indication that anything had happened in those contacts of significance to the Foreign Office or the Ministry of Defence.

JG: So you are not prepared to make any sort of concession in this regard then?

RH: No, I am not. I think it is a fundamental failing in what he did.

JG: You told the inquiry yesterday that you thought that the support which was provided for Dr Kelly was outstanding?

RH: I did.

JG: Do you think it was outstanding support by the MoD not to warn him on question and answer material and its contents so that he was wholly unaware of the process?

RH: I don't accept he was wholly unaware of the process.

JG: Do you consider it outstanding support by the MoD not to inform him of the decision to confirm his name if suggested by a journalist?

RH: I think he knew all along that if we were faced with a serious statement that they knew it was Dr Kelly that we would have to confirm the name because the MoD cannot deny things that are true.

JG: It is your view, is it not, that there was no need to obtain his consent to naming him?

RH: No.

JG: You told us that yesterday. Would you like to be treated like that, Mr Hatfield?

RH: I have been treated like that.

JG: Have you?

RH: Yes, I have.

JG: In comparable circumstances?

RH: In very comparable circumstances. The media have made all sorts of statements about what I did and did not do. They have attempted to say that I am going to be moved at the end of my job. All this is, you know, deduction from the basis of nothing.

Pam Teare

Director of news, Ministry of Defence (also appeared on day 5)

● It was highly likely that Geoff Hoon, the Defence Secretary, was told of the controversial Q and A naming process of Kelly by his own head of press at a meeting on the morning of 9 July.

cont'd p.254

Lesson for QC by man from the ministry

Sketch
Simon Hoggart

There was a splendid face-off at the Hutton inquiry yesterday. Richard Hatfield, the personnel director at the Ministry of Defence (or anti-personnel director, as Dr David Kelly's family no doubt think of him) became the first witness to fight back against one of the majestic briefs who are now doing the cross-examinations.

He faced Jeremy Gompertz, the QC who is appearing for the Kelly family. I don't think I have seen two people simultaneously patronise each other, so successfully too.

Mr Hatfield spoke to Mr Gompertz as if he were a clever but hopelessly inattentive schoolboy. Mr Gompertz spoke to Mr Hatfield as if he were a junior clerk who had split an important infinitive.

The QC had all the top brief's devices: incredulity, sarcasm, long and meaningful pauses. Mr Hatfield stared over his gold-rimmed glasses as if wondering why this person was asking him such impertinent questions.

Mr Gompertz had to use all his tricks because Mr Hatfield wasn't going to give anything away. It was like seeing a man try to open an oyster with a butter knife.

In fact, the man from the ministry could give a masterclass in how to hold your own against a top barrister. Civil servants, tax dodgers and even car radio thieves would pay good money.

I'd say the main elements are these:

1 Condescend. Say in a plonking voice 'as I think I made clear yesterday' or 'quite obviously, that is the case'.

2 Stand your ground. Asked 'would you adhere to that?' reply, 'I would,' in a firm voice. When the brief says in exaggeratedly incredulous tones, 'You would?' riposte, 'Yes, I would!'

3 Do a lot of staring. If you don't like the question, peer at your opponent as if you cannot

quite believe anyone would ask anything so silly.

4 Repeat phrases back at your tormentor. For instance Mr Hatfield had claimed that the MoD had given Dr Kelly 'outstanding' support. Faced with a suggestion that this is nonsense, describe everything you did, adding the word 'outstanding' at each point.

5 If you don't like a question, decline to answer. Or answer another one. This is an old politician's trick.

6 Here's the cunning one. Flip the charges back. If someone suggests you acted harshly, claim that, on the contrary, you didn't act harshly enough. For example, Mr Hatfield accused Dr Kelly of 'a fundamental failing in what he did' – which was talking to the press.

Asked whether the ministry had therefore treated him badly, Mr Hatfield said that, by contrast, if he'd known then what he knew now, he would have suspended Dr Kelly forthwith and started disciplinary proceedings.

Here's another example of chucking the ammo back. Mr

Gompertz: 'Would you like to be treated like that?'

Mr Hatfield: 'I have been treated like that!'

7 Let your opponent get the sniggers. Mr Gompertz said Dr Kelly had been obliged to leave home at very short notice, to stay in a hotel in [dramatic pause] Weston-super-Mare! As if that resort were one of the outer circles of hell. We all giggled.

Later a couple of computer experts came in to interpret the contents of Andrew Gilligan's personal organiser. There are some curiosities to be found in there. One of the boffins said: 'Because we had not decompressed the upload file, evidence in these memos might not have been in contiguous form.' He tried to explain what a 'hexadecimal format' was. The inquiry's QC interrupted him: 'Don't bother!'

But this is the future of the trials, in which judges will be laughed to scorn if they ask, 'And what, may I ask, is a hexadecimal format?' ■

Guardian, 19 September 2003

- In seemingly contradictory evidence Teare admitted that there was 'not a standard practice' and 'no rules that govern the release of civil service names', while claiming that for Kelly it was 'highly likely that as a civil servant he would be aware of the Q and A procedures'.

- Under aggressive cross-examination by Jeremy Gompertz, the Kelly family QC, Teare denied there had been any 'change' in the three consecutive Q and A drafts, despite the fact they evolved from saying there would be 'nothing to be gained' from naming Kelly to pre-emptively informing journalists that a correct guess would be confirmed.

- Teare at one point said that the point of pre-emptively telling journalists that a correct name would be confirmed was so 'the media would check with us before printing or broadcasting a name'.

- Asked how it had come about that after she had confirmed the name to the *Financial Times*, *FT* journalist Christopher Adams was briefed by an anonymous Whitehall official with further details about Kelly, she said she had 'no knowledge at all' about that matter.

- In a minor new revelation, Teare insisted that the confirmation strategy was only pre-emptively told to 'one or two' journalists but she was not asked, and did not reveal, who they were.

On the rationale behind the Q and A

'I wanted to ensure a system where the media would actually check with us before they printed a name or broadcast a name.'

On whether Kelly would have known about the strategy to name him.

'Dr Kelly, I think it is highly likely, as a civil servant, would be aware of the Q and A procedure. I do not know that for a fact but I think it is likely. There is nothing in the Q and A with which he could disagree.'

On the different drafts of the press office Q and A
'I will accept it reflects a different approach.'

About the press meeting on 9 July 2003, also attended by Geoff Hoon
'I do not recall there being a long discussion about the Q and A ... I cannot recall the detail, though I think it is highly likely that I would have outlined some of the material in the Q and A, but I cannot give you a verbatim account ... He may have already had it.'

On the need to consult Kelly about the Q and A
'I felt that Dr Kelly's name was likely to emerge because he was quite well known in media circles anyway. But on the substance of the Q and A material, I do not see that there was anything there that we needed to consult him about in any way . . . I believe that the issue of the statement certainly accelerated the process of journalists wanting to identify the unnamed individual. I do not believe that the Q and A did.'

Edward Wilding

Computer investigator

- The computer expert told the inquiry there were anomalies in two sets of notes that Andrew Gilligan had made on an electronic organiser of his meeting with the weapons expert, who was his only source.
- Four differences could be explained by technical factors, said the computer investigator, who was hired by Gilligan's lawyers to scour the organiser's memory.

- The fifth difference between notes Gilligan submitted to the Hutton inquiry and a file recovered from the electronic organiser at first produced alarm, said Wilding. It had no mention of Alastair Campbell.
- The date stamp on the notes read 21 May, possibly because the organiser's internal clock was wrong by up to 40 hours, a common occurrence, according to Wilding.

Key quote

'This has worried me quite a lot. The version of kelly.txt dated 21 May 2003 is different to the version produced by Mr Gilligan to the inquiry.'

Professor A. J. Sammes

Professor of computer science and director, Centre for Forensic Computing, Cranfield University

- Instructed by the inquiry to look at the report from Wilding.
- Recovering files from the reporter's organiser may have damaged their contents, but Gilligan had back-up copies on a computer.

Andrew Gilligan

BBC Journalist (also appeared on days 2 and 18)

- Recalled for the third time to give evidence, Gilligan said the set of notes without Alastair Campbell's name had been typed as Kelly talked. He had saved those notes, saving a copy in the organiser's memory, then gone through the notes with the weapons expert to agree what quotes could be used. Some quotes were deleted at the scientist's request, some were added in as Gilligan asked further questions.

- During this quote-checking the scientist had mentioned Campbell as having 'sexed up' the dossier, Gilligan said. He then saved this version on the organiser.

Heather Rogers QC [for Andrew Gilligan]: If it is to be suggested that you might have made the notes at . . . some time after you left the Charing Cross Hotel, how would you respond to that?

Andrew Gilligan: I would say no.

On when Campbell's name was first raised
'I am not quite sure when the word "Campbell" was mentioned during the conversation. I know it was mentioned by David Kelly. But it may have come towards the end.' ∎

Day 20
22 September 2003

Geoff Hoon's claims that he was only marginally involved in the outing of Dr Kelly appeared to be dramatically contradicted by extracts from Alastair Campbell's personal diary released by the inquiry. It was another bad day for the Defence Secretary, at least so far as the inquiry exchanges and subsequent media comment were concerned.

Geoff Hoon
Secretary of State for Defence (also appeared on day 10)

- The Defence Secretary admitted he did nothing to correct newspaper reports that Iraq could launch its weapons of mass destruction over long distances against British troops, though he knew the stories were wrong.
- He admitted that at the time of publication he knew that the 45-minute claim referred only to 'battlefield munitions' such as shells. Press reports, however, assumed the weapons related to strategic, or long-range missiles.
- The Defence Secretary argued that Kelly knew his name would emerge, and said officials told him the scientist 'accepted' that.
- Said he played no part in preparing the dossier, but admitted agreeing that Kelly's name would be confirmed.

Key Exchanges
Jeremy Gompertz [for the Kelly family]: What I suggest to you is that there was a deliberate government strategy to leak Kelly's name into the public arena without appearing to do so, by a combination of

the press statement, the question and answer material, the Prime Minister's official spokesman's press briefing and other leaks which appear to have taken place to the press. That is what I suggest.

Geoff Hoon: Well, you have put that point to a number of witnesses; they have all denied it; and I deny it.

JG: His name was leaked, was it not?

GH: Not by me.

JG: You did overrule Sir Kevin Tebbit's advice [for Dr Kelly not to appear before both the FAC and the ISC]?

GH: I would not put it that way. Civil servants give advice to ministers, it is not always accepted . . . It is part of the process of taking decisions. 'Overrule' is – perhaps it might be good for a headline but it does not describe the process that takes place in government. No one was suggesting Kevin Tebbit's advice was definitive. I considered it and I decided to take a different course.

* * *

Andrew Caldecott [for the BBC]: Are you aware that on 25 September a number of newspapers had banner headlines suggesting that this related to strategic missiles or bombs?

GH: I can recall, yes.

AC: Why was no corrective statement issued for the benefit of the public in relation to those media reports?

GH: I do not know.

AC: It must have been considered by someone, must it not?

GH: I have spent many years trying to persuade newspapers and journalists to correct their stories. I have to say it is an extraordinarily time-consuming and generally frustrating process.

AC: I am sorry, are you saying that the press would not report a corrective statement that the dossier was meant to refer, in this context, to battlefield munitions and not to strategic weapons?

GH: What I am suggesting is that I was not aware of whether any consideration was given to such a correction. All that I do know from my experience is that, generally speaking, newspapers are resistant to corrections. That judgement may have been made by others as well.

AC: But, Mr Hoon, you must have been horrified that the dossier had been misrepresented in this way; it was a complete distortion of what it actually was intended to convey, was it not?

GH: Well, I was not horrified. I recognised that journalists occasionally write things that are more dramatic than the material upon which it is based.

Alastair Campbell
Downing Street director of communications and strategy (also appeared on day 6)

- Extracts from Alastair Campbell's personal diary were released.
- The portrayal by Campbell in his diaries of the Defence Secretary apparently contradicts Mr Hoon's evidence to the inquiry.
- He distanced Tony Blair from the exercise, saying in several

diary entries that the Prime Minister wanted to leave the handling of Kelly to MoD officials.

● Denied that he had 'sexed up' parts of the dossier. He was pressed on why he had not mentioned all the changes he proposed when he gave evidence to the Commons Foreign Affairs Committee.

On the idea of leaking Kelly's name to the press

'I hesitate even to call it a proposal, it was a thought which was very quickly rejected by the Defence Secretary. Godric [Smith] and Tom Kelly both though it was a bad idea. But more importantly I raised it with the Prime Minister, he thought it was a bad idea and nothing came of it.'

Asked to confirm it would be 'bad' for Gilligan if the source was revealed – or as the diary puts it 'fuck Gilligan'

'I do not deny and I did not deny when I was questioned by Mr Sumption that I was very, very angry and frustrated about this whole situation and the BBC were saying that the source for their story was a senior intelligence official, somebody centrally involved in the drawing of the dossier.'

James Dingemans [for the inquiry]: 'GH wanted to get up [the] source . . .' That is not what I recollect Mr Hoon tells us this morning. He said it was your suggestion.

Alastair Campbell: I think in relation to that that does risk being unfair to Mr Hoon.

On whether he 'sexed up' the dossier

'I was keen, and this is the job the Prime Minister asked me to do, to make sure that the dossier as presented to parliament was a strong, clear, consistent document that allowed him effectively to

cont'd p. 264

Dear Diary, this isn't what is going on

Sketch
Simon Hoggart

Alastair Campbell's diaries exploded on top of the Hutton inquiry like a shellburst over the chateau where the officers are billeted.

They were sensational! Right in the very first paragraph he wrote: G[eoff] H[oon] and I agreed it would fuck Gilligan if that was his source.'

We gasped. We reeled. The thought that a senior official in the British government would use that word only once in the pages of his diaries was unimaginable!

This is a man who probably reads his children stories like *Now We Are Fucking Six* and *The Wind in the Fucking Willows*. Were the diaries a forgery? It seemed likely.

But then why was he there to launch them? For a launch is what it was. They had everything except warm white wine and cheesy nibbles.

The inquiry clerk began by describing them. 'They were written not for publication, or indeed for anyone except Mr Campbell to see,' he said, to cynical laughter. They might use that bit on the dustjacket.

Authors these days tend to offer publishers a 'proposal' for their book. It includes a summary, plus a few teasing extracts. This is what Mr Campbell has done. But few writers get to do it in front of umpteen barristers and the world's press. Ka-ching! went the cash register with each evasion. 'Kuh-chung!' it went as he tried to make us believe that he hadn't actually meant what he wrote.

I suspect that in the course of one short hour, he doubled his advance. It was superb!

Mr Campbell was trying hard to make out that he didn't want Dr Kelly's name to be published. But the diaries said that he wanted to get it out through the papers. What could that mean?

'This is diary writing - it doesn't actually express what is going on,' he said. There it was, the Blair spin machine - never actually expressing what is going on.

He persisted. He hadn't wanted 'it' to happen. Lord Hutton asked in a baffled way if he had any idea what 'it' was. 'It is me, at the end of the day, scribbling whatever comes into my head,' Mr Campbell replied.

So that's how the dossier was prepared. I think we'd already guessed.

Earlier Geoff Hoon produced some fine obfuscation. Asked by Jeremy Gompertz QC, for the Kelly family, if he thought the govern- ment had done anything wrong, he replied: 'Having followed your cross-examination carefully, I can see that there may be judgments about the precise timing of partic- ular decisions, the precise point at which those decisions had an effect which are within what I would describe as the reasonable range of judgments people can make, when confronted with this situation.'

So that's all right, then. No one got anything wrong!

He told us that he could not admit the government had been mistaken on the 45-minute claim, because we journalists hate to retract something we've got wrong.

He's right that we are terrible hypocrites. But because we are hypocrites we just love pointing out the government got it wrong. We'd have leapt on the chance, Geoff!

He even insisted that the ministry had not released Dr Kelly's name, which took some tortuous reasoning. In short he was both ingenious and ingenuous.

For Dr Kelly's outing wasn't 20 Questions, as one QC put it. It was *Give Us A Clue*, with Lionel Blair, in which each player is desperate for the others to get it right.

'Fingers in his ears, is it 'quiet'? No, I know, he's got a stethoscope! He's a doctor!

'Now he's cupping his ear, so it's 'sounds like'. Rubbing his tummy. I know, Dr Stomach!'

'No, no, it's belly. Is it that bloke off the telly?'

'I've got it, Gilligan's source was George Melly!' ■

Guardian, 23 September 2003

explain to the British public the reality of the threat posed by Saddam Hussein's WMD. That is my job in these circumstances; and I think if you are saying 'strong' equals 'sexed up', I do not accept that at all. If you are saying 'strong' equals a good, solid piece of work that does the job that the Prime Minister wants it to do, then I agree with that.'

On his diary entry of 15 July 2003 where Kelly giving evidence proved to be a 'disaster'

'It has obviously been terrible and far worse for Dr Kelly and his family than for anybody else but what has been terrible from our perspective is that at every stage of this we have felt as it were to be the wronged party and yet nothing has really ever gone according to the outcome that we might have wished, and frankly I think it just reflected in the mood that then existed in Downing Street that this was something which we were just going to have to sort of put behind us and forget.'

On his diary

'This is diary writing which . . . does not accurately express what is going on . . . At the end of the day, it is not an account of the day, it is me sitting down and scribbling whatever comes into my head.' ■

Key Document

Extracts from Alastair Campbell's diary
4 July 2003

Spoke to [Defence Secretary Geoff] Hoon who said that a man had come forward who felt he was possibly [the BBC reporter Andrew] Gilligan's source had come forward [sic] and was being interviewed today. GH said his initial instinct was to throw the book at him, but in fact there was a case for trying to get some kind of plea bargain. Says that he'd come forward and he was saying yes to speak to AG, yes he said intel. went in late, but he never said the other stuff. It was double-edged but GH and I agreed it would fuck Gilligan if that was his source. He said he was an expert rather than a spy or full-time MoD official. GH and I agreed to talk tomorrow.

6 July

Spent much of weekend talking to TB [Tony Blair] and GH re the source, man who felt he was the source because his colleagues said he sounded like what AG was saying. Came forward earlier in the week to confide that he'd seen Gilligan in a hotel, that he'd made some of these comments, but not others, eg re me. GH, like me, wanted to get it out that the source had broken cover to claim that AG misrepresented him. TB and I had a long chat about it and TB was worried that we (TB or GH) ought to tell FAC about it. His worry was that it could lead to them reopening the inquiry. I wanted, and GH did, to get it to the BBC governors that we may know who the source was, that he was not a spy, not involved in the WMD dossier and was a WMD expert who advised departments. TB was fine about that but backed off after speaking to [Sir David] Omand [the Prime Minister's security co-ordinator], who felt the guy had to be treated properly and interviewed again. GH and I felt we were missing a trick. I suggested to GH, to speak to TB to try to persuade him we should do this and maybe GH should speak to [BBC director of news Richard] Sambrook and tell him that it was re the dossier, nobody. GH said he was almost as steamed up as I was. TB said he didn't want to push the system too far. But my worry was that I wanted a clear win not a messy draw and if they presented it as a draw that was not good enough for us. GH and I both wanted to get the source up but TB was nervous about it. Felt that we should not push K Tebbit [Kevin Tebbit, permanent secretary at the MoD]/Omand too hard, and could maybe bring it out tomorrow if we needed it. TB also feeling that we had to have something for the ISC to go for and that could be this.

[Later entry] Source idea went nowhere as he had to be interviewed again by Martin Howard [deputy head of defence intelligence], DIS and personnel.

The evidence

7 July

Then round with JS [Foreign Secretary Jack Straw], John S [Scarlett, chairman of the Joint Intelligence Committee] to see TB who was meeting Kevin Tebbit, Omand and others re 'the source'. He was ex-inspector, who advised the government, was aware of information going into the dossier but not involved in drawing it up. He'd once sat next to Jack as expert at select committee. Kevin said the guy claimed he never mentioned me, he was a bit of a show-off though. Felt that maybe Gilligan just lied about the stuff about me. It was agreed he should be interviewed again, and then we should get it out that the source was not in the intelligence community, not involved drawing up dossier. Again we should be saying source was misrepresented by [Gilligan]. TB was keen for the officials (KT and DO) to be in control of the process.

[Later entry] Several chats with MoD, Pam Teare [MoD head of communications], then Geoff H re the source. Felt we should get it out through the papers, then have line to respond and let TB take it on at liaison committee. TB felt we had to leave it to Omand/Tebbit judgement and they didn't want to do it. Had to go for natural justice. GH said there was a problem that he [Kelly] once gave evidence alongside Jack Straw, we were briefing that they [BBC] would eventually apologise. Wall to wall all day, source issue not moving.

[Later entry] Source going better but not necessarily him.

[Later entry] GH wanted to get up source, TK [Tom Kelly, Prime Minister's spokesman], GS [Godric Smith, Prime Minister's spokesman], felt best to wait until tomorrow and 'had to do it right'.

8 July

Meeting with TB, JS, Scarlett, DM [David Manning, Prime Minister's foreign affairs adviser], etc to go over liaison committee. Still not clear how we were going to handle the case of the MoD official.

[Later entry] Said he [GH] should get going on the source issue, TB clear that we should leave the bureaucracy to deal with it.

[Later entry] TB . . . came back [from liaison committee] and continued to try to sort the source issue. He met Scarlett and Omand and agreed try to resolve through letter from Ann Taylor. Word then came back she didn't want a letter on it. That meant do it as a press release. JoP [Jonathan Powell, No. 10 chief of staff], AC, PMOS [Prime Minister's official spokesmen], John S and Kevin Tebbit went GS room and wrote press release. Tebbit wrote letter from GH to [BBC chairman] Gavyn Davies offering to give him the name of the source. Martin Howard had interviewed David Kelly and was pretty convinced that he was the source . . . Tebbit took it away to MoD and had to clear it with David Kelly who was on a motorway. Then out by 6 and briefing mainly on fact BBC put out a non-denial denial within two hours.

9 July

BBC story moving away because they were refusing to take on the source idea. There was a big conspiracy at work really. We kept pressing on as best we could at the briefings, but the biggest thing needed was the source out. We agreed that we should not do it ourselves, so didn't, but later in the day the *FT*, *Guardian* after a while [Michael] Evans [defence correspondent of *The Times*] got the name.

15 July

Looking forward to Kelly giving evidence, but GS, CR and I all predicted it would be a disaster and so it proved. Despite MoD assurances he was well schooled . . . ■

Day 21
23 September 2003

Another bad day for the government. A document was released showing how Jonathan Powell, the Prime Minister's chief of staff, instructed intelligence chiefs to change the government's Iraqi weapons dossier to make it appear the threat posed by Saddam Hussein was much greater than they really believed.

Tom Kelly
Prime Minister's official spokesman (also appeared on day 7)

- Admitted that Downing Street released personal details about Kelly to the media in an attempt to undermine the BBC.
- A BBC statement, which gave a false impression of its reporter Andrew Gilligan's relationship with David Kelly, could only be challenged by outlining biographical details about the scientist, Kelly said.
- Kelly 'categorically' denied that there was a strategy to get the name of the source out. He explained that he had released details about Dr Kelly, such as how his salary was paid and the basis on which he worked for the government, because of the BBC's misleading statement.

On the process that ensured Dr Kelly's identity became a crucial element in the battle with the BBC
'I and I do not believe others that I worked with lost sight of that there was an individual caught up in this controversy, in the middle

of it, and that therefore we had to respect that individual. At the same time, there was a logic of events which stretched back to 29 May which unfortunately . . . which was working its way through.

. . . There was a chain of events . . . that in terms of the source, once a claim is made we would challenge that claim. If the BBC did not address that challenge in a way which allowed the public record to be set straight, then we had to maintain the challenge.'

Jeremy Gompertz [For the Kelly family on the Campbell diaries]:
. . . Because the whole purpose of the statement, the lobby briefings and the Q and A material is demonstrated in these notes, is it not, Mr Kelly? Namely, that there was a strategy to reveal Dr Kelly's name without appearing to do so?

Tom Kelly: Categorically not.

On the pressure to reveal the name
'I genuinely wanted to try to protect Dr Kelly's identity as much as possible but I had to explain the discrepancies between the BBC statement and the MoD statement; and I had to do so without misleading the lobby, which is the golden rule for prime minister's official spokesman, you cannot mislead the lobby.'

Godric Smith
Prime Minister's official spokesman (also appeared on day 7)

- Questioned over a recently discovered email attachment sent to Clare Sumner, a Downing Street official, that appeared to be a draft Commons Foreign Affairs Committee press release announcing that Andrew Gilligan would be recalled to give evidence.

269

- Also asked if Campbell's diary entry about getting the source out reflected the director of communication's views.

On why he sent the email
'It was my personal view that the FAC would inevitably wish to see those involved in this development and to revisit this issue, but given the complexity of the argument and the fact that I think she had other things to do, I said I would put something in writing to her . . . I understand why on first sight this looks curious . . . I hope people recognise that it is benign.'

Asked if Campbell's diary entry about getting the source out reflected the director of communication's views
'I think there is a qualitative difference between a desire for something to happen and actually taking concrete steps to make it happen.'

John Scarlett
Chairman of the Joint Intelligence Committee (also appeared on day 9)

- Jonathan Powell, Tony Blair's chief of staff, asked the Joint Intelligence Committee to redraft a passage in the dossier to state that Saddam had plans to use chemical or biological weapons against the west.
- Scarlett insisted that concerns expressed by weapons experts about the government's dossier on Iraq were fully taken into account and that he agreed all the changes hardening up the language of the controversial document.
- He welcomed advice about how to describe intelligence in the dossier from the Prime Minister's advisers, including Alastair Campbell, Tony Blair's communications chief. He was in control, he insisted, through 'delegated authority' from his full

committee, which included the heads of all the security and intelligence agencies, including MI6, MI5 and GCHQ.

- Many of the changes in the dossier were made by him personally, he insisted. Even the change in the title, from *Iraq's Programme for Weapons of Mass Destruction* to the harder title of *Iraq's Weapons of Mass Destruction* was his.
- Asked about headlines suggesting that Britain was under threat from chemical and biological weapons fired by Saddam Hussein's forces, Scarlett said he was not responsible for correcting them.
- Dismissed any hint in documents provided to the inquiry which suggested there was dissent within the intelligence community or tension between his Whitehall committee and No. 10.
- Said he took on board Campbell's comment that a reference to Iraqi forces deploying chemical or biological weapons within 45 minutes of an order to do so was 'weaker' in the text. But that was only because of a 'clear inconsistency'.

On a memo which said that ownership of the dossier lay with No. 10

'Since this was a document that was going to be presented by the Prime Minister to Parliament on behalf of the government, its ownership, in that sense, looking ahead to that moment, lay with No. 10 and the JIC itself does not produce documents for public dissemination and there had never been any intention that it would do so. So it is ownership in that sense and it is a forward-looking statement.'

Andrew Caldecott [for the BBC]: Your position in intelligence matters is plainly far superior to that of Campbell, is it not?

John Scarlett: It is indeed.

AC: He may not agree with you, but I do. You, presumably, regarded it as important to get across the message that you were in charge of this dossier?

JS: I did, yes.

AC: And you asked Mr Campbell, as we know – I think you said to him: it would be helpful if you set out the process, and that was one of the points he was to include in it?

JS: Yes.

AC: Why did you not chair that first planning meeting in order to get across the clear message that you were in charge and not the communications side of Downing Street?

JS: That meeting was held to discuss the overall structure, format, presentation of the dossier; and Alastair Campbell, as the Prime Minister's representative and very clearly representing his views – and the Prime Minister was commissioning this document – chaired that meeting in that role. At that meeting we did not in any way discuss intelligence matters or anything in terms of intelligence content, intelligence reports, intelligence items, which fell within my area of responsibility. Therefore it was natural for him to chair it.

AC: Strategic weapons have a far longer range, they could reach British bases in Cyprus, for example, which is what the newspaper said on 25 September.

JS: A small number of newspapers said it on 25 September and not thereafter.

AC: A small number of newspapers with a readership of millions.

JS: On the 25 September there were a small number of headlines about that; and afterwards virtually no reference to it.

AC: Were you concerned that that should be corrected, Mr Scarlett?

JS: No, I was not and I will tell you why not. First of all, as regards my own assessment staff, we were ready to field inquiries from the press offices of No. 10, the MoD, the FCO with anything relating to issues of this kind. We received no inquiries whatsoever about the 45-minute point. The second point was I was of course following the press coverage of the dossier and I was interested to note that immediately after the headline flurry on various points on 24 and 25 September the press coverage fell quickly into assessing the dossier as a sober and cautious document that most explicitly did not make a case for war, if anything it made a case for the return of the inspectors and it focused in particular, quite rightly in my view, on the importance of what the dossier had to say about the nuclear issue. I was content with the way that coverage came out; and that is – that was my attitude over many months indeed.

His reaction to an email from Jonathan Powell (see below)
'This email did prompt me and the assessment staff to look again at that particular passage.'

Assistant chief constable Michael Page
Thames Valley Police (also appeared on day 14)

- Police have interviewed around 500 people during their inquiry, taken 300 statements and seized in excess of 700 documents.

- Could find no evidence of a 'criminal dimension'.
- Kelly's dentist had been concerned the family would be distressed if they received a routine reminder of his check-up. When she went to the files, the records were missing. They reappeared two days later. Police then ran a DNA test on the body, which confirmed it was Kelly. ■

Key Documents

Email from Godric Smith to Clare Sumner, 9 July 2003

In the light of the new evidence from the MoD last night and the BBC own statement in response we believe we need to see AG [Andrew Gilligan], RS [Richard Sambrook] and source . . . AG said in answer to John Maples Q422 that he had only discussed the WMD dossier with one source before the story was broadcast. We now know from the MoD statement that, if this individual is not the source, that statement cannot be correct. This too would be material to our inquiry.

Either way there are important questions that need to be addressed in order for us to try and resolve this issue.

Email from Jonathan Powell to Alastair Campbell and John Scarlett, 19 September 2002, 15.45

I think the statement on page 19 that 'Saddam is prepared to use chemical and biological weapons if he believes his regime is under threat' is a bit of a problem. It backs up the . . . argument that there is no CBW threat and we will only create one if we attack him. I think you should redraft the para. My memory of the intelligence is that he has set up plans to use CBW on western forces. ■

Day 22
24 September 2003

As the BBC chairman was recalled for cross-examination, the inquiry heard more details about the treatment of Dr Kelly by senior MoD officials. It heard how the scientist was told he was about to be exposed in a snatched 46-second mobile phone conversation cut off because the caller was on a train.

Gavyn Davies
Chairman of the BBC (also appeared on day 11)

- The BBC refused to give an inch at the height of the dossier row with Downing Street because it was determined not to bow to 'intolerable' pressure from the government.
- The inquiry was shown a draft script of Andrew Gilligan's *Today* programme report where claims that Iraq could launch WMD in 45 minutes were attributed to experts instead of 'members of the intelligence community'.
- Davies rejected a suggestion that the governors should have seen Gilligan's notes before they discussed his story on 6 July, saying they accepted the assurances of the news director, Richard Sambrook, that the source was 'credible and reliable'. He said the governors would not be able to function unless they trusted BBC executives and knew nothing about the source other than the 'credibility and reliability of the source as attested by several editors'.
- Conceded there had been a 'great deal of concern' among the governors about an article by Andrew Gilligan in the *Mail on*

cont'd p.278

Godzilla, QC takes on the BBC titan

Sketch
Simon Hoggart

When titans of the establishment fall out! It's fantastic entertainment to watch these giants trying to tear each other to bits. I'm reminded of those old Japanese movies with titles like *Godzilla versus Mothra*: you might not care who wins, but those special effects make for a terrific 90 minutes.

Yesterday saw the fabulously rich Gavyn Davies, the chairman of the BBC, in deadly combat with the almost as fabulously rich Jonathan Sumption, a QC beside whom a mere criminal brief defending a pub brawler at Snaresbrook resembles a sparrow pecking at a burger box in the shadow of a soaring eagle.

These two men – Davies, the boy from Balliol, and Sumption, the Magdalen mauler – are at the very height of their profession.

Yet they managed to treat each other as if they were not only beneath contempt but barely visible on the radar of human regard.

From my seat I couldn't see Mr Sumption's face, but I could hear his voice, smooth and yet sodden with scorn, like a Victoria sponge soaked in embalming fluid.

Mr Davies responded with basilisk glances, each more supercilious than the last.

It was as if all the majesty and splendour of his office had to be expressed with total and utter disdain.

It says a lot about British society that two people with so much in common – Oxford degrees, enormous wealth, men at the pinnacle of their careers – should be treating each other like squabbling cats.

Yet since this is the establishment, were they to meet again, they'd be the epitome of courtesy towards each other, lavishly praising each other's performance.

So these grandees are the opposite of the average backbiter. They are nasty in public, all right, but they're incredibly nice behind their backs. Or at least behind our backs.

Mr Sumption was trying to show that the BBC governors had decided to support their version of events come what may, in order to protect their own executives.

They couldn't care less, he implied, whether the Gilligan story was true, or whether the government had a case against the BBC at all.

It was heavy going. Mr Sumption tried a series of jabs about naming the source.

Then he shuffled round, and demanded to know if the governors were happy with the decision to stand by the Gilligan broadcasts.

'I see,' said Mr Davies, his lip curled. 'We have moved off the source at this point, have we?'

'Just answer the question as asked,' snapped back Mr Sumption.

Lawyers have a special way of talking in which the words 'you bastard' are unspoken but clearly implied.

The BBC was so worried about appearing to cave in that they had decided not 'to give an inch' whatever new facts came to light, he said.

'That is absolutely NOT the position, Mr Sumption,' he barked back.

Little lead pellets were loaded into the gloves. 'As I have made clear before ... as Mr Sambrook has correctly told you ...'

The phrase 'Mr Sumption' was used lavishly, the impression being given of the local toff speaking to a dense rural constable who nevertheless has the power to make his life difficult.

At one point Mr Davies let rip with a superb 'funff' noise, like a belch stifled by a pillow, a vast expression of contempt and despair.

'I think that is a very tendentious way of putting it,' he said of something, then the superb: 'I have never heard such nonsense!' (What, never? Working in the Treasury and the BBC?)

We judges met at lunchtime and compared scores.

We agreed it had been a tremendous bout which we would not have missed for anything, but we unanimously made Mr Davies the winner on points. ∎

Guardian, 25 September 2003

Sunday, in which he named Alastair Campbell in connection
with the insertion of the 45-minute claim into the September
dossier.

- He said that two reports by Susan Watts on BBC2's *Newsnight*
provided the governors with 'important corroboration' for
Gilligan's report, but conceded that most governors believed
No. 10 should have been given advance warning of Gilligan's
story.

Key quotes and exchanges

Jonathan Sumption [for the government]: What you were saying was
that whatever details might emerge about the precise facts about
the 45-minute claim, (1) there should be no compromise of the
kind you refer to at the beginning of that paragraph, and (2) the
governors must not give way but must be seen to support the
management.

Gavyn Davies: Absolutely not saying that whatsoever . . .

JS: You were so concerned about creating the outward appearance
of succumbing to political pressure that you were urging the
governors that they should not give an inch whatever a further
investigation of the facts might show. Is that not the position?

GD: It is absolutely not the position, Mr Sumption. I do not, at any
stage in my life, ignore the facts. And the most important thing,
undoubtedly, is to tell the truth to the public. But what I was
concerned about here – and I can tell you it was in the face of
absolutely unprecedented pressure from the director of communications at 10 Downing Street, not an insignificant figure in the
government at the time. In the face of that pressure, I then believed
and I now believe, and I had the full support of all of the board in

saying that it was a legitimate public duty of the board to say that that pressure was intolerable.

JS: Was it the governors' view that notice should have been given to No. 10 in advance?

GD: It was not a unanimous view.

JS: Was it the majority view?

GD: It was the majority view, although when we described it in the statement we said 'could'.

JS: Yes, you watered it down in the statement because you did not wish to be seen to let down the executives. That was the reason for that, was it not?

GD: I have never heard such nonsense. We watered it down in the statement because one of our most senior and most respected governors [shorthand notes of the meeting appear to show he was referring to Sarah Hogg] thought it was actually actively wrong to give prior notification to No. 10, and in order to ensure that unanimity was maintained among the governors, not among the executive, among the governors, I put the word 'could' instead of 'should'.

Patrick Lamb

Deputy head of the counter proliferation department, FCO (also appeared on days 1, 4 and 14)

- Official who worked closely with Kelly struggled to hold back tears as he described how the scientist had wanted to be accompanied by him for support as he gave evidence to the Commons Foreign Affairs Committee.

- Since Kelly was giving evidence as the government's Iraqi weapons expert seconded from the FO to the MoD, he could not do as asked.
- The inquiry has heard how tense and nervous Kelly was before testifying in a televised session of the committee.
- Kelly knew he needed authorisation before speaking to Mr Gilligan. Although speaking to the media was part of his job, there was 'an element of self-discipline and judgement involved', he said.

On Kelly's request for him to attend the FAC with him – a request Lamb had to turn down

'Dr Kelly asked me if I could attend the FAC hearing, which was the first occasion – this was a man I looked up to. As a policy person you are sometimes an interloper in the areas of the experts, in particular experts such as Dr Kelly, and you feel an interloper and you wonder what their reaction and attitude to you is. This was the first occasion when I instinctively understood that he valued my opinion, valued and had certain respect for my judgement, and also would have appreciated my personal presence at that hearing. Excuse me.'

On Kelly's relationship with the press

'There is an element of self-discipline and judgement involved in all of these matters, and that self-discipline is imposed on all of us involved, including Dr Kelly.'

On how Kelly would have received the media attention

'These were comments that referred to him as the MoD mole. This was a man who I knew had been largely responsible for taking down the Soviet biological weapons programme, he had been heavily involved in dealing with the Iraqi BW programme, and to refer to him casually as a "mole" I knew was something that I found hurtful and I knew he would find hurtful. There were comparisons with Harold Shipman. There were comparisons of a sort that I found personally distasteful. I knew that he was a sensitive man and I was deeply offended personally and all his colleagues similarly offended by the treatment he received at that time.'

Bryan Wells

Director of Counter Proliferation and Arms Control, MoD (also appeared on day 4)

- Kelly was told he was about to be exposed in a snatched 46-second mobile phone conversation that was cut off because the caller, Bryan Wells, was on a train.
- Wells called Kelly at 7.03pm on 9 July 2003, an hour after the MoD had confirmed his name to journalists.
- At 7.54pm, after Wells arrived at his home station, he again called Kelly. 'I wanted to make sure David understood and made preparations to go,' he told the inquiry.
- Wells changed his witness statement to say Kelly was not told in his first interview on 4 July 2003 that his name 'may' become public. He said he was only told this three days later.

The call to Kelly at 7.03pm
'I said that I had been asked to pass on the message that the press office had confirmed his name to the press; and I recall that I advised him to get in touch with the press office . . . It was a bad line. I think we were cut off, and I suspect that we were trying to get in touch with each other after that.'

281

Jeremy Gompertz [for the Kelly family]: Were you ever given the opportunity to talk to Dr Kelly about it [press statement] before it was released?

BW: I was not, sir.

JG: You were his line manager.

BW: The press arrangements were being dealt with by other people. I was not involved in this.

JG: So nobody thought it right that you should be involved in this process.

BW: I had other business to attend to. We have a press office.

James Harrison,

Deputy director Counter Proliferation and Arms Control, MOD (also appeared on day 10)

- Confirmed he had forwarded four parliamentary questions to Kelly on 17 July 2003.
- Said he did not believe these would have increased the pressure on Kelly and that he thought it was easing.

Wing Commander John Clark

Counter Proliferation and Arms Control Secretariat (also appeared on day 10)

- Questioned on the four parliamentary questions (PQs) sent to Kelly by James Harrison.

- Said he was aware of the questions (though not the contents, he said he checked the deadline and ignored them) but could not recall discussing then with Kelly, or Kelly having spoken to him about them.
- He said that there was no reason why he should not have been sent them, adding that 'it would have been unfair if elements of the investigation or the PQs were kept from him'.
- Wing Cdr Clark was also questioned on a call Kelly made to his office telephone at 1.36pm on 17 July 2003 but said he had no recollection of it, and that he had probably popped out for a sandwich.

Nicholas Rufford

Sunday Times journalist (also appeared on day 8)

- Testified on his meeting Kelly and the offer of an article for the *Sunday Times*.
- Confirmed that he had made an offer of hotel accommodation to Kelly – but said he did not link the offer of hotel accommodation to the writing of an article.
- Said that Kelly acknowledged him and that he did not believe it was an unwelcome visit. Said they parted amicably. 'I had been talking to him for about 15 minutes, he had not invited me into the garden or into the house so I felt that I did not want to stay any longer.'

Professor Keith Hawton

Psychiatrist (also appeared on day 13)

- David Kelly believed that his mother, Margaret, committed

suicide, killing herself after suffering a stroke and had told his wife, Janice, about it.

- A death certificate stated the cause of death as broncho-pneumonia. Prof Hawton said: 'That is, chest infection due to barbiturate poison.' He claimed that documents he had seen since first testifying had confirmed the suicide of Kelly's mother.
- An MoD vetting file showed the weapons expert had said in an interview in 1985 that his mother had suffered from depression before her death.

Key quote

'If a person is in a situation in which they are faced by apparently insurmountable problems and are feeling hopeless and suicidal, having had a family member commit suicide might possibly make them somewhat more comfortable with the idea of suicide. On the other hand, such a person is likely to have intimate knowledge of the terrible impact that suicide very often and usually has on families, which may indeed actually serve to decrease the likelihood of suicide in that individual.'

Richard Hatfield

Personnel director, MoD (also appeared on days 1, 18 and 19)

- Kelly stopped at a lay-by on 8 July 2003, as Richard Hatfield read over by mobile phone a carefully drafted MoD press statement. The press statement, crafted in Downing Street, did not name Kelly but detailed his background and what he said he told Andrew Gilligan.
- Hatfield in his earlier appearance at the inquiry claimed he had spent 10 minutes reading the press statement to Kelly, but

phone records obtained by the inquiry only the day before showed this could not have happened.

- He also admitted he was not clear why the press statement needed to be issued. ■

Key Documents

Draft script for Andrew Gilligan's *Today* programme report

Doubts about the reliability of Tony Blair's assertion last September that Iraq could deploy WMD within 45 minutes have been confirmed by this programme.

What do they say: Evidence that experts felt their work was being misrepresented to justify an attack on Iraq to fit in with the US-led timetable for overthrowing Saddam Hussein.

Email from Gavyn Davies to BBC governors, 29 June 2003

I remain firmly of the view that, in the big picture sense, it is absolutely critical for the BBC to emerge from this row without being seen to buckle in the face of government pressure . . . This, it seems to me, really is a moment for the governors to stand up and be counted. ■

Day 23
25 September 2003

It was the day for the QCs to sum up. Jeremy Gompertz, the Kelly family's lawyer, delivered a blistering attack on the government, and the MoD in particular. Jonathan Sumption, for the government, said it was 'exceptionally unfair' to blame MoD officials and implied no lessons could be learned from the affair. Andrew Caldecott, for the BBC, said Geoff Hoon's view that it was not his responsibility to correct media reports exaggerating the message of the weapons dossier 'borders on cynical indifference'. The inquiry QC James Dingemans had a go at everyone, saving Dr Kelly. He referred to one of Kelly's last emails, in which he spoke of 'many dark actors playing games'. He suggested wider issues the inquiry had thrown up should be investigated by 'other institutions' – a reference to parliament.

Jeremy Gompertz QC
Counsel for the Kelly family

- Made an excoriating attack on the government's treatment of the dead weapons expert, accusing it of duplicity and 'a cynical abuse of power' which deserved 'the strongest possible condemnation'.
- Government accused of making a 'deliberate decision to use Kelly as part of its strategy in its battle with the BBC'.
- Defence Secretary, Geoff Hoon, accused of hypocrisy and 'false' denials about his role in the unmasking of Kelly.
- With the exception of what he called the 'Walter Mitty slur' – a

reference to comments by Tom Kelly, the Prime Minister's official spokesman – the government, unlike the BBC, 'did not accept any criticism' of any action by any individual involved in the events leading to Kelly's death,' said Gompertz.

Key quotes

'The principal aims of the family in this inquiry are: (1) that the duplicity of the government in their handling of Dr Kelly should be exposed, and (2) that the systemic failures at the Ministry of Defence should be identified and remedied so as to ensure, as far as is humanly possible, that no one else should suffer the ordeal endured by Dr Kelly. If, however, in order to achieve their goal it is required that there should be some criticism of individuals then the family accept this as a necessary step towards their objective.'

'Never again should someone be put in such a position. Never again should a civil servant be publicly named if there is an alternative route to a legitimate objective which can be achieved without naming him. Never again should there be such feeble support for an employee in a time of crisis.'

'The family also wish me to mention the contribution of the culture of the media to the tragedy of Dr Kelly's death. The style of the *Today* programme in apparently making news as opposed to reporting it, the conduct and confrontational approach of some investigative and political journalists and the conduct of some of the photographers all played a part in the harassment of both Dr Kelly before his death and of the family after it.'

'The government and the nation have lost their greatest expert in biological weapons of mass destruction, yet he was characterised by his employers to suit their needs of the hour as a middle-ranking official and used as a pawn in their political battle with the BBC. His public exposure must have brought about a total loss of self-esteem, a feeling that people had lost trust in him. No wonder Dr Kelly felt betrayed after giving his life to the service of his country. No wonder he was brokenhearted and, as his wife put it, had shrunk into himself. In his despair he seems to have taken his own life.'

Jonathan Sumption QC

Counsel for the government

- Rejected any criticism of the government's handling of the affair and implied that no lessons could be learned from it.
- Kelly's death was undoubtedly a tragedy for his family and a great loss 'for the service for which he worked', Sumption said. It was perfectly possible to express genuine sympathy to his family, 'without at once turning aside in order to hunt for other people to blame'.
- Sumption said Andrew Gilligan's 'scandalous' allegations had to be rebutted, and defended details about Dr Kelly given by Tom Kelly, Tony Blair's own spokesman, on 9 July 2003 which one reporter testified helped to identify him. The government barrister said this was the fault of the BBC which issued a statement the evening before.
- Once named, the weapons expert did not reveal the pressure he was under to government officials, said Sumption.
- Sumption branded as 'unjustified' claims that two committees of MPs were used to out Kelly. It could not be kept secret, he said.
- It was right for the Prime Minister's closest aides, Jonathan Powell and Alastair Campbell, to be involved with the dossier, and dismissed criticisms from some in the Defence Intelligence

Staff, saying they had been 'out of the loop', rejecting claims of a government 'crusade'.

Key quotes

'The essential point broadcast by Gilligan was that No. 10 had overruled the advice of the intelligence services. That meant that the fact that his source was said to be a senior member of the intelligence services was an extremely important factor in making his reported allegations appear credible.'

'If the government wanted Kelly's name to be in the public domain, they did not need to be devious in order to get it there. Since all of them believed that it would inevitably come out anyway, they only had to wait on events.'

'It was simply not possible for a democratic government to dismiss charges like these as part of the ordinary currency of political debate.'

'Of course Mr Campbell put the points forcefully and articulately on behalf of the government and in the kind of direct language that was calculated to make people listen. That is what Mr Campbell is there for.'

'A government is as much entitled to defend itself against falsehoods as anyone else. If that means disclosing the truth, then it not only can do it but ought to.'

'Looking at the whole of this issue we are, I suggest, in danger of trying to learn general lessons from appalling but wholly exceptional and unpredictable events. What is much worse than that is we are in danger of learning the wrong lessons. Dr Kelly's death is undoubtedly a tragedy for his family. It is also a great loss for the service for which he worked but it is perfectly possible to recognise those facts and to express genuine sympathy to his family, as we do, without at once turning aside in order to hunt for other people to blame.'

Andrew Caldecott QC
Counsel for the BBC

- Hoon's view that it was not his responsibility to correct misleading media reports exaggerating the message of the weapons dossier 'borders on cynical indifference'.
- The corporation had acted in the public interest by airing reports on 29 May 2003 of Kelly's criticisms.
- Said Jonathan Powell, the Prime Minister's chief of staff, had had part of the dossier changed. In a 19 September email to John Scarlett, chairman of the Joint Intelligence Committee, he asked for a change in a reference to Saddam Hussein using WMD if his regime was threatened.
- He also said Alastair Campbell, Downing Street's director of communications, had caused a 'gear change' in the language of the 45-minute claim after another email to Scarlett.
- He said Kelly had told three BBC journalists of the dossier's alleged flaws.

Key quotes
'There can be few subjects of greater public interest than reasons presented by a government to its own people as possible grounds for war.'

'He was clearly a principled man. If he thought in an area where his two special subjects converged, Iraq and WMD, that the public were being misled, he would most likely have deeply resented it. For these various reasons Dr Kelly was and appeared to be an important and credible source.'

'Several mass circulation newspapers understandably interpreted the 45-minute claim as referring to strategic missiles or bombs . . . The reaction of Mr Hoon and Mr Scarlett borders on cynical indifference. The government's failure to correct is wholly indefensible.'

'The BBC anticipates criticism of the 6.07 broadcast in particular and its treatment thereafter, but they do ask the inquiry to have in mind the public interest in the remainder of its extensive coverage of Dr Kelly's concerns about the dossier, which the BBC believes the public had a right to know.'

Heather Rogers QC
Counsel for Andrew Gilligan

- The Defence Secretary, Geoff Hoon, and the No. 10 director of communications, Alastair Campbell, were described as being like 'playground bullies'.
- Described Gilligan as a 'working journalist' and said everyone made mistakes.
- Lord Hutton interrupted her several times, noting that it had not been an ordinary story, given the enormity of the charge against the government.
- She said Kelly had told Gilligan that 'most people in intelligence were unhappy with the dossier because it did not reflect their views'. Lord Hutton interrupted to inquire whether she had meant 'most people in intelligence'. She replied that she stood by that.

Key quotes

'What I will seek to do is to address you from the perspective of Andrew Gilligan, which is that of the working journalist, the working journalist who has an essential job to do in a democracy.'

'We now know, because we have seen Alastair Campbell's diary extracts, that he and Geoff Hoon agreed . . . to get Gilligan. Of course, 'get' is not exactly the word Mr Campbell used in his diary. The response is like that of a playground bully.'

'Of course, Andrew Gilligan did not have a verbatim note of the conversation. He is not a court transcriber who records every word. He is a journalist, and like most journalists he made notes.'

James Dingemans QC

Counsel for the inquiry

- As well as being an investigation into the events surrounding Kelly's death, the inquiry is also acting as the official inquest.
- Criticised Alastair Campbell, for losing a sense of perspective in his battle with the BBC over the Iraq dossier.
- Ran through 15 questions that he considers Lord Hutton would have to answer, one of them relating to Campbell's role. He said that Campbell's response to a BBC letter on 27 June 2003, in which it replied to his complaints, 'was, as he himself accepted, not measured'.
- He said that it was plain that Kelly was involved in the final stages of the dossier.
- He noted that there was confusion over the inclusion in the dossier of a claim that Iraq could deploy its biological and chemical weapons within 45 minutes: it left the incorrect

impression that these would be delivered by long-range missiles rather than fired by artillery or mortars.

- Dingemans expressed scepticism over Andrew Gilligan's account of his meeting with Kelly.
- The government was criticised for failing to inform Kelly about its media strategy that would lead to his name being made public.

Key quotes

'The evidence points overwhelmingly to the fact that Dr Kelly had taken his own life and there was no involvement of third parties.'

'There are two phrases which have been used throughout this inquiry which are certainly capable of more than one interpretation. One is "weapons of mass destruction" and the other is "sexing up".'

'It is plain that Dr Kelly was involved in the final stages of the dossier.'

'It might be thought unfortunate that if government communications experts were involved, because of the lack of experience of JIC members at public presentation, such confusion was allowed to occur.'

'The absence of Mr Campbell's name in the first set of notes may suggest that it was more likely to be Mr Gilligan's question than Dr Kelly's answer.'

'It is plain from the evidence that Dr Kelly was not aware of the media maelstrom which was about to descend upon him.'

'Somewhere along the way we lost a summer. I hope we exchange it for understanding.' ■

Day 24
13 October 2003

Sir Kevin Tebbit, the top official at the MoD, was the last witness at the inquiry, his appearance having been delayed because he had had an eye operation. Coming well after the formal ending of the inquiry, his evidence did not have the impact it would otherwise have done. He disclosed that all the key decisions leading to Dr Kelly's unmasking were taken at a meeting in Downing Street chaired by the Prime Minister.

Sir Kevin Tebbit
Permanent secretary at the Ministry of Defence

- Key policy decisions were taken at a Downing Street meeting chaired by Tony Blair.
- Sir Kevin emphasised the importance of the meeting, which took place on 8 July 2003, the day before Kelly's name was identified by the media.
- The meeting also approved a question and answer briefing paper whereby the MoD would give out more details of Kelly leading to the confirmation of his name.
- Mr Gompertz asked Sir Kevin about an email sent by the BBC diplomatic correspondent James Robbins giving an account of a conversation with an MoD official who described Kelly as being 'rather eccentric' and 'a bit weird'. Sir Kevin admitted he had spoken briefly to Mr Robbins at a reception but said his words 'were not intended as a smear'.
- He said that he had not discussed, and would have objected to

leaking Kelly's name to a particular newspaper, an option mentioned in the diaries of Alastair Campbell.

On the Downing Street meeting which approved the press strategy
'The change in stance, as you put it, was a decision taken by a meeting chaired by the Prime Minister.'

Asked if Kelly approved the naming strategy
'He was never asked that question because that was not the question that we were seeking to establish ... the problem here is you are assuming – there was some process to reveal Dr Kelly's name. There was not a process to reveal Dr Kelly's name. There was a process to release the information which the government believed it could not sit on any longer.'

Referring to Andrew Gilligan report
'There was also the right of government here to decide how to proceed to correct the record; and while I wanted and we all wanted to do this cooperatively with Dr Kelly, because he would need to stand by whatever was said, this does not mean to say that we simply had to follow as opposed to lead in this respect.'

Insisting that if he had in fact spoken to Mr Robbins at the buffet table, his remarks were not intended as a smear
'My light comments were made, as I say, in the context of anybody who talks to Andrew Gilligan like this must be off their head. That was the context. It was not about my view about Dr Kelly – it was not intended as a smear. It was in the context of: why would anyone do this – I said, you know, frankly anyone who talks to Andrew Gilligan in these circumstances must be a bit odd.'

Asked to comment on the diary entries

'I understand that Alastair Campbell has a very racy diary style.' ■

Key Documents

Email from BBC diplomatic correspondent James Robbins to Richard Sambrook, titled Snippet from MoD, 17 July 2003

He sought me out to whisper a few thoughts 'confidentially' and 'off the record'.

For what it's worth, he was very keen to stress that Dr Kelly came forward because he was alarmed that the idea was gaining currency among friends/colleagues that he was the sole source, and they advised him to dispel it.

[Blanked out] wouldn't be led as to why Downing Street presented him in that way, and only rolled his eyes and looked pained when I mentioned Downing Street's involvement.

He volunteered that Dr Kelly was regarded as a 'bit weird' and 'rather eccentric'. . . not quite clear what this smear was intended to achieve.

He earnestly hoped the summer recess would bury all this. He was 'very tired' and so was most of Whitehall. ■

The odd couple: intelligence meets New Labour

Richard Norton-Taylor and Ewen MacAskill

One of the most intriguing, illuminating, and disturbing insights thrown up by the Hutton inquiry was the relationship between Downing Street and the intelligence agencies.

At the apex was an odd couple – Alastair Campbell, Tony Blair's director of communications, and John Scarlett, chairman of Whitehall's Joint Intelligence Committee. The Whitehall establishment shuddered when they heard Campbell describe Scarlett as his 'mate' in his evidence to the Commons Foreign Affairs Committee.

The close relationship between the two men was illustrated in an extract of Campbell's diary which Blair's chief communications adviser read out to the inquiry counsel, James Dingemans. He recorded Scarlett telling him: 'You are the brutal political hatchet man and I am the dry intelligence officer and we've been made to accord to our stereotypes.'

The curious thing about the last part of this entry is that it was written in early June, only a short time after the row provoked by the original Gilligan broadcast about the government's Iraqi weapons dossier. Though Campbell had already been firing broadsides, Scarlett was hardly a public figure. But his name had been prayed in aid by Blair and Campbell in their attack on the Gilligan allegations.

The intelligence community believed that the two men had overstepped the line separating party politics and their professional role as providers of secret information. Scarlett, who works in the Cabinet Office adjoining Downing Street, had 'gone native', seduced by being a member of an unaccountable cabal around the Prime Minister – a cabal including Sir David Manning, then Blair's foreign policy adviser, now British ambassador to Washington, and Sir David Omand, security and intelligence coordinator in the Cabinet Office, and Jonathan Powell, Blair's chief of staff. Also in the cabal were the Downing Street press officers and Campbell's propaganda staff.

The Hutton inquiry disclosed not only the cosy relationship between the Downing Street cabal and the head of the joint intelligence staff but confirmed the extent to which Blair had become even more presidential than his predecessors. In the run-up to the war in Iraq and the preparation of the September dossier on Iraq's (alleged) weapons of mass destruction, what is notable is the extent to which Downing Street largely ignored two of the great departments of state: the Foreign Office and the Ministry of Defence. So minimal was the role of the Foreign Office that the Secretary of State, Jack Straw, was not called to give evidence before Hutton, and few of his staff were either. The Defence Secretary, Geoff Hoon, was called but claimed either not have been consulted or not to have been involved in much of the decision-making. The cabinet too was remarkable for its lack of debate over the dossier, the decision to go to war and the post-war controversy.

The myth is that the British civil service is supposed to be anonymous, impartial and non-partisan. But that has survived neither the impact of the Labour party nor of Hutton. All those senior civil servants were brought to the courtroom and their thoughts and working practices exposed. What was remarkable was the haphazard nature of so much of the decision-making, partly a result of the retention of power in a few hands. Far from a streamlined service – a Rolls-Royce civil service, as they often prided themselves – the view that emerged at Hutton was of pettiness, of being malleable and, in some cases, lacking in basic humanity when faced with an individual in distress such as Dr David Kelly. Even the intelligence community, with its much-prized reputation for objectivity and cool assessment, proved not to be beyond the reach of Campbell and his colleagues.

Labour was scarred by the length of its time in opposition – from 1979 to 1997 – and came back to power with an undue amount of faith in its strategists and press team. The party wanted to transfer into government its ability to control the news agenda, which it did brilliantly in the years immediately prior to the 1997 election. But it anticipated that the civil service would not be able to react as swiftly as the party machine – and so it turned out to be. Campbell and others would ask departmental press officers what was going to be in the next day's papers, to which they replied that they did not know. That was not the Labour way: its press officers were on the phone throughout the day, trading information with journalists and asking what was going to lead tomorrow's front pages. They wanted to know so they could try to influence the final decision, either through cajoling or bullying editors and senior journalists, or at the very least so they had responses ready when the papers hit the streets. Labour, unhappy with the quality of many existing departmental press officers and special advisers, gradually replaced them with either party staffers or journalists known to have Labour sympathies. Presentation was all-important, frequently at the expense of substance.

This over-reliance on presentation and on a handful of trusted advisers was eventually going to come unstuck and it did spectacularly with the so-called 'dodgy dossier' released by the government in February 2003.

With the help of the Coalition Information Centre the government published a dossier entitled *Iraq's Infrastructure of Concealment, Deception and Intimidation*. Part of it was copied from the internet. It included, almost word for word but with significant embellishments, extracts from a PhD thesis written by Ibrahim al Marishi, a Californian student.

Marishi wrote that the Iraqi Mukhabarat – secret intelligence service – aided opposition groups in hostile regimes. The government's dossier said the Mukhabarat supported terrorist organisations in hostile regimes – a significant change.

The concern about the media was well illustrated on 19 September when Powell emailed Campbell and Scarlett expressing concern about the dossier suggesting 'there is no CBW [chemical and biological weapons] threat and we will only create one if we attack him'. He asked Campbell: 'What will be the headline in the [*Evening*] *Standard* on day of publication? What do we want it to be?'

The inquiry heard that Downing Street did apply pressure on Scarlett to harden up the language of the dossier. Scarlett, Blair, and Campbell, all of them in their evidence insisted the dossier was under Scarlett's 'ownership', a word they emphasised. Campbell and Scarlett were asked why Campbell chaired a meeting of Joint Intelligence Committee members. The response was that the meeting was discuss presentation rather than substance.

Yet Brian Jones, a former senior member of the Defence Intelligence Staff, asked by Lord Hutton about the concerns of his colleagues, replied: 'They were about language but language is the means by which we communicate an assessment, so they were about the assessment, yes'.

In the end, the intelligence agencies, notably MI6, whose raw material was used in the dossier, accepted it through gritted teeth. Scarlett said later that he had had a 'debate' with Campbell during the whole exercise, but not a 'bust-up'.

Sir Richard Dearlove, known as C, for Chief, of MI6, after much anguish adopted the view that he could live with the language of the dossier and what politicians did with it was their affair. It drew a sort of constitutional dividing line. However, he got his own back – to some extent at least – when at the Hutton Inquiry he described as 'valid' criticism from the Commons Foreign Affairs Committee that the claim Iraqi forces could fire chemical and biological weapons within 45 minutes was given 'undue prominence' in the dossier.

'Valid' too, he said, was criticism by the parliamentary Intelligence and Security Committee, which said the dossier should have made clear the 45 minutes referred to battlefield weapons and that the failure to explain this was 'unhelpful'.

Sir Richard dismissed the 45-minute claim – one of the issues at the heart of the Kelly affair – as unsurprising and, by implication, insignificant.

Sir Richard also made clear he strongly objected to attempts by Downing Street to exaggerate the threat posed by Saddam Hussein's nuclear programme in the government's Iraqi weapons dossier. He told the inquiry that MI6 delivered a 'rigorous response' to a memo Campbell sent to Scarlett about Iraqi nuclear ambitions. MI6 insisted that the dossier should 'stick to [the] original intelligence'.

Whenever he was questioned about his close relationship with the security and intelligence agencies, Campbell argued that it was important for him to know what terrorist and other threats Britain faced so that he could brief the media and prepare for a possible attack.

The truth is MI6 did not want a dossier in the first place. It had nothing new to say about Iraq. There are few certainties in the world of intelligence. Kelly, a scientist who preferred dealing with evidence and facts told the BBC reporter, Susan Watts: 'It was an interesting week before the dossier was put out because there were so many people saying, "Well, I'm not so sure about that", or in fact that they were happy with it being in, but not expressed the way that it was – because the word-smithing is actually quite important. The intelligence community are a pretty cautious lot on the whole

– but once you get people presenting it for public consumption then of course they use different words.'

It was the first time Britain went to war on the basis of intelligence claims. Intelligence officers are the first to agree that intelligence has a part to play in decision-making. But it should never be decisive, not least because it is so rarely certain, black and white. Even if it discloses hitherto secret and significant facts, judging how human beings – the potential enemy, in this case Saddam Hussein – respond, what their intentions are, is a very different exercise.

Furthermore, British security and intelligence agencies were against war. The main reason was spelt out in a warning from the Joint Intelligence Committee in February 2003 – a month before the invasion of Iraq – that 'al-Qaeda and associated groups continued to represent by far the greatest threat to western interests, and that threat would be heightened by military action against Iraq'.

The intelligence chiefs added: 'Any collapse of the Iraqi regime would increase the risk of chemical and biological warfare technology or agents finding their way into the hands of terrorists, including al-Qaeda.'

The agencies had self-interested reasons – war, with Britain fighting alongside American troops would make it more difficult for them to gather intelligence, to recruit informants from the Muslim community, as well as increase the threat of terrorist attacks.

The point was made succinctly by Ann Taylor, chair of the Intelligence and Security Committee who told Scarlett after she was given a sneak preview of the dossier: 'The hardest questions in the debate, not fully answered in the dossier, remain, why now and why Saddam?'

In his summing up, James Dingemans, the inquiry counsel, said many issues had been raised some of which were for 'other institutions' to pursue. He was referring to parliament. Many MPs say they want to investigate just how it came to be that intelligence and partisan politics had been allowed to get entangled so dangerously, and why it was not allowed to see documents which saw the light of day only because of the suicide of a government scientist.

If Scarlett and the intelligence service were badly damaged by its closeness to Campbell, the Foreign Office did not fare well either. Iraq policy was formally the responsibility of the FCO. With twenty-odd Arab countries, the Foreign Office had many Arab speakers and many diplomats who had served either in Iraq or neighbouring countries. They prided themselves on their expertise, and their overwhelming message was to avoid war with Iraq. Conflict could destabilise Iraq, and possibly lead to its break-up, with a Kurdish north, Sunni centre and Shia south. In terms of the region, that meant a strong Iraq would be replaced with what was effectively a vacuum, one that neighbours such as Iran and Syria might want to exploit. These Arabists also warned that though support for Saddam was brittle and the Iraqis would be glad to see the back of him, they did not want the Americans – in part because of the country's support for Israel – to do it. Their preference was to continue the policy of containment, hoping that eventually Saddam would be overthrown.

Blair, like Thatcher and other prime ministers, did not trust the Foreign Office and employed Lord Levy, a Labour fundraiser, as his personal Middle East envoy, one who was contemptuous of much Foreign Office thinking. The Foreign Office disliked him as much as he disliked it. Downing Street ensured he had a desk in the Foreign Office, which further angered its diplomats.

Straw, the Foreign Secretary, heard the warnings from the Foreign Office about the dangers of war but opted to pursue the line that emerged from Downing Street. That came from Blair's own conversations with Bush, from the almost daily contact between Sir David Manning and the US national security adviser,

Condoleezza Rice. These close contacts meant that Downing Street had higher connections – the highest – in the US administration than the Foreign Office.

The cabinet, in which Blair was supposed to be the head of a group of equals, was neutered by Thatcher but hers began to look like a lively debating club compared with the passive team of ministers that Blair ruled over. The decision to go to war, one of the most serious any state can make, was barely discussed. There was a debate in February 2002 in which ministers expressed hostility towards war but, apart from two cabinet members, Robin Cook and Clare Short, there was little further discussion or debate. The cabinet nodded through the dossier on Iraq's WMD and, finally, war itself. In earlier governments, foreign policy was often discussed and debated in detail not before the full cabinet but at the defence and overseas policy committee, which included all the ministers directly involved with foreign and defence issues. But, in a sign of the extent of Blair's control, that committee did not meet once from January 2001 through to the outbreak of war.

One element of the civil service that survived the Labour onslaught on its traditional way of working was its 'Sir Humphrey' culture. This manifested itself in an unwillingness to take responsibility for awkward decisions and to speak at length without answering questions. Sir Kevin Tebbit, permanent secretary at the MoD, told the inquiry – in relation to the treatment of Kelly: 'This was a case where an individual had caused a great deal to happen, operating, as it were, outside his official responsibilities and the only way, in a sense, that he could deal with that was under his own responsibility. So there was a different sense of accountability here.' In reply to a question on whether Kelly should have been subjected to a more thorough grilling, Sir Kevin paused before telling the inquiry: 'That is rather an interesting question. It is not one of the yes or no answers that I can provide.'

That was comical. There was nothing comical about the way Whitehall responded to the news that Kelly had come forward to volunteer to the Ministry of Defence that he might have been the source of Gilligan's story. There was much else to occupy the government that weekend, a whole range of domestic issues. Instead, Campbell, Blair, Hoon and some of the highest and best-paid civil servants in the country were discussing how best to exploit this news. An abiding memory of the Hutton inquiry is the revelation that, on the Monday after Kelly came forward, senior Downing Street and defence staff were all huddled round the computer screen of the deputy Downing Street press officer, Godric Smith, as he composed a press release to announce that someone had come forward. The revision process took at least four hours. Round the computer at various times were Smith himself, Campbell, Powell, Sir Kevin Tebbit, and one of Campbell's press deputies, Tom Kelly. The line-up and time involved is telling enough: that policy-making had taken a poor second place to a battle with the BBC. What is equally telling is that such was the dominance of Downing Street that it was composing a statement for release under the name of the Ministry of Defence. Powell told Hutton: '[We] worked on a draft of the MoD press statement. This was [finished] around 2.30pm [on 8 July]. At the end of the exercise I said to him [Tebbit] he should take it back to the MoD.' The MoD could not even be trusted with that.

The final submissions

If the witnesses to the Hutton Inquiry came to agree on anything, it was the importance of presentation. Their final submissions, delivered after the close of formal proceedings and published only when the report itself appeared, offered little fresh evidence, but boosted their cases by restating them more plainly.

While Dr David Kelly's relatives declined to comment on Lord Hutton's findings, final submissions to the inquiry suggest that they drew diametrically opposing conclusions from the same evidence.

The Law Lord cleared the government of an 'underhand' or 'devious' strategy to identify the weapons expert. His family accused it of an 'improper' plan to name him. 'The government made a conscious decision to cause Dr Kelly's identity to be revealed and it did so in order to assist it in the battle with the BBC,' their lawyers wrote, citing newspaper articles that gave clues to Andrew Gilligan's source.

Those indicated that government sources had briefed journalists about Kelly before the decision to issue a press statement was made, they said. 'It is improbable in the extreme this was an 'indiscretion' committed by a person within Whitehall who was a rogue element and who was on a frolic of his or her own,' the submission added.

But the 'smoking gun', the Kelly family claimed, was Alastair Campbell's diary, in which he wrote: 'The biggest thing needed was the source out.' 'Alastair Campbell's diary reveals that it was his desire and the desire of others, including the Secretary of State for Defence, that the fact and identity of the source should be made public,' their lawyers added.

The government's statement denied any attempt to disclose the scientist's name, adding that such allegations of 'bad faith or underhand conduct are . . . inherently implausible' and went on to explain how the dossier had been drawn up.

But it also went on the attack, focusing on errors in Gilligan's report and the BBC's handling of criticism. Anticipating just such tactics, the BBC devoted the bulk of its submission to a pre-emptive strike, setting out and knocking down potential criticisms of Greg Dyke, the director general, Gavyn Davies, the chairman, and Richard Sambrook, the corporation's director of news.

Those defences would not be enough to save the jobs of the first two men when Lord Hutton launched his stinging attack on the BBC's 'defective' management.

The document accepted that editors had responsibility for their journalists' shortcomings, but argued that the sheer volume of material broadcast by the BBC made it unrealistic to suggest that Dyke 'could or should' have known of the report's failings prior to transmission. In hindsight, he would have conducted a fuller investigation; but it would be wrong to blame him for the implementation of systems.

It went on to suggest that the governors' ultimate responsibility for the BBC was distinct from 'direct management responsibility' and dismissed suggestions that Davies had put pressure on the other governors into 'backing the executive's line'.

But it also underlined the way in which the BBC had distanced itself from Gilligan in its defence of Sambrook. It pointed out that the journalist had not initially conceded there were errors in his report, adding, 'The position between the defence correspondent of the *Today* programme and the BBC's director of news is ultimately one of trust.'

Gilligan himself admitted making mistakes in his unscripted 29 May report, but argued that reporters should be given a 'margin of error' when dealing with matters of public interest because the central issue was freedom of expression in a democracy.

'If criticism were to be confined to what can be proved to be true, then freedom of political debate would be illusory,' wrote Paul Jones, his solicitor, in a final submission to Lord Hutton. 'In the context of political reporting, it can be right to report matters, even if it later turns out that they are untrue.'

And he insisted that Gilligan's report 'accurately reported the burden of what Dr Kelly had told him', citing his evidence to parliamentary committees and discussions with other journalists.

The government had placed disproportionate emphasis on Gilligan's comment in an unscripted report for *Today* that the government 'probably knew' its claim that Iraqi weapons of mass desctruction could be used within 45 minutes was wrong, said the submission. It was precisely the allegation on which Lord Hutton focused – and which he dismissed as 'unfounded'. Gilligan and the BBC cannot have been helped by Susan Watts's final letter. It accused the corporation of misrepresenting her evidence, insisting that she had never described 'political interference' with the dossier.

Yet the most significant submission may have been the most understated: that of Sir Kevin Tebbit, the permanent secretary at the Ministry of Defence. His evidence had embarrassed the government; he appeared to testify that the decisions leading to Kelly's identification were made at a No. 10 meeting chaired by Tony Blair.

When asked whether this included a decision to issue question-and-answer material that offered journalists details on the scientist, as well as a less detailed press statement indicating a possible source had come forward, Sir Kevin replied: 'Yes.'

But in his submission he backtracked, stating that he had been referring solely to the statement, adding: 'The Q&A material itself was neither approved nor considered at that meeting.' That might not, of course, have precluded discussion of what a Q&A should include. Once again, it was all about the wording.

Tania Branigan

Lord Hutton's summary of his conclusions

Extract from the Report published 28 January 2004

I am satisfied that Dr Kelly took his own life and that the principal cause of death was bleeding from incised wounds to his left wrist which Dr Kelly had inflicted on himself with the knife found beside his body. It is probable that the ingestion of an excess amount of Coproxamol tablets coupled with apparently clinically silent coronary artery disease would have played a part in bringing about death more certainly and more rapidly than it would have otherwise been the case. I am further satisfied that no other person was involved in the death of Dr Kelly and that Dr Kelly was not suffering from any significant mental illness at the time he took his own life.

On the issues relating to the preparation of the government's dossier of 24 September 2002 entitled Iraq's Weapons of Mass Destruction, *my conclusions are as follows:*

- The dossier was prepared and drafted by a small team of the assessment staff of the JIC. Mr John Scarlett, the Chairman of the JIC, had the overall responsibility for the drafting of the dossier. The dossier, which included the 45 minutes claim, was issued by the government on 24 September 2002 with the full approval of the JIC.

- The 45 minutes claim was based on a report which was received by the SIS from a source which that service regarded as reliable. Therefore, whether or not at some time in the future the report on which the 45 minutes claim was based is shown to be unreliable, the allegation reported by Mr Gilligan on 29 May 2003 that the government probably knew that the 45 minutes claim

was wrong before the government decided to put it in the
dossier, was an allegation which was unfounded.

- The allegation was also unfounded that the reason why the 45
minutes claim was not in the original draft of the dossier was
because it only came from one source and the intelligence
agencies did not really believe it was necessarily true. The reason
why the 45 minutes claim did not appear in draft assessments or
draft dossiers until 5 September 2002 was because the intelligence report on which it was based was not received by the SIS
until 29 August 2002 and the JIC assessment staff did not have
time to insert it in a draft until the draft of the assessment of 5
September 2002.

- The true position in relation to the attitude of 'the intelligence
services' to the 45 minutes claimbeing inserted in the dossier
was that the concerns expressed by Dr Jones were considered by
higher echelons in the intelligence services and were not acted
upon, and the JIC, the most senior body in the intelligence
services charged with the assessment of intelligence, approved
the wording in the dossier. Moreover, the nuclear, chemical and
biological weapons section of the Defence Intelligence Staff,
headed by Dr Brian Jones, did not argue that the intelligence
relating to the 45 minutes claim should not have been included
in the dossier but they did suggest that the wording in which the
claim was stated in the dossier was too strong and that instead
of the dossier stating 'we judge' that 'Iraq has: military plans for
the use of chemical and biological weapons, including against
its own Shia population. Some of these weapons are deployable
within 45 minutes of an order to use them', the wording should
state 'intelligence suggests'.

- Mr Alastair Campbell made it clear to Mr Scarlett on behalf of
the Prime Minister that 10 Downing Street wanted the dossier
to be worded to make as strong a case as possible in relation to

the threat posed by Saddam Hussein's WMD, and 10 Downing Street made written suggestions to Mr Scarlett as to changes in the wording of the draft dossier which would strengthen it. But Mr Campbell recognised, and told Mr Scarlett that 10 Downing Street recognised, that nothing should be stated in the dossier with which the intelligence community were not entirely happy.

- Mr Scarlett accepted some of the drafting suggestions made to him by 10 Downing Street but he only accepted those suggestions which were consistent with the intelligence known to the JIC and he rejected those suggestions which were not consistent with such intelligence and the dossier issued by the government was approved by the JIC.

- As the dossier was one to be presented to, and read by, parliament and the public, and was not an intelligence assessment to be considered only by the government, I do not consider that it was improper for Mr Scarlett and the JIC to take into account suggestions as to drafting made by 10 Downing Street and to adopt those suggestions if they were consistent with the intelligence available to the JIC. However I consider that the possibility cannot be completely ruled out that the desire of the Prime Minister to have a dossier which, whilst consistent with the available intelligence, was as strong as possible in relation to the threat posed by Saddam Hussein's WMD, may have subconsciously influenced Mr Scarlett and the other members of the JIC to make the wording of the dossier somewhat stronger than it would have been if it had been contained in a normal JIC assessment. Although this possibility cannot be completely ruled out, I am satisfied that Mr Scarlett,the other members of the JIC, and the members of the assessment staff engaged in the drafting of the dossier were concerned to ensure that the contents of the dossier were consistent with the intelligence available to the JIC.

- The term 'sexed-up' is a slang expression, the meaning of which lacks clarity in the context of the discussion of the dossier. It is capable of two different meanings. It could mean that the dossier was embellished with items of intelligence known or believed to be false or unreliable to make the case against Saddam Hussein stronger, or it could mean that whilst the intelligence contained in the dossier was believed to be reliable, the dossier was drafted in such a way as to make the case against Saddam Hussein as strong as the intelligence contained in it permitted. If the term is used in this latter sense, then because of the drafting suggestions made by 10 Downing Street for the purpose of making a strong case against Saddam Hussein, it could be said that the Government 'sexed-up' the dossier. However in the context of the broadcasts in which the 'sexing-up' allegation was reported and having regard to the other allegations reported in those broadcasts, I consider that the allegation was unfounded as it would have been understood by those who heard the broadcasts to mean that the dossier had been embellished with intelligence known or believed to be false or unreliable, which was not the case.

On the issues relating to Dr Kelly's meeting with Mr Andrew Gilligan in the Charing Cross Hotel on 22 May 2003 my conclusions are as follows:

- In the light of the uncertainties arising from Mr Gilligan's evidence and the existence of two versions of his notes made on his personal organiser of his discussion with Dr Kelly on 22 May it is not possible to reach a definite conclusion as to what Dr Kelly said to Mr Gilligan. It may be that Dr Kelly said to Mr Gilligan that Mr Campbell was responsible for transforming the dossier, and it may be that when Mr Gilligan suggested to Dr Kelly that the dossier was transformed to make it 'sexier', Dr

Kelly agreed with this suggestion. However I am satisfied that Dr Kelly did not say to Mr Gilligan that the government probably knew or suspected that the 45 minutes claim was wrong before that claim was inserted in the dossier. I am further satisfied that Dr Kelly did not say to Mr Gilligan that the reason why the 45 minutes claim was not included in the original draft of the dossier was because it only came from one source and the intelligence agencies did not really believe it was necessarily true. In the course of his evidence Mr Gilligan accepted that he had made errors in his broadcasts in the *Today* programme on 29 May 2003. The reality was that the 45 minutes claim was based on an intelligence report which the SIS believed to be reliable and the 45 minutes claim was inserted in the dossier with the approval of the JIC, the most senior body in the United Kingdom responsible for the assessment of intelligence. In addition the reason why the 45 minutes claim was not inserted in the first draft of the dossier was because the intelligence on which it was based was not received by the SIS in London until 29 August 2002. Therefore the allegations reported by Mr Gilligan that the government probably knew that the 45 minutes claim was wrong or questionable and that it was not inserted in the first draft of the dossier because it only came from one source and the intelligence agencies did not really believe it was necessarily true, were unfounded.

- Dr Kelly's meeting with Mr Gilligan was unauthorised and in meeting Mr Gilligan and discussing intelligence matters with him, Dr Kelly was acting in breach of the civil service code of procedure which applied to him.

- It may be that when he met Mr Gilligan, Dr Kelly said more to him than he had intended to say and that at the time of the meeting he did not realise the gravity of the situation which he was helping to create by discussing intelligence matters with Mr

Gilligan. But whatever Dr Kelly thought at the time of his meeting with Mr Gilligan, it is clear that after Mr Gilligan's broadcasts on 29 May Dr Kelly must have come to realise the gravity of the situation for which he was partly responsible by commenting on intelligence matters to him and he accepted that the meeting was unauthorised, as he acknowledged in a telephone conversation with his friend and colleague Ms Olivia Bosch after his meeting with Mr Gilligan.

On the issues relating to the BBC arising from Mr Gilligan's broadcasts on the BBC Today programme on 29 May 2003 my conclusions are as follows:

- The allegations reported by Mr Gilligan on the BBC *Today* programme on 29 May 2003 that the government probably knew that the 45 minutes claim was wrong or questionable before the dossier was published and that it was not inserted in the first draft of the dossier because it only came from one source and the intelligence agencies did not really believe it was necessarily true, were unfounded.
- The communication by the media of information (including information obtained by investigative reporters) on matters of public interest and importance is a vital part of life in a democratic society. However the right to communicate such information is subject to the qualification (which itself exists for the benefit of a democratic society) that false accusations of fact impugning the integrity of others, including politicians, should not be made by the media. Where a reporter is intending to broadcast or publish information impugning the integrity of others the management of his broadcasting company or newspaper should ensure that a system is in place whereby his editor or editors give careful consideration to the wording of the

report and to whether it is right in all the circumstances to broadcast or publish it. The allegations that Mr Gilligan was intending to broadcast in respect of the government and the preparation of the dossier were very grave allegations in relation to a subject of great importance and I consider that the editorial system which the BBC permitted was defective in that Mr Gilligan was allowed to broadcast his report at 6.07am without editors having seen a script of what he was going to say and having considered whether it should be approved.

- The BBC management was at fault in the following respects in failing to investigate properly the government's complaints that the report in the 6.07am broadcast was false that the government probably knew that the 45 minutes claim was wrong even before it decided to put it in the dossier. The BBC management failed, before Mr Sambrook wrote his letter of 27 June 2003 to Mr Campbell, to make an examination of Mr Gilligan's notes on his personal organiser of his meeting with Dr Kelly to see if they supported the allegations which he had made in his broadcast at 6.07am. When the BBC management did look at Mr Gilligan's notes after 27 June it failed to appreciate that the notes did not fully support the most serious of the allegations which he had reported in the 6.07am broadcast, and it therefore failed to draw the attention of the governors to the lack of support in the notes for the most serious of the allegations.

- The email sent by Mr Kevin Marsh, the editor of the *Today* programme, on 27 June 2003 to Mr Stephen Mitchell, the head of radio news, which was critical of Mr Gilligan's method of reporting, and which referred to Mr Gilligan's 'loose use of language and lack of judgment in some of his phraseology' and referred also to 'the loose and in some ways distant relationship he's been allowed to have with *Today*,' was clearly relevant to the complaints which the government was making about his broadcasts on 29 May, and the lack of knowledge on the part of Mr Sambrook, the director of news, and the governors of this critical email shows a defect in the operation of the BBC's management system for the consideration of complaints in respect of broadcasts.

- The governors were right to take the view that it was their duty to protect the independence of the BBC against attacks by the government and Mr Campbell's complaints were being expressed in exceptionally strong terms which raised very considerably the temperature of the dispute between the government and the BBC. However Mr Campbell's allegation that the BBC had an anti-war agenda in his evidence to the FAC was only one part of his evidence. The government's concern about Mr Gilligan's broadcasts on 29 May was a separate issue about which specific complaints had been made by the government. Therefore the governors should have recognised more fully than they did that their duty to protect the independence of the BBC was not incompatible with giving proper consideration to whether there was validity in the government's complaints, no matter how strongly worded by Mr Campbell, that the allegations against its integrity reported in Mr Gilligan's broadcasts were unfounded and the governors failed to give this issue proper consideration. The view taken by the governors, as explained in evidence by Mr Gavyn Davies, the chairman of the board of governors, that they had to rely on the BBC management to investigate and assess whether Mr Gilligan's source was reliable and credible and that it was not for them as governors to investigate whether the allegations reported were themselves accurate, is a view which is understandable. However this was not the correct view for the governors to take because the government had stated to the BBC in clear terms, as had Mr Campbell to the FAC, that the report that the government probably knew that the 45 minutes claim was wrong was untruthful, and this denial was made with the authority of the Prime Minister and the chairman of the JIC. In those circumstances, rather than relying on the assurances of BBC management, I consider that the governors themselves should have made more detailed investigations into the extent to which Mr Gilligan's notes supported his report. If they had done this they would probably have discovered that the notes did not support the allegation that the government knew that the 45 minutes claim was probably wrong, and the Governors should then have questioned whether it was right for the BBC to maintain that it was in the public interest to broadcast that allegation in Mr Gilligan's report and to rely on Mr Gilligan's assurances that his report was accurate. Therefore in the very unusual and specific circumstances relating to Mr Gilligan's broadcasts, the governors are to be criticised for themselves failing to make more detailed investigations into whether this allegation reported by Mr Gilligan was properly supported by his notes and for failing to give proper and adequate consideration to whether the BBC should publicly acknowledge that this very grave allegation should not have been broadcast.

On the issue whether the government behaved in a way which was dishonourable or underhand or duplicitous in revealing Dr Kelly's name to the media my conclusions are as follows:

● There was no dishonourable or underhand or duplicitous strategy by the government covertly to leak Dr Kelly's name to the media. If the bare details of the MoD statement dated 8 July 2003, the changing drafts of the Q and A material prepared in the MoD, and the lobby briefings by the Prime Minister's official spokesman on 9 July are looked at in isolation from the surrounding circumstances it would be possible to infer, as some commentators have done, that there was an underhand strategy by the government to

317

leak Dr Kelly's name in a covert way. However having heard a large volume of evidence on this issue I have concluded that there was no such strategy on the part of the government. I consider that in the midst of a major controversy relating to Mr Gilligan's broadcasts which had contained very grave allegations against the integrity of the government and fearing that Dr Kelly's name as the source for those broadcasts would be disclosed by the media at any time, the government's main concern was that it would be charged with a serious cover up if it did not reveal that a civil servant had come forward. I consider that the evidence of Mr Donald Anderson MP and Mr Andrew Mackinlay MP, the chairman and a member respectively of the FAC, together with the questions put by Sir John Stanley MP to Dr Kelly when he appeared before the FAC, clearly show that the government's concern was well founded. Therefore I consider that the government did not behave in a dishonourable or underhand or duplicitous way in issuing on 8 July 2003, after it had been read over to Dr Kelly and he had said that he was content with it, a statement which said that a civil servant, who was not named, had come forward to volunteer that he had met Mr Gilligan on 22 May.

- The decision by the MoD to confirm Dr Kelly's name if, after the statement had been issued, the correct name were put to the MoD by a reporter, was not part of a covert strategy to leak his name, but was based on the view that in a matter of such intense public and media interest it would not be sensible to try to conceal the name when the MoD thought that the press were bound to discover the correct name, and a further consideration in the mind of the MoD was that it did not think it right that media speculation should focus, wrongly, on other civil servants.

- It was reasonable for the government to take the view that, even if it sought to keep confidential the fact that Dr Kelly had come forward, the controversy surrounding Mr Gilligan's broadcasts was so great and the level of media interest was so intense that Dr Kelly's name as Mr Gilligan's source was bound to become known to the public and that it was not a practical possibility to keep his name secret.

On the issue whether the government failed to take proper steps to help and protect Dr Kelly in the difficult position in which he found himself my conclusion is as follows:

● Once the decision had been taken on 8 July to issue the statement, the MoD was at fault and is to be criticised for not informing Dr Kelly that its press office would confirm his name if a journalist suggested it. Although I am satisfied that Dr Kelly realised, once the MoD statement had been issued on Tuesday 8 July, that his name would come out, it must have been a great shock and very upsetting for him to have been told in a brief telephone call from his line manager, Dr Wells, on the evening of 9 July that the press office of his own department had confirmed his name to the press and must have given rise to a feeling that he had been badly let down by his employer. I further consider that the MoD was at fault in not having set up a procedure whereby Dr Kelly would be informed immediately his name had been confirmed to the press and in permitting a period of one and a half hours to elapse between the confirmation of his name to the press and information being given to Dr Kelly that his name had been confirmed to the press. However these criticisms are subject to the mitigating circumstances that (1) Dr Kelly's exposure to press attention and intrusion, whilst obviously very stressful, was only one of the factors placing him under great stress; (2) individual officials in the MoD did try to help and support him in the ways which I have described and (3) because of his intensely private nature, Dr Kelly was not an easy man to help or to whom to give advice.

Lord Hutton's summary of his conclusions

On the issue of the factors which may have led Dr Kelly to take his own life I adopt as my own conclusion the opinion which Professor [Keith] Hawton, the Professor of Psychiatry at Oxford University, expressed in the course of his evidence:

James Dingemans: Have you considered, now, with the benefit of hindsight that we all have, what factors did contribute to Dr Kelly's death?

Keith Hawton: I think that as far as one can deduce, the major factor was the severe loss of self esteem, resulting from his feeling that people had lost trust in him and from his dismay at being exposed to the media.

JD: And why have you singled that out as a major factor?

KH: Well, he talked a lot about it; and I think being such a private man, I think this was anathema to him to be exposed, you know, publicly in this way. In a sense, I think he would have seen it as being publicly disgraced.

JD: What other factors do you think were relevant?

KH: Well, I think that carrying on that theme, I think that he must have begun – he is likely to have begun to think that, first of all, the prospects for continuing in his previous work role were diminishing very markedly and, indeed, my conjecture that he had begun to fear he would lose his job altogether.

JD: What effect is that likely to have had on him?

KH: Well, I think that would have filled him with a profound sense of hopelessness; and that, in a sense, his life's work had been not wasted but that had been totally undermined.

Lord Hutton: Could you just elaborate a little on that, Professor, again? As sometimes is the case in this inquiry, witnesses give answers and further explanation is obvious, but nonetheless I think it is helpful just to have matters fully spelt out. What do you think would have caused Dr Kelly to think that the prospects of continuing in his work were becoming uncertain?

KH: Well, I think, my lord, that first of all, there had been the letter from Mr Hatfield which had laid out the difficulties that Dr Kelly, you know, is alleged to have got into.

Lord Hutton: Yes.

KH. And in that letter there was also talk that should further matters come to light then disciplinary proceedings would need to be instigated.

Lord Hutton: Yes.

KH: And then of course there were the parliamentary questions which we have heard about, which suggested that questions were going to be asked about discipline in Parliament.

Lord Hutton: Yes. Thank you.

JD: Were there any other relevant factors?

KH: I think the fact that he could not share his problems and feelings with other people, and the fact that he, according to the accounts I have been given, actually increasingly withdrew into himself. So in a sense he was getting further and further from being able to share the problems with other people, that is extremely important.

321

JD: Were there any other factors which you considered relevant?

KH: Those are the main factors that I consider relevant.

* * *

I wish to record my gratitude and thanks to Mrs Kelly and her daughters for the great assistance which they have given to the inquiry in a time of great sorrow and stress for them . . .

The circumstances leading up to Dr Kelly's death were wholly exceptional and I have decided that it is unnecessary for me to make any express recommendations because I have no doubt that the BBC and the government will take note of the criticisms which I have made in this report.

Dr Kelly was a devoted husband and father and a public servant who served his country and the international community with great distinction both in the United Kingdom and in very difficult and testing conditions in Russia and Iraq. The evidence at this Inquiry has concentrated largely on the last two months of Dr Kelly's life, and therefore it is fitting that I should end this report with some words written in Dr Kelly's obituary in the *Independent* on 31 July by Mr Terence Taylor, the President and Executive Director of the International Institute of Strategic Studies, Washington DC, and a former colleague of Dr Kelly:

'It is most important that the extraordinary public attention and political fallout arising from the events of the past month do not mask the extraordinary achievements of a scientist who loyally served not only his government but also the international community at large.'

Brian Hutton
28 January 2004

The verdicts

David Kelly

- Kelly took his own life and he was not suffering from any significant mental illness at the time.
- Kelly did not tell Andrew Gilligan that the government probably knew the 45-minute claim was wrong before it was inserted in the dossier.
- Kelly's meeting with Gilligan was unauthorised and by discussing intelligence matters with him, he breached the civil service code.
- There was no underhand or duplicitous strategy by the government to covertly leak Kelly's name to the media.
- Kelly's exposure to press attention was a factor placing him under stress.
- Because of his intensely private nature Kelly was not an easy man to help, although individual Ministry of Defence officials did try to support him.
- The factors which led Kelly to take his life included loss of self-esteem resulting from a feeling that people had lost trust in him and dismay at media attention, and fear he would lose his job and that his work had been undermined.

Sexing up

- The allegation that the government's September dossier was 'sexed up' was unfounded.
- The 45-minute claim was based on a report from a source regarded as reliable. The allegation the government knew the claim was wrong before it went in the dossier was unfounded.
- The 45-minute claim was not in original drafts because the intelligence was not received until 29 August.

- Alastair Campbell wanted wording of the Saddam threat to be as strong as possible, but said nothing the Joint Intelligence Committee was unhappy with should be in the dossier.
- The JIC may have been 'subconsciously' influenced by Downing Street, but had made sure the contents of the dossier were consistent with the intelligence.

MI6 and John Scarlett

- Lord Hutton said his terms of reference did not include weapons of mass destruction in Iraq.
- John Scarlett, chairman of the Joint Intelligence Committee, had the overall responsibility for the drafting of the dossier, which was issued by the government and approved by the JIC.
- Concerns expressed by the intelligence services over the way the 45-minute claim was included in the dossier were not acted on.
- Scarlett accepted some of the drafting suggestions made to him by 10 Downing Street but rejected those suggestions which were not consistent with intelligence.

Tony Blair

- The Prime Minister was involved in discussions about handling Kelly's admission that he may have been Gilligan's source.
- He was party to the decision to issue a statement which said an unnamed civil servant had come forward as a possible source.
- Downing Street was not, however, involved in the preparation of briefing material within the Ministry of Defence that led to Kelly's name being confirmed to broadcasters.
- Lord Hutton read a transcript of Blair's comments to journalists shortly after Kelly's death denying any involvement in the leaking of his name. But the Law Lord makes no comment on this beyond repeating that there was no 'dishonourable or underhand or duplicitous' strategy to expose Kelly.

Alastair Campbell

● Alastair Campbell made it clear to the JIC that the wording of the September dossier should be as strong as possible. But he also said that nothing should be stated in the dossier with which the intelligence community was not entirely happy.

● Campbell's complaints about the BBC and the Gilligan broadcast were expressed in exceptionally strong terms which raised very considerably the temperature of the dispute between the government and the BBC.

● It is unnecessary to express an opinion on the BBC's criticism of Campbell's evidence to the Commons Foreign Affairs Committee about his involvement in preparing the dossier.

Geoff Hoon

● Hoon was not untruthful when he gave evidence that he had not seen the MoD's question and answer material for the press.

● His decision not to resist pressure for Kelly to appear before MPs cannot be subject to valid criticism.

● It would not have been possible for him to refuse to permit Kelly to appear before the Commons Intelligence Committee and there would have been a political storm had he barred him from appearing before the Foreign Affairs Committee.

The naming strategy

● It was reasonable for the government to think that the identity of Gilligan's source was bound to become known because of media interest, and that it was not practically possible to keep Kelly's name secret.

● There was no 'dishonourable or underhand or duplicitous strategy' by the government to covertly leak Kelly's name to the media.

● The MoD's decision to confirm Kelly's name if it was put to officials by a reporter was not part of a covert strategy to leak his name but was based on the view that it would not be sensible to try to conceal his identity.

- Lord Hutton criticised the MoD for not telling Kelly its press office would confirm his name if a journalist suggested it.
- The MoD was at fault in not setting up a procedure whereby Kelly would be informed as soon as his name had been confirmed to the press.
- Kelly's exposure to media attention was only one of the factors placing him under great stress.
- Individual officials in the MoD did try to help and support him.

The BBC

- The BBC's editorial system was defective.
- Gilligan was allowed to broadcast his 6.07am report without editors having seen a script.
- Editors should have given careful consideration to the report's wording and whether it was right to broadcast. They did not.
- The BBC management failed to examine Gilligan's notes and failed to draw attention of the governors to the discrepancies between them and his early morning broadcast.

Andrew Gilligan

- Gilligan's allegations aired on the *Today* programme at 6.07am on 29 May 2003 about the government's 'sexing up' of its dossier on Iraq's alleged WMD were 'very grave' – and drew Kelly into the row that ensued.
- His allegation that the government probably knew the 45-minutes claim was wrong before it went in the dossier was unfounded.
- His allegation that the 45-minutes claim was absent from the original draft because it only came from one source and the intelligence agencies were not sure of its accuracy was also unfounded.

- Neither of these allegations could be justified by pointing to Kelly as their source as Kelly did not say either of them to Gilligan.

Gavyn Davies

- Gavyn Davies, as chairman of the BBC governors, was wrong to state that it was not feasible for them to investigate for themselves the accuracy of the 6.07am Radio 4 broadcast.
- The governors, led by Davies, should be criticised for failing to investigate whether the 6.07am broadcast was supported by Gilligan's notes and for failing to acknowledge that the allegation should not have been broadcast.

Richard Sambrook

- BBC managers, led by Richard Sambrook, the director of news, failed to check Gilligan's notes to see whether they supported allegations made in the 6.07am broadcast.
- When managers did check the notes, they failed to appreciate that they did not fully support the most serious allegations, and therefore failed to draw this to the attention of the governors.
- Sambrook's lack of knowledge of an email written by the editor of the *Today* programme which was critical of Gilligan's reporting methods showed a defect in the management system's handling of complaints.

Greg Dyke

- Dyke is not named directly in Lord Hutton's findings – but the BBC's management, which he heads, was criticised for failing to properly investigate government's complaints on the 6.07am broadcast.
- Senior management also failed to appreciate the gravity of the allegations, which were so serious that it was unreasonable to expect the government to complain through the usual channels.

'Bring back Greg'
Matt Wells

It is perhaps inevitable that it should have ended as it had begun –
with a leak. Late in the evening before the Hutton report was due to
be published, the first editions of Britain's biggest-selling newspaper,
the *Sun*, hit the London newsstands. Emblazoned across the front
page was a picture of the newspaper's cerebral political editor, Trevor
Kavanagh, with a telephone pressed to his ear, under a headline
declaring that the he had uncovered the story that everyone else had
been chasing: the long-awaited and much-anticipated conclusions of
the investigation into the death of David Kelly.

By morning on Wednesday 28 January, every newspaper had
picked up on the story, with most crediting the *Sun* for its scoop.
The breakfast news programmes were full of it – and by lunchtime,
when Lord Hutton eased himself into his courtroom chair, it was
confirmed. The report could not have been worse for the BBC had
it been written by Alastair Campbell himself

The protagonists were by now aware of its devastating contents. All
had received advance copies at 12.30pm the day before. Downing
Street staff could scarcely believe it – even Geoff Hoon, the battered
Defence sScretary whose political demise had been deemed a
certainty even by his closest supporters, escaped with barely a scratch
to his body armour. But as the sheen of innocence descended on the
government, the BBC was sinking into a pit of despair.

The previous monday, Gavyn Davies, the BBC chairman, had come
in to the editor's office at the *Guardian* to brief senior journalists on
the corporation's position. He was on good form, bullish even,
looking forward to putting the nightmare of the previous six months

behind him and getting on with seeing out his term. He appeared to be confident that the BBC would be credited for having identified its mistakes and made efforts to ensure they would not happen again: editorial systems had been strengthened and procedures for dealing with complaints would be comprehensively overhauled. The worst-case scenario? That Hutton would declare the entirety of Gilligan's Iraq dossier story untrue. That, he admitted, would put the BBC in a very tricky position. But it seemed an unlikely proposition, given that weapons of mass destruction had not been found; the evidence from David Kelly's colleagues of their concern about the use of intelligence; and the crucial recording by *Newsnight*'s Susan Watts of the former weapons inspector himself, expressing concern about No. 10's role in the dossier and even fingering Alastair Campbell for the alleged embellishments. Hutton commentators, he said, had failed to appreciate the weight attached by the BBC to the tape's corroborative attributes. The trouble was, so had Hutton.

The former Law Lord had it in for the BBC at every level. From Andrew Gilligan at the bottom to Greg Dyke and Gavyn Davies at the top, the BBC was found to have failed at all turns. Editorial systems were defective, the response to government complaints was unsatisfactory, and, most damning of all, the story that triggered the cataclysmic row with Downing Street was itself ruled to be unfounded.

Under a previously agreed plan, the worst-case scenario demanded that Davies would take the flak and resign, at a governors' meeting planned for the following day. But it was much worse than even them most pessimistic projections of the BBC disaster planners: not only had Hutton declared the Gilligan report unfounded, he had completely exonerated the government. Davies was devastated. When Tony Blair stood up the Commons that afternoon to open the debate on the report, he watched in despair. In what may turn out to have been a crucially damaging decision, Davies decided to throw in the towel there and then. In the late afternoon, he picked up the phone to the BBC's political editor, Andrew Marr, and told him he was quitting as chairman of the BBC's board of governors. Marr immediately broadcast the revelation on BBC News 24, just after it had played out Greg Dyke's recorded statement of apology in which he hoped a line would now be drawn under the affair. At the highest level of the BBC at this crucial moment, there was disarray.

Davies was Dyke's chief cheerleader on the board: now, with his key ally gone, Dyke's fate was sealed. He knew the game was up, and tendered his resignation. That night, the board gathered at Broadcasting House in central London for their traditional eve-of-meeting dinner. But convivial gossip was replaced by sombre discussion; food was cast aside as the governors – stunned by the gravity of the situation and facing enormous political pressure – discussed what to do. Three governors argued for the offer to be refused: Sir Robert Smith, the BBC governor for Scotland, Professor Fabian Monds, his Northern Ireland counterpart, and Dermot Gleeson, a businessman, argued that to ditch Dyke at such a critical moment would be unwise. Some even argued that the whole board should quit. They were deeply split, even panicked. Eventually, the board agreed to accept Dyke's resignation, eight against three.

The next morning, Friday, Dyke told his executive colleagues of his imminent departure. The decision was ratified at the govenors' formal meeting in Broadcasting House, just as the Downing Street spokesman used the daily 11am briefing to political journalists to denounce Dyke's apology of the previous day as insufficient, nailing the lid on the director general's coffin. Word was spreading to the reporters and news crews shivering in the freezing temperatures outside. BBC News 24 was the first to stand up the story; BBC1 quickly turned its airwaves over to the news network. As its reporter June Kelly was delivering the news to camera, Dyke emerged from the building behind her, and the assembled media scrambled to get a position; Kelly was overwhelmed and by the time the BBC camera was hitched off its tripod, its operator could barely get a clear shot through the scrum of photographers and reporters gathered to hear Dyke's resignation statement.

It was classic Dyke. Not for him a sombre press conference in a dull BBC boardroom; his old hack instincts preferred the drama of the 'doorstep' – the raw, impromptu energy of a statement delivered off the cuff. After a few prepared paragraphs, he smiled as he fielded questions, waving sheaves of emails printed from his computer earlier in the day from supportive BBC staff. He was emotional, but bouncing with energy, a burden lifted from his shoulders. He was quitting, he said, to save the BBC. The crisis would be over, the organisation could get on with doing what it did best. With that, he darted back inside.

After a few minutes, the reporters wandered back to their offices, bewildered by the scale of the story – the country's public broad-caster, an icon abroad, robbed of its two top men in as many days.

But the drama of the day was only just beginning. News of Dyke's enforced departure and the 'unreserved' apology issued by acting chairman Lord Ryder spread quickly among the BBC's 28,000 staff, linked by Gateway, the corporation's internal communications system. The message boards whirred with fury, staff outraged at the 'grovelling' climbdown and the deposing of their charismatic and popular boss, who signed his resignation email – as he did every other communication – 'Greg'. Within hours, there was word of a walkout at Broadcasting House; soon, a few dozen were gathered on the Portland Place pavement. Over at Television Centre in west London, a crowd of hundreds was growing. Dyke was told, and headed out to acknowledge their adulation.

It was a spontaneous, extraordinary outpouring of emotion. Waving banners hurriedly copied on the photocopiers, they chanted 'Bring Back Greg' as his chauffer-driven Lexus slid into Wood Lane for the last time. Senior executives such as the controller of BBC1, Lorraine Heggessey, and the head of drama Jane Tranter, joined reporters, producers, editors and administrative staff in the throng.

Dyke struggled to get through the reception area, bombarded by shouts and hugs. The *Newsnight* presenter Kirsty Wark thrust her microphone at him, recording the mellée for that evening's programme. When he entered the newsroom, a great cheer went up. For the BBC's journalists, this was the man who had stood up for them against a bullying government, who had refused to give in to the incessant hectoring of Alastair Campbell. They all knew Gilligan's story was flawed, but they knew too that Greg would stand by them even if they made mistakes. There are few companies in the land, let alone organisations dominated by cynical journalists, where the resignation of the chief executive would lead to such an emotional outburst. After clambering onto a table to address the staff – he urged them not to be cowed and to continue making challenging and probing programmes – he paid a symbolic visit to the *Today* office, at the heart of the crisis. It was something, he said later, that he had to do. There, he agreed to appear on the programme the following morning. When he left the BBC, they urged him to reconsider. 'When you screw up,' he told them, 'you've got to go.'

Back at Downing Street, there was mounting horror. What had appeared hours earlier as a stunning victory was quickly turning messy. This had not been predicted: 28,000 staff rising up in support of their deposed leader in scenes played out across the television news bulletins all evening. Suddenly, it was Dyke who appeared the hero, the BBC the victim of government triumphalism. Britain hates a gloater, and public sympathy swung towards the underdog.

Day three of the 'BBC crisis', as it was now being described in journalistic shorthand, was no less dramatic than the first. On the *Today* programme, Dyke accused Campbell of being ungracious in his response to the Hutton report, and suggested that some of Lord Hutton's conclusions, if adopted in law, would place worrying restrictions on press freedom. Among BBC staff, despair was turning to anger, and much of it directed at Gilligan. Motions criticising the

Hutton report and Lord Ryder's reaction to it were passed at union meetings around the country, but attempts by the National Union of Journalists to rally support in Gilligan's favour were given the cold-shoulder. It was clear, too, that he had lost the confidence of his managers: he was a 'rogue reporter', said one, more suited to the flyers of Sunday newspaper journalism than the rigorous, robust processes of the BBC. By the evening, he was out, firing a broadside at Hutton and despairing of the 'chill' that had descended on journalism. The statement did not go down well within the BBC, where many regarded it as arrogant and self-serving. Yet undoubtedly the previous seven months had been a personal nightmare for Gilligan, and he did not want to leave, believing still that he had done little wrong. Still, the blow was cushioned by a five-figure offer from the *Sunday Times* to tell the story of the 'worst week of my life'. BBC staff, meanwhile, chan-nelled their frustration through a newspaper advert: again co-ordinated via the internet, 10,000 staff each paid £5 towards a newspaper advert that expressed their dismay at the departure of Dyke. It said: 'Greg Dyke stood for brave, independent and rigorous journalism that was fearless in its search for the truth. We are resolute that the BBC should not step back from its determination to investi-gate the facts in pursuit of the truth. Through his passion and integrity, Greg inspired us to make programmes of the highest quality and creativity. We are dismayed by Greg's departure, but we are deter-mined to maintain his achievements and his vision for an independent organisation that serves the public above all else.' BBC managers attempted to bring closure by announcing a swift internal investigation that will decide whether any institutional changes need to be made, and whether any individuals should face action.

At the end of the first day of the rest of the BBC's life, it seemed the bloodletting was over.

* * *

It is hard to underestimate the scale of the calamity that befell the BBC in the last week of January 2004. Never in its long history had the corporation had such a battering. Around the world there was disbelief that an organisation that prided itself on political impartiality and independence from state control had, apparently, been crushed by politicians. (And Labour ones at that.) How big is the damage to its reputation? How serious is the fall-out with government? And what will be the long-term ramifications, with the process of renewing its royal charter – which sets out its role, remit and method of funding – already under way? Is it the beginning of the end?

As for the effect on the corporation's journalism, it is impossible to gauge. One senior BBC executive said that the corporation badly needed to break a hard-hitting, agenda-setting story that would cause discomfort to the government, such as the *Secret Policeman* documentary that uncovered racism in the police force in 2003.

Politically, and despite ministerial protestations to the contrary, it is hard to imagine that the government will not allow the Kelly affair to influence the charter review process. After all, few can deny that it exposed in dramatic fashion the fundamental contradiction inherent in the role of the board of governors, charged simultaneously with defending the integrity and independence of the corporation from political pressure, and regulating the BBC executive's performance against its objectives and editorial standards. At that fateful meeting on 6 July 2003, it seems that Gavyn Davies made a catastrophic error of judgment, in taking on trust his managers' assurances instead of launching an investigation of his own. In his defence, Davies insists he had no option: the BBC was on the back foot, the Foreign Affairs Committee was due to report on the government's use of Iraq intelligence the next day and there was no time to lose. But that defence shows up the impossibility of squaring the governors' circle: Davies was damned either way.

The call for bringing the corporation under independent regulation has now become a political hot potato. In earlier charter renewal processes, there would be some Westminster hand-wringing about whether to put adverts on the BBC, perhaps fuelled by a dense report from a politically appointed commission, before the minister responsible and the BBC chairman would lock themselves in a room and reconcile how much the corporation wanted with how big a rise in the licence fee the government felt it could sell to the public. This time, everyone has heard of the Office of Communications, the new media regulator for the commercial broadcasting and telecommunications industry. 'Send for Ofcom!', goes the cry. Some have even more dramatic solutions for the BBC: 'Privatise it!' cries Siôn Simon, a Labour – yes, Labour – backbench MP.

Whatever happens, it is clear that Hutton signals a critical stage in the corporation's history. It is unlikely that the present system of regulation can survive. It was established when broadcasting was in its infancy and the BBC held a monopoly; now, in the days of 250 television channels, interactivity and the proliferation of the internet, it seems not only inappropriate, but woefully inadequate. At the very least, the governors are likely to be reconstituted, and given a position of greater independence from the BBC's executive.

The staff, meanwhile, will take time to get over their hurt. Even the government appears to realise this: the day after Dyke's departure, one minister was quoted, anonymously, in the *Guardian* as expressing frustration with the government's handling of the aftermath. 'Alastair is a bully who likes to grind people's faces into the ground. That is not what you should do when people are crying, as they are at the BBC at the moment. We should be putting our arms around the BBC, but how can you do that when it has been decapitated?'

The end of the poisoned embrace

David Aaronovitch

'Hutton came down on the side of politicians and officials, and he came down against the BBC and journalism.'

Andrew Marr, BBC political editor, Wednesday 28 January.

'If they [the public] knew the truth about politicians they would be pleasantly surprised. If they knew the truth about [the media] they would be horrified.'

Alastair Campbell, former journalist and
No. 10 director of communications, Wednesday 28 January.

It was appropriate that, the night before the publication of the Hutton Inquiry, it was revealed by the *Sun* that someone had leaked the closely guarded report's summary. The co-chairman of the Conservative party immediately claimed that the leak carried 'the fingerprints of a government which is willing to say or do anything to save its own skin', a claim that simultaneously dominated the late evening news bulletins. No 10 promptly and vehemently denied the accusation.

Next morning – with only seven hours to go before publication – on the BBC's *Today* programme, the presenter John Humphrys, himself a figure in the inquiry, interviewed the political editor of the *Sun*, Trevor Kavanagh, about who had given the *Sun* the story. Humphrys' probings suggested strongly that he suspected Alastair

Campbell, though he couldn't say so, and Kavanagh certainly wouldn't. Later, in the programme's round-up of the British newspapers, listeners were also told that the *Daily Mirror* was running an editorial that pinned the blame for the leak firmly on the government. Headlined 'Blair and spin: the corrupting obsession', the *Mirror* accused No. 10 of leaking the summary of the report to win headlines away from its near-defeat over tuition fees the night before.

This was, according to the *Mirror*, a 'dodgy, underhand act', typical of the government's 'scheming and duplicity'. It admitted though (in a passage that was not carried on the *Today* programme) that the evidence for its accusation was 'circumstantial' amounting to nothing more than its belief that the government had a motive for the leak, while other recipients of the report – who it only partly listed – did not. The government, however, had form.

This one incident, arising from an inquiry into the death of a man who was the secret source for a story supposedly concerning government skulduggery, and culminating in a BBC journalist interviewing a print journalist about the source for his story about the leak of the report of that inquiry, amid speculative statements about political guilt – all to the probable bewilderment of the ordinary listener – was a perfect illustration of the parasitic circularity of the relationship, the poisonous embrace in which journalism and politics hold each other. It is an embrace that can smother those who find themselves pressed between the writhing bodies.

Politicians and journalists simultaneously need each other, and suspect each other; their relationship in a democracy is always fraught. Where politicians do not possess their own TV and radio stations or enjoy the automatic support of a section of the press – as they often do on the continent, and as Margaret Thatcher did for a while in Britain – they find themselves completely at the mercy of the media to tell their story to the voters. Journalists depend partly upon the actions and knowledge of politicians as a source of stories.

The motive for a series of symbiotic trade-offs is obvious. I give you the story, you write it up the way that suits me.

Despite the scope for cosiness, and even in the days when newspaper editors and politicians went to the same clubs and married each others' nieces, there was room for bitter conflict. In the 1930s the Conservative Prime Minister, Stanley Baldwin, found himself under attack from Tory proprietors ideologically committed to the gold standard. This led to his famous speech encapsulating the politician's generic view of the press. The papers owned by Lord Rothermere and Lord Beaverbrook were, said Baldwin, 'engines of propaganda for the constantly changing policies, desires, personal wishes and personal dislikes of two men. What are their methods? Their methods are direct falsehood, misrepresentation, half-truths ... What the proprietorships of these papers are aiming at is power, and power without responsibility – the prerogative of the harlot throughout the ages'. Amen to that, say Tony Blair and John Major.

The trouble is that politicians have no option but to ride the tiger. Or, in the era of 24-hour news, to 'feed the beast', and as politics and the media have evolved and changed, so the ways in which the two forces have accommodated each other have changed too. The Wilson governments became famous for using certain sympathetic journalists to get stories into the public domain, the privileged papers being dubbed the 'white Commonwealth'. This was a practice that was resented by rival journalists but – presumably – enjoyed by the lucky recipients of this conditional largesse. Nowadays such goodies tend to be spread around.

Then things changed, mostly because of the onset of an intense period of media competition in which new newspapers were set up, the number of TV and radio channels multiplied and the hours of news coverage increased so that news became an all-day operation. At the same time the ancient allegiances of newspapers could no longer be guaranteed to provide a bedrock of support for either of the two large political parties.

In the 1992 general election Labour was expected to win the largest number of seats. That it didn't was ascribed to a number of factors, of which the most frightening was implacable newspaper hostility. As the *Sun* put it on election day itself, 'If Kinnock is elected, will the last person to leave Britain, please turn out the lights'. But something else had happened during that campaign: the derailing of a major part of the Labour critique of Tory policy by a sudden media storm over one of Labour's campaign broadcasts. The use of the case of 'Jennifer's ear' in a broadcast ended up with press conferences hijacked by questing journalists interviewing each other about Jennifer, her family and her glue-ear. Suddenly, said the BBC political correspondents, amid the campaign disciplines, we have a real story. It became the number one issue for several days in the middle of the campaign.

The loss of its health agenda to an unpredictable firestorm shocked a Labour party that was thought to be newly adept at dealing with a hostile media. But the same thing was happening in spades in America. The journalist Joe Klein in *The Natural*, his book on Bill Clinton, devotes a number of pages to the phenomenon of what Klein called 'frenzy journalism'. Klein sees its psychological origins in the Watergate scoop. One was the self-perception of the journalist as hero. The journalists had 'brought down a president. But that precedent caused a severe distortion in the culture of journalism – a new generation of reporters and editors were obsessed with replicating the *Post*'s feat during the Clinton presidency.'

A second factor, according to Klein, was the internal culture of journalism. 'There was a considerable peer pressure,' he writes, 'to stay cynical: reporters who wrote favourably about politicians were considered to be 'in the tank'. A negative story about a politician was the safest story.' Ring a bell? Klein then goes on to quote a Harvard political scientist, Bill Kovach. 'Over the past two decades,' Kovach argues, 'political reporters have become more concerned with how other political reporters judge their work. Not wanting to look soft leads to a negative spin: no matter what position is taken by a politician, the journalistic tendency is to examine it in a negative light – to emphasise political calculations rather than substance.'

When the US frenzies struck Clinton with waves of successive '-gates' (Whitewater, Trooper, etc.), his reaction at first, according to Klein, was a 'furious, self-defeating defiance'. Alastair Campbell striding into the studio of *Channel 4 News* springs to mind here. The motives of some rightwing journalists were obvious enough, but what had happened to the judgment and fairness of the rest? As Democrat politician Barney Frank put it: 'The media love hate. In Washington excessive cynicism is the most prevalent form of naivete. I just wish reporters were as sceptical about bad news as they are about good news.'

When this cynicism was helping to destroy the premiership of John Major it was encouraged by New Labour. They did not protest as David Mellor was forced out of office for the crime of having a talkative mistress or as sexual infidelities were wrongly rolled together with brown envelopes in an all-encompassing narrative of sleaze. They were probably simply glad that it wasn't them in the headlines. Glad, but afraid. Meanwhile they tolerated the potent myth of their own media cleverness. Like Clinton New Labour had a war room, instant rebuttal, a computer called Excalibur, stories for friendly hacks, and brickbats for unfriendly ones. Even in 1989 I recall a senior figure at the Mirror, on its political staff (and there still), praising Peter Mandelson to me. 'He's the real leader of the Labour Party,' said this chap admiringly, 'not Kinnock.' Ten years on and this man was damning spin and all its works.

In December 2002 I went to America and Japan for two weeks and lost sight of the British press. On returning I discovered that there had been a scandal of bulletin-hogging dimensions involving the prime minister's wife, and dubbed Cheriegate. I asked a colleague at the *Independent*, still excited about the whole thing, to explain exactly who had committed what crime. It was a comic conversation. Cherie had used some advice in buying a flat for her son from a dubious Australian who was her adviser's boyfriend. And then, when it was splashed across the *Mail on Sunday* ('Blairs used fraudster to buy flats') had denied it. Or something like that.

The result? A full-page in the *Mirror* on 'Cherie's cranks', and the opinion that what she had done 'may not be illegal, but it is wrong', though without quite saying why. A retired judge appeared on the *Today* programme, then edited by Andrew Gilligan's boss, Rod Liddle, with some bizarre argument about how Cherie could not now be a judge, and concluded his comments, 'In my opinion, she's far too overdressed.' Broadsheets justified their involvement in this coverage in quite ingenious ways. A *Guardian* editorial gave it all a progressive gloss. 'One can tut-tut all one likes about the unfairness of all this. But . . . the early feminists were right: the personal is the political . . . Cheriegate is not just about Mrs Blair, her role and judgment. It is also, in a resonant way, about New Labour as a whole.'

But if it was about New Labour it was also (in a resonant way) about New Journalism. Cherie, argued a *Guardian* writer, had been found wanting 'before the court of public opinion'. But who, the politicians might ask, appointed that court, provided it with evidence and interpreted its verdict? And who, if there was ever to be a dispute between those elected by the people and those self-appointed to be its tribunes, would adjudicate?

So a government, fearful of the press but believing in the case for war, amassed and published its evidence of weapons that seem not to have been there. The very least that can be said about the September dossier is that it was designed to use the information that the government had in order to persuade the country of the case for war. In other words it made the best case it could, and not the truest. Not much of a surprise there.

Had Andrew Gilligan been the defence correspondent of Yes FM's *Breakfast With Bunty* Show, there would have been no Hutton Report because nobody would have cared what he broadcast on 29 May 2003, even though he did – repeatedly, in my opinion – effectively accuse the government (through his nameless intelligence source) of telling deliberate lies in order to 'sex up' the dossier. Had he been defence editor of the *Sunday Times* his story might have earned an angry letter and a denial from a minister, but would have been accepted in Whitehall with a fatalistic shrug. The BBC, however, is different: it is effectively state-funded, non-partisan, widely trusted, international, and constitutes the gold standard of balanced journalism in Britain. Which is why so much effort is expended by just about everyone on complaining about its broadcasts. The defection of the BBC to the camp of antagonistic commitment journalism was a very real problem for the government. It was exemplified in the way some presenters would act as impartial Olympians and then moonlight as columnar mud wrestlers in the most partisan newspapers. As Andrew Gilligan did.

Over Iraq, opinions have become so polarised that BBC balance matters more than ever. For example, the weekend before the Hutton Report was published the *Independent on Sunday* carried a full-page list of what it headlined, 'The fifty lies, half-lies, distortions and exaggerations that took Britain to war'. In fact it was a highly selective list of statements about the war from US and British government sources, none of which were lies, some of which were exaggerations, some of which have turned out to be wrong, several of which were true and half of which were made after the war. For the government it was always going to be intolerable if the BBC joined a chorus that was so unreasonable and unreasoning.

The BBC itself has been under several different pressures in recent years. It is under pressure to 'compete', to provide a show-business element to its news coverage (as Richard Sambrook, director of news, told Ian Hargreaves for his book *Truth or Dare*), to break stories. Andrew Gilligan had been brought to the BBC from Sunday newspaper journalism specifically with the remit to break stories and to make waves. And this he had done, often to the chagrin of the Ministry of Defence and, occasionally, to that of his less excitable colleagues.

And the BBC was, in times of national emergency, under pressure from government. The onset of an unpopular war was always going to be problematic. How did one reflect the feeling at home while covering events themselves? Whenever the tone was even slightly questionable, there would be a note or an email or a phonecall from the government complaining about inaccuracy or bias. The complaints became part of the background noise – an occupational hazard. When, at last, the complaint was about a matter of substance, the BBC failed to spot the specific seriousness of the situation. This was not entirely its fault.

So, there was a story that the journalist said was fair because he had been told it by a particular type of person, and that the government said was a slander. The only possible way of finding out who was right was by discovering who the source for the story was, and that is where the feeding frenzy began, the one that ended up with journalists questioning each other about who told them what; that ended up with a nervous man in front of a noisy committee.

The BBC thought that the government's ire was confected and unreal, though it was warned often enough that this perception was wrong. The government further damaged its case by making its criticism of the corporation general rather than keeping it specific. It looked and sounded like bullying. Writing in the *Sunday Telegraph* the then-chairman of the BBC, Gavyn Davies, wrote,

'Alastair Campbell's recent attack on the BBC was not mainly about Andrew Gilligan's story on the *Today* programme, but amounted to a full-frontal assault on the motivation, skill and professionalism of the entire news operation.' Attack one of us, and you attack all of us, he seemed to be saying. So he 'bet the shop' on Gilligan, and lost. Hutton was specific where the BBC was general. 'False allegations of fact, impugning the reputations of others should not be made,' he judged.

Immediately after Hutton reported, the public was being invited to take sides again. Would you agree with the judge and the politicians, or with the press? The general secretary of the National Union of Journalists, Jeremy Dear, called Hutton's conclusions 'selective, grossly one-sided and a serious threat to the future of investigative journalism', defended the 'essential truth' of the original story and then threatened journalism himself by telling the BBC that any action against Gilligan could lead to strike action. 'The real final judgment,' Dear told the *Today* programme, 'will be with the public. All the evidence is that they trust BBC journalists more than politicians.' And more, presumably, than judges.

Us versus them, and be careful anyone caught in the middle.

Hutton and
the history books
Michael White

The dignified and authoritative manner in which Lord Hutton conducted his inquiry into the death of Dr David Kelly was too good to last. Tony Blair drew comfort and quiet optimism from observing the proceedings. So did every rightwing politician and leftwing pundit, who would have been delighted – but hardly surprised – if the venerable law lord concluded that the prime minister had murdered the Iraq weapons scientist with his own bare hands.

So it was inevitable that one side would be disappointed, possibly both sides, if the report proved equally hard on all concerned. But no one expected Lord Hutton to come down quite so hard on the BBC, or to be so understanding of the difficulties that attend the badly oiled machinery of government.

Lord Hutton clearly handled publication of his inquiry the way he did because he has read the history books. They are not very comforting and must have left the former Lord Chief Justice of Northern Ireland determined to try to avoid repeating mistakes made by those conducting investigations into assorted governmental crises that littered the twentieth century.

Take Lord Denning's inquiry into the conduct of the security services and John Profumo, the war minister who had been caught lying to the Commons about sharing the favours of Christine Keeler with the Soviet military attaché. Harold Wilson, then Labour's modernising opposition leader, publicly insisted 'this is not a moral issue'. But no one took much notice. It remains one of the juiciest sex-and-politics scandals in modern British history.

Appointed after a turbulent Commons debate in June 1963, Lord Denning reported that September. But the distinguished law lord heard 160 witnesses in private over 49 days of testimony, double Lord Hutton's. So we only have Lord Denning's word for it that when Keeler's irrepressible chum, Mandy Rice-Davies, was told that Lord Astor had denied sexual misconduct, she coined what became an instant catchphrase: 'He would, wouldn't he?'

Though modestly entitled *Lord Denning's Report,* the official findings were written in what the veteran commentator, Anthony Howard, has called 'a style halfway between a Mills & Boon romance and a schoolboy's adventure story' with chapter headings such as 'The Slashing and the Shooting' and 'Christine Tells Her Story'. Little wonder it became a bestseller.

But Lord Denning was notably discreet, both about the murky role of the security services and about two other unnamed ministers who might have been judged a security risk. His report reeked of respect for the good sense and humour of the decent chaps upholding the existing order, an orthodoxy which was, even then, changing rapidly. It is startling to discover that Lord Denning was allowed to hand his report to the embattled prime minister, Harold Macmillan, in mid-September along with full discretion as to the timing of its publication. By the time it went on sale on 26 September, the pro-Macmillan *Daily Mail*'s leak (ministers cleared) had inevitably been countered by the hostile *Telegraph*'s counter-leak (Mac blamed). By the time MPs got to debate the report in December, Macmillan had long since resigned, pleading prostate trouble, though he lived another twenty-three years. The future Lord Hutton was thirty-two during these shenanigans and his attempt in 2004 to minimise news management – spin – must owe much to their youthful impact on his fastidious character.

When Lord Hutton was plucked from near-retirement by Tony Blair in July 2003, what quickly impressed many old hands in the narrow, lawyer-infested world where Whitehall and Westminster meet the law courts is that his inquiry was not been set up under the powerful Rolls-Royce procedures established by the Tribunals of Inquiry (Evidence) Act of 1921. Yet he appeared to conduct himself as if it had.

Barristers did the cross-examinations in proper legal fashion and confident demands were made for 'persons and papers' which even the prime minister answered. Only later, when Lord Hutton was accused of cherrypicking his own evidence, did critics argue that he had failed to insist on more paperwork from the government side. Yet it was all done quickly and adapted to the new technology at the inquiry's fingertips. TV cameras were rightly excluded. The Hutton website was a triumph of modernity and transparency.

That change owes something to Dame Janet Smith, who headed the Dr Harold Shipman inquiry. She had a rapid-fire website for evidence and under pressure she later allowed TV companies to take a feed from the inquiry's own coverage.

The tribunals process was discredited by two failed reports in the 1970s: a long and costly one into the mismanagement of the Crown Agents (1978) and Lord Chief Justice Widgery's own horribly flawed 1972 inquiry into Bloody Sunday. Old and ailing, guided by a sense of duty to the state, the former soldier delivered what was indisputably a whitewash on the shooting of thirteen civilians in Derry. Lord Saville's fresh look at that afternoon – also appointed under the 1921 act – has not restored the legislation's standing. He has been groping with the festering consequences of Widgery since January 1998, with no end in sight.

As with Sir Richard Scott's departmental inquiry (1993–6) into arms sales to Iraq and the collapse of the Matrix-Churchill trial, the choice of judge is always a gamble. The liberal, independent-minded Scott was not familiar with the workings of government or with the media – and quickly became bogged down. His five-volume report, replete with confusing double-negatives, damaged John Major's government, but did not decisively clarify the issues.

Scott was promised the powers of a 1921 investigation if he needed them, but managed with an inquiry of the ad hoc departmental variety. It was established under powers held by the Department of Trade and Industry because of its role in export licensing. Departmental tribunals of inquiry, dozens of them, are the norm these days.

They range from Professor Sir Ian Kennedy's penetrating report into the retention of children's organs at the Bristol Royal Infirmary to Lord Philips's BSE investigation. They too remain a hit-and-miss arrangement, some admired, some scorned and ignored. The Macpherson report's charge of institutional racism over the Stephen Lawrence murder investigation still rankles within the Metropolitan Police. But it has not been ignored, far from it.

The Kennedy report led directly to the Human Tissue Bill which was passing through the Commons as Hutton reported. Lord Nolan's committee into standards in public life, set up by John Major at the height of the mid-1990s cash for questions furore, was created to be a permanent fixture on the Westminster landscape, to the annoyance of many MPs.

The historic alternative model for broader, wide-ranging inquiries was the Victorian royal commission, usually on great policy issues of the day. About 150 royal commissions were appointed in the twentieth century. Harold Wilson liked them as a means of kicking an issue into the long grass – 'they take minutes to set up, years to report,' he joked. For that reason Margaret Thatcher hated royal commissions and let the concept wither.

The last royal commission to report was Lord John Wakeham's review of the House of Lords, its terms of reference tightly controlled by Tony Blair ('rigged', said the critics) to exclude serious consideration of the relative powers of Lords and Commons. Even so Blair rejected the great fixer's cautious formula for a part-elected upper house. The stalemate continues.

Ministers are anxious to be seen to tackle an issue of public controversy in a manner that restores public confidence and refocuses public policy. Nowadays they tend to opt for the ad hoc version of a judicial inquiry. It is a flexible instrument, set up without recourse to parliament under existing legislation, its terms and appointments susceptible to the needs of the moment and political will.

Few judges are immune to pressure about who staffs their inquiry, which witnesses to see – and where – according to Professor Phil Scraton of Queen's University, Belfast. He has studied a clutch of inquiry reports from the Hillsborough disaster and Bradford stadium fire to the Dunblane killings and *Marchioness* and Southall disasters. After one, he told the *Guardian*: 'The decision to hold an inquiry, who chairs it, the remit, rules of engagement, selection of civil servants and interested parties, can all be shaped by political expediency and opportunism.'

Thus Lord Cullen, who did the Piper Alpha oil rig, Dunblane massacre and Ladbroke Grove rail inquiries, becoming known as 'Mr Disaster', caused outrage among some victims' families at Dunblane by the way he handled evidence from police (gently) and social workers (not so gently) and locked up some evidence for 100 years.

Ditto Lord Taylor's verdict on the Hillsborough stadium disaster where, Scraton says, police evidence was extensively coordinated in advance. It still rankles on Merseyside. 'Public inquiries are an essential part of the democratic process, to examine acts or omissions of state institutions. But they must clean up their act,' he insists.

As a salutary warning against manipulation the most spectacularly successful pre-Hutton inquiry in recent history must surely be the Franks Report on events leading up to Argentina's short-lived capture of the Falkland islands in April 1982.

Whitehall had ignored the signals from Buenos Aires, a political, diplomatic and intelligence failure. Margaret Thatcher dispatched her 40,000-strong taskforce and won her war. But she deemed it prudent to concede the six-man inquiry chaired by Lord Oliver Franks, brilliant Oxford-to-Whitehall warrior, veteran of many such exercises. Franks too took evidence in private, much of it from the spooks. The result was an elegant insider's assessment of the system's weaknesses which pulled its punches in the final paragraph to protect an elected government – much as Lord Hutton seems to have done.

Labour's former prime minister, Jim Callaghan complained that Lord Franks had 'got fed up with the canvas he was painting and . . . chucked a bucket of whitewash over it' on the last page. Needless to say it was the last page that was leaked to the press on the Sunday before publication. It always helps to get your own spin published first. What was it Callaghan is supposed to have said years earlier: 'You leak, but I brief .'

In the Falklands affair Lord Carrington had honourably insisted – within twenty-four hours of the invasion – on taking the blame and resigning as foreign secretary. There is a little-known link here to an earlier ministerial resignation, famous in its day – that of Sir Thomas Dugdale as Churchill's minister of agriculture in 1954.

Dugdale fell foul of the inquiry into Whitehall's refusal to sell back to its own pre-war owners the Crichel Down farm in Dorset which it had requisitioned as a bombing range in 1938. Ostensibly he gallantly took responsibility for the failures of his officials – the classic doctrine – though subsequent research showed that Dugdale quit in disgust because the rejected policy had been right.

Either way, Lord Carrington is the link. He was Dugdale's aristo-junior minister, the one who actually saw the policy papers. He too offered to resign, Churchill dissuaded him. He duly rose to dizzy heights. But insiders believe that it was the memory of Dugdale which made him walk the plank, despite Thatcher's entreaties to stay in 1982.

Lord Hutton must have read the story behind Crichel Down and the Franks report too. But he will also have had his attention drawn to two model public inquiries conducted by Lord Scarman that were widely, if not universally, admired. After the Brixton riots of 1981 he was fair and constructive. A few years earlier he had distributed blame to both sides when a demonstrator was killed in clashes with police in Red Lion Square.

Blair announced the Hutton inquiry on a plane over Asia. That may not have left him time to consider two options for the handling of public controversy. One is to tough it out and do nothing at all. That is what Anthony Eden and Macmillan did in the face of calls for an independent inquiry into the Suez crisis of 1956, a disastrous and illegal invasion of an independent Arab state that many critics liken to the 2003 invasion of Iraq.

In perilous circumstances in 1986 Thatcher, like Blair this time, got herself too closely involved in the details of a highly partisan policy. In the sale of the Westland helicopter firm to a US or European consortium, like Blair again, she took the US side. But, as the sitting prime minister, she avoided a formal inquiry.

Toughing it out is what Blair has been trying to do for months over the wider causes of the Iraq war. To critics Hutton's inquiry into Dr David Kelly's death was a distraction from the larger issues.

The second option is the parliamentary investigation. Some MPs bemoan the fact that they, not Lord Hutton, should have been holding the executive branch of government to account. The unhappy truth is that the foreign affairs select committee, which got in on the act first, proved itself inadequate to the task.

It lacked the lawyers and procedures to protect witnesses from each other and themselves. Its members lacked the forensic skills to follow up questions effectively. There were leaks, grandstanding interventions and surreptitious acts of partisanship on both sides. The committee failed to grasp what was common knowledge in the Westminster village, that Kelly was almost certainly Andrew Gilligan's main source.

If the foreign affairs committee failed in public, the intelligence and security committee, made up of senior peers and MPs, did better in getting to grips with the problems, albeit without Lord Hutton's access. But it failed to command public trust because its hearings were in private and its report delivered to Blair, not to the waiting world.

Openness and transparency are vital to restoring public confidence, as Lord Salmon, the law lord who staged a tribunal on tribunals noted long ago. There are stirrings at Westminster, where Tony Wright's public administration select committee is also inquiring into inquiries.

Select committees can and sometimes do make a difference, though not often enough. They lack the staff and the powers of a Hutton. But scandal is a major engine of change and reform, as Nolan showed over sleaze. Alas, the Commons liaison committee, made up of all the select committee chairmen, is a slow and conservative body.

So Lord Huttons, past present and future, are left to do their imperfect best. How strange that Lord Hutton should pay so much attention to defective reports of the past yet fail to deliver a verdict that both sides, however grudgingly, would accept as more or less fair.

Instead, like Diego Maradona's hand of God goal in Argentina's World Cup win over England, his report becomes an event remembered as something that was not quite right – but had profound consequences too.

Tugging back the veil

Jonathan Freedland

By a strange coincidence, on the very day that Lord Hutton delivered his report a different verdict was being handed down some 3,000 miles away. On Capitol Hill in Washington DC, Dr David Kay – a former colleague of the late Dr David Kelly in the small, global fraternity of weapons inspectors – was testifying before the Senate armed services committee.

He had been called there to explain his resignation the previous week as head of the Iraq Survey Group, the body that had been combing the country for evidence of weapons of mass destruction from the moment Saddam was toppled. When he quit Kay said he no longer wanted to search for Iraqi WMD because, he concluded bluntly, 'I don't think they existed'.

Now he sat before the Senate committee and spoke of a systemic intelligence failure. Multiple agencies had judged Saddam to hold a serious WMD arsenal and events had proved otherwise. 'It turns out we were all wrong, probably, in my judgment,' Kay told the committee. 'And that is most disturbing.'

Meanwhile, amid the modern, Ikea-blond wood of his room at the Royal Courts of Justice the white-haired Lord Hutton sat, hunched over his text, reading aloud in his gentle Ulster brogue. He had spoken for just a few minutes, reading only the fourth of his 80 numbered paragraphs when he acknowledged that there had been 'a great deal of controversy and debate' on precisely the question Kay was raising: whether the intelligence that had guided Britain and America to war had been accurate. 'This controversy and debate has continued because of the failure, up to the time of writing this report, to find weapons of mass destruction in Iraq,' he said. But he would not rule on this matter, nor even consider it. '[A] question of such wide import . . . is not one which falls within my terms of reference.'

In that sentence, Lord Hutton may have consigned his report to the footnotes of British military and political history (though it will certainly loom large in the annals of the BBC). For it consciously steered clear of the 'big picture' question – Did the country go to war on a false basis? – preferring to stick to the narrower business of the accuracy or not of Andrew Gilligan's report for the *Today* programme and the battle royal of government against BBC that it triggered. That contest dominated British politics in 2003 and its reverberations might be felt for years within the BBC and the wider media. But compared with the larger question of the rights and wrongs of going to war, it almost looked like a sideshow.

And yet, despite that, the Hutton inquiry shed enormous light both on the justification for the war and on a topic that was entirely unrelated to the judge's remit: the very way Britain is governed.

Start with the question of war. For those summer weeks leading up to the inquiry and in the few months that preceded it, there was a curious unreality about the whole Kelly affair. Alastair Campbell and the BBC traded barbs about the precise meaning of individual words in a dispatch heard on BBC Radio 4 at 6.07am; a parliamentary committee grilled David Kelly as to whether he had been the source of that report; finally a judge probed deep into the engine room of Downing Street, seeking to learn how a September 2002 dossier setting out the Iraqi threat had been drawn up. Throughout it all, fresh word came every day from Iraq of the reality on the ground, news that should have cast the whole rumpus into relief: no weapons of mass destruction had been found.

But these two things never connected. As Lord Hutton declared when he published his report, he was not interested in the reality of the Iraqi threat – merely whether the government was honest and sincere when it had assessed it in September 2002. It made for a strange kind of row – one in which the current reality was not the issue, only the perception of reality a year earlier.

Even so, Hutton's investigations did go some way in explaining how we travelled from a dossier confidently setting out the full terror of Saddam's arsenal in September 2002 to an admission, in January 2004, from George Bush's own handpicked weapons inspector, David Kay, that there were no WMD after all. Lord Hutton may not have highlighted it in his final conclusions – indeed he all but ignored it – but he heard evidence that offered key clues as to how the government got it so badly wrong.

First was the testimony of Dr Brian Jones, a colleague of Kelly, who confirmed that there was indeed some disquiet in the intelligence community at the government's depiction of the threat from Iraq. He and his colleagues thought the data needed to be framed more cautiously. The claim that Iraq had weapons of mass destruction deployable within 45 minutes was the clearest example. Jones and those like him wanted the relevant sentence in the dossier to be phrased as 'intelligence suggests . . .' The final version declared instead, 'we judge', a much stronger formulation. Cautious experts wanted the dossier to state that such weapons 'could be' deployed within 45 minutes; the final version said instead that 'these weapons are deployable' within that period. Yet there is no doubt which of the two versions would have read more credibly a year later.

The 45-minute claim, the inquiry soon revealed, was part of a pattern in which the intelligence services were pressured to present their findings in the strongest form possible. That much we know from Alastair Campbell's now infamous correspondence with John Scarlett, the joint intelligence committee chairman, seeking and getting no fewer than fourteen changes to the wording of the dossier, each one proposing a toughening of language.

Even beyond the question of wording – and Jones made the crucial point that, when it comes to intelligence assessments, wording is substance – the proceedings made clear that the security services were not quietly making their own inquiries into the situation in Iraq and then simply presenting their best guess as to what was really going on. On the contrary, the evidence showed that the intelligence agencies were under pressure to find information that would cast the worst possible light on Baghdad and its intentions. Witness the joint intelligence committee's 'last call' to all agencies to come up with something juicy to enliven the September 2002 dossier. (In the United States there was similar pressure, typified by the Office of Special Plans set up in Donald Rumsfeld's Pentagon. Former official Karen Kwiatowski told a Channel 4 documentary, *What Hutton Won't Tell You*, that that body was specifically tasked with 'cherrypicking' from the raw intelligence data to find items that might harden the case for a pre-emptive war.)

None of these actions – overriding intelligence officers' caution, beefing up the presentation of their research and sending them looking in a specific, pre-conceived direction – are crimes. But they do undermine the claim that the government was simply making a cool, disinterested judgment based on the evidence laid before it. And they show how the government ended up with such a gloomy view of Iraq's military capability, one that subsequent events did not bear out. The Hutton process revealed all this, even if the Hutton report made so little of it.

This was not the only area in which the judge shed light almost despite himself. For the Hutton Inquiry illuminated one topic entirely outside its remit: the state of British democracy.

The lead-up to war, long before anyone had heard of David Kelly, should already have prompted some concern for the state of Britain's democratic health. A steady run of opinion polls showed public opposition to military action against Iraq without United Nations approval, yet this was precisely the path taken by Tony Blair's government. Of course, representative democracies do not govern by plebiscite; they do not always do everything the public wants them to do. Still, many Britons did feel frustrated that, even when between a million and two million people gathered for an anti-war rally on the streets of London on 15 February 2003, the biggest demonstration in the country's political history, they were still ignored. Many wondered in despair: what do you have to do to be heard around here?

But Britain is not a direct democracy; we rely on representatives to express our will. Yet here too there was frustration. Besides the Liberal Democrats and a couple of other minor parties, there was no formal anti-war voice in parliament. More than 100 Labour MPs were against the war, but such is the magnitude of the Labour government's majority in the House of Commons – it won the 2001 election by 165 seats – all those backbenchers could rebel and still have no hope of stopping the war, not least because the official Conservative opposition was for it. If parliament's prime task is to reflect the will of the people who elect it, in the case of Iraq it badly failed.

These facts were known before Hutton began his proceedings on 1 August. But once he did, yet more of the deficiencies of British democracy were exposed – starting with secrecy. Hutton had the right to demand forests of paper – internal memos, confidential letters and private emails from any government department the noble lord fancied. There they were, posted on large screens in court 73 and relayed by closed circuit TV to the marquee where most of the press were housed. Here was the business of power laid bare.

This sudden avalanche of open government represented a delightful novelty. The default position in Britain remains that official papers are locked up for 30 years, sometimes 50 or more.

Secrecy is the rule, openness the exception. Britons have come quietly to accept that, noticing it, if ever, only on New Year's Day when the secrets of an earlier era are ritually set free and published in the 1 January papers – like news breaking three or more decades too late.

Now, thanks to Hutton, political observers could wallow in paper that would normally be seen only by the historians of the future. The documents were live and fresh, some just a few weeks old. Historians and Whitehall buffs were thrilled, but it set other Britons thinking. Was this not a legitimate expectation all the time, not just for the duration of an extraordinary, one-off judicial inquiry? After all, some Britons asked, we pay the government's wages; ministers and civil servants work for us. Why shouldn't we be able to see how they, the hired help, reach the decisions they take in our name, and according to which they risk our blood and treasure?

What Hutton proved was that only a crisis, in this case an apparent suicide, could tug the veil back. The rest of the time, government would take place in the dark. Labour had once understood this argument, when it was the humble opposition before 1997. Back then, it promised a robust Freedom of Information Act as the solution. In office, they delivered only a watery imitation which, in January 2004, was yet to kick in.

Hutton shone a torch into another aspect of British governance that remains shadowy: not paper, but people. Watching the parade of powerful witnesses that came to testify, one was struck by how few of them had ever been seen before, how few of them the public had ever heard of. Yes, the Prime Minister and his bulldog of a spokesman – the director of communications Alastair Campbell – were big names, along with a government minister or two. But the rest were civil servants who no one sees, no one has heard of and, most certainly, no one ever elects. Yet these people, Hutton soon revealed, wield significant power. Whether it was Jonathan Powell, the Prime Minister's chief of staff, or Sir Richard Dearlove, the head of the intelligence agency MI6 (who, fittingly, testified in the dark, via audio link from an undisclosed location), these unelected men were exposed as mighty players in the land. Advice from them or their counterparts had not only helped 'out' David Kelly but had shaped the government's case for war. They described the way their business was done, encountering each other at Whitehall cocktail parties, trading gossip, passing on titbits of high-grade information – and the impression grew of a closed world of unelected mandarins who, bereft of any public mandate, nevertheless make decisions that can end up as matters of life and death.

If there was one theme that rivalled secrecy as a constant thread throughout the Hutton inquiry it was the phenomenon of the over-mighty executive. Other democracies concluded long ago that an essential underpinning of any democracy is the separation of powers. Yet Britain has an oddly skewed system of checks and balances in which the executive almost always outweighs the other component parts. To an extent, that had already been illustrated by the inability of parliament to resist the will of an executive deter-mined to go to war. But Hutton offered further proof.

We saw, for example, that the intelligence agencies – so energeti-cally promoted as an 'independent' and therefore trustworthy source of guidance on the Iraqi menace – had been effectively co-opted by the current government. Campbell perhaps erred by admitting in his own testimony that he regarded John Scarlett, the evocatively named head of the Joint Intelligence Committee, as a 'mate'. But Scarlett himself, whose testimony to Hutton stuck dili-gently to the Downing Street line on every detail, only confirmed the impression that he had become a paid-up ally of the New Labour project. Correspondence between Scarlett, Campbell and Blair's chief of staff also exposed the close involvement of political aides in the writing of what purported to be a cold, non-political assessment of intelligence.

Hutton illuminated too the feebleness of parliament in its attempts to scrutinise the executive. The inquiry heard how the Foreign Affairs Committee had wanted to take testimony from David Kelly but the Defence Secretary Geoff Hoon granted permission for Kelly to speak only on condition that he not be asked his wider views on Iraq's military capacity. When the same committee asked to see Scarlett, it was refused by the intelligence chief's notional boss, the Foreign Secretary Jack Straw. One MP on the committee called such unhelpfulness 'monumental cheek' but that slightly misses the point. The problem is a constitutional one: in Britain the legislature, parliament, which should have its own authority to scrutinise the government, the executive, does not. It has to go cap in hand, as a supplicant, to the very people it is meant to be watching over.

Indeed, Hutton exposed the entire select committee system of parliamentary scrutiny as toothless. To investigate one man's death, the judge was allowed access to all the paper and witnesses he needed. A humble select committee, weighing the rights or wrongs of going to war, had to ask nicely for the right to ask questions at all. Not that it was ever going to press the executive too hard. Under British rules, every committee of parliament is weighted according to strength in the chamber – which means the governing party of the day always has a built-in majority.

The lesson was clear. Real scrutiny only happens in exceptional cases, like that triggered by the death of David Kelly. Even then, the hand of the executive is not absent. For who appointed the noble Lord Hutton? None other than the prime minister himself.

Ordinarily this scrutiny gap is filled by the fourth estate, with a lead role played by the government's chief antagonist in the Kelly affair: the BBC. If ever Britain was to have a written constitution, which it lacks to this day, a formal place would have to be allocated to John Humphrys and Jeremy Paxman, the inquisitors-general of radio and television respectively. Frequently it is the probing, often rude, interrogations of these interviewers which has exposed key flaws in government policy. Where parliament fails, very often the media succeeds.

According to Downing Street loyalists, this kind of thinking has congealed into a swollen media arrogance. Before he left his post, Alastair Campbell often complained that too many journalists now regarded themselves as the official opposition. It was this culture, alleged Campbell, which infected the BBC and led to what he believed was a series of journalistic lapses committed in the story of the 'sexed-up' dossier. Once the verdict was in, Campbell made the point more forcefully than ever – calling on the BBC and the wider media to drop its cynical suspicion of politicians and governments, and behave.

So the Hutton process taught Britons a few lessons about themselves. They saw how their country was governed and learned a thing or two about how politics really works. They gained some valuable insight, too, into how a supposedly expert assessment of the threat posed by Saddam's Iraq got it so badly wrong. But these still looked like diversions from the core question: did the country go to war on a false basis, even if that false basis was an honest mistake? After the long, hot weeks of the Hutton inquiry, the 700-plus pages of his report and a bruising year in British politics – that question still remained unanswered.

The trust fund
Polly Toynbee

The Hutton report has been a curious lesson in how a prime minister can win – and lose at the same time. Did ever a politician receive such a ringing endorsement from a judge? Did ever journalism come under such savage bombardment? And yet, as the polls suggest in the days immediately after the war, it was Tony Blair who took most of the damage. The public trust the BBC a lot less than they did, but they still trust it a lot more than they trust their prime minister. The spectacle of the BBC so devastatingly demolished and its leadership decapitated was an ugly sight and the people seemed to blame the government for bullying it.

Whatever becomes of him next, the Iraq war and its aftermath changed the relationship between the prime minister and his voters. As the failed search for weapons of mass destruction slowly ground to a halt and the surprised world came to accept that Iraq had none after all, this uncomfortable truth bled into the whole process of the Hutton Inquiry. Lord Hutton may have found the prime minister and his team innocent of all wrongdoing associated with Dr David Kelly's death – but the trauma of those post-war summer months still marked a watershed in the remarkable career of Tony Blair.

So did the country lose faith in him? Although, by a narrow margin, people believe Blair was right to go to war in Iraq, a strong undertow still suggests a reluctant nation was dragged there against its will, despising George Bush profoundly. Unrealistic expectations were stoked up that Lord Hutton would investigate every aspect of why we went to war. As month followed month and the report was delayed, those expectations swelled. But he was only an ordinary judge, by nature inclined to reduce the issues in front of him to a containable minimum.

The growing realisation over the months that there were no weapons came as a shock to most observers. Most of us who were against the war – the *Guardian* and this commentator included – thought Saddam probably had them: it was one reason to fear attacking him and provoking their use.

Hutton may have handed Tony Blair innocence on a plate. But the fraught history of his attempt to persuade the voters of his cause has left him damaged none the less. Confronted with the gargantuan task of persuading his party and his country, Blair pulled out every stop and he overstepped the mark: even if Hutton glossed over that, the voters did not.

However, at the time, it worked. By the eve of combat, according to the polls, the country was ready and willing to fight. Despite mighty anti-war demos flooding the streets of London, most people did in the end support it. There was a brief Baghdad bounce in Blair's ratings the week after the rapid victory but it began to seep away. With Kelly's death, his ratings plunged. It was a sudden and catastrophic haemorrhaging of confidence that has never been restored. To be sure his ratings improved by the time Hutton reported. The number of people saying it was right to fight was finally tipped – just – in Blair's favour by the sight of Saddam Hussein dragged bedraggled out of his hole. Ever since then, despite the non-existence of WMD, a narrow majority have told pollsters that the war was justified.

Yet trust in the Prime Minister himself never returned to the phenomenal levels he enjoyed before Iraq. For the whole of 2003 he slipped into negative ratings he had never had before, except for a brief blip in the week of the fuel protests. Whatever Hutton said, too many people still thought Blair lied minus 45 per cent, which was only a three-point improvement on what they said before Hutton reported. Trust in Blair's honesty had evaporated.

Would they forgive him? That's another matter altogether, for the only question that counts is will they vote for him and his party – and the answer is still yes, with an extraordinary five-point lead intact. Trust, it turns out, is not the most important quality: expectations of political truth were never high. People are hard-headed about choosing between the political options on offer at elections – and for this usually low point in the electoral cycle, it still looks overwhelmingly likely that they will choose him again next time.

So what did Iraq and its fallout in the Kelly affair do to change perceptions of Tony Blair? Start by looking back to 1997 when his approval ratings in the early days stood at a staggering plus 68 per cent. All his hapless opponents could do was to call him Phony Tony, mocking him as a man too eager to please. That ready smile and winning informality, those casual 'y'knows' and his air of hopeful honesty could force rooms full of hardened enemy journalists into something like glum submission. He was the great persuader.

John Prescott had teased him memorably as Bambi – all round-eyed innocence and charm but wobbly-legged and fundamentally unstable. Unstable, Prescott was suggesting, on the fundaments of Labour ideological belief, direction and purpose. However, no one doubted Blair had one unerring purpose born of 18 years in the wilderness – for Labour to win – and win he did for them as Labour had never won before, in two landslides.

How had he done it? His critics used to say it was done by appealing to whatever the people wanted in whatever language they wanted to hear it. His focus groups held a mirror up to the public and he reflected back to them whatever they wanted. Or so the story went. He appeased his enemies, wooed the City and Whitehall mandarins. Above all, he neutralised the deadliest enemy – the hostile press that had kept Labour out of power for most of the last century. Rupert Murdoch was his first visitor to No. 10, an honour bestowed for his newspapers' support in the election. The emollient art of being all things to all people was seen as both his besetting sin and his winning trick. He sucked the oxygen out of all opposition, drawing every opposing idea into his own body politic. To fight him, the Conservatives found, was to wrestle with an octopus. Amorphousness and indefinability were his trademarks. Like Ruby Tuesday, no one pinned a name on him.

How long ago those days seem now. Over Iraq, he became one man alone at the prow of the ship of state, making his lonely decisions with precious little consultation among his cabinet colleagues. Had they known at the outset that UN diplomacy would fail, few of them would have signed up to going to war alone with George Bush. They hoped until the last minute there would be an escape, until it was too late to pull back: only two resigned but other ministers wriggled wretchedly in their seats. There was certainly no question of his listening to his deeply unhappy party.

But the real change was this: Blair was not stopped in his tracks by a country consistently opposed to going to war in every opinion poll until the eve of battle. He was convinced that he was doing the right thing – regardless of what anyone else thought. Most of the press of left and right was deeply dubious. No one could accuse Tony Blair of obsession with focus groups now.

It cost him undoubted personal strain: look how he became thinner, greyer, gaunt – and his heart tremor episodes happened soon afterwards. No one any longer spoke or wrote of a man blown about by the weathervanes of public opinion. Strong, decisive war leadership looked as if it paid off. But did it really?

Consider the shape of the polls: a month before the war the BBC's 'Britain Decides' poll showed that when asked 'Do you believe Britain should take part in a war against Iraq?' 40 per cent said we should only go to war with a fresh UN mandate and 45 per cent said we should not go to war with or without that mandate. Asked to give the main reason why the US and the UK wanted to attack Iraq, top of the list of reasons was to secure oil supplies – sheer cynicism. But as soon as the fighting began, 82 per cent told pollsters we should see it through, while only 13 per cent wanted to pull out. By April the *Guardian* poll showed that 63 per cent of voters approved of the military attack on Iraq, with only 23 per cent disapproving. Straight after the war Blair's Baghdad bounce gave him for the first time in a while a positive rating for 'doing a good job'.

But then in July came the shocking news of David Kelly's death. In the cacophony of an impromptu press conference, one journalist asked him' 'Why did you authorise the naming of David Kelly?' to which he replied, 'That is completely untrue'. On this one denial Michael Howard, leader of the opposition, hoped to pin a charge that the prime minister lied. Polls said that if Hutton found he had indeed lied, then he should resign. But Hutton found nothing of the sort. All the same, there was that one shouted question at that early press conference that stuck in people's minds: 'Prime minister, have you got blood on your hands?'

Hutton exonerated him. The intelligence was there – even if it was wrong. There was added poignancy when the key US weapons inspector, Dr David Kay, head of the Iraq Survey Group, resigned in the very week before the Hutton report was published, declaring he thought there never had been a weapons programme initiated after the first Gulf war: 'I don't think they existed'. This remains the wicked question. Even if Blair did not fabricate the facts, everyone thought he had rhetorically exaggerated what intelligence evidence there was: Hutton finding him innocent does not dispel that impression. The great persuader had pulled out every stop to swing the nation round to war – and he did it, with remarkable success, against all the odds. But that meant he alone carried the burden for all that happened thereafter.

The real damage done to Tony Blair was that he expended most of his credit in the bank of public trust in the effort – and it will always be emptier now as a result. It will never be easy again for him to persuade people of anything against their will. He may have won the Commons vote on university tuition fees, by a whisker of five votes, but he did not win the support that really matters: 60 per cent of voters are still against top-up fees.

ICM pollsters for the *Guardian* reported that the people now found him 'out of touch', 'too concerned with spin' and 'untrustworthy'; 61 per cent were dissatisfied with the job he was doing. Teflon Tony no more. Pollsters talked of a 'seismic loss of trust' in the prime minister as the Gilligan/Campbell/Kelly drama followed by the Hutton inquiry dominated bulletins and headlines through three long hot summer months.

But even so, how bad was that? According to MORI, the polling organisation, Margaret Thatcher at the height of her unpopularity during her first term clocked up an unpopularity rating of minus 50, but went on to win her second election. At the equivalent time in her second term, her government was scoring a net dissatisfaction rating of minus 45 and for two years suffered ratings far worse than Blair's, yet she went on to win again in 1987. John Major managed even worse, reaching a minus 63 dissatisfaction score besides which Blair's mere minus 29 pales into insignificance.

However, 2003 marked a sharp fall from grace for Blair, even if this was only the end of a honeymoon that had lasted longer than for any prime minister in recent times. So to seasoned political observers this still does not look dangerous, let alone fatal. He was simply returning back to earth into the zone of unpopularity most prime ministers inhabit much of the time, even when they are about to go on to win the next election.

Nick Sparrow, ICM's chief political pollster, says: 'Escaping blame by Hutton, he comes through as a strong war leader, a man who faced a crisis alone and survived. He was a leader determined against the odds. Yes, he lied – but he's a politician and all politicians lie. Choose between him and Michael Howard? They still choose him.'

There has never been much trust in politicians: they have always inhabited the bottom of the most trusted tables, alongside journalists. Trust may not be the quality voters seek, for Iain Duncan Smith still scored a good 53 per cent as 'honest' right up to his fall. A stronger indicator stayed in Blair's favour: a majority still thought him 'competent', 'tough' and 'standing by his principles'. That mattered more, for Labour stayed resolutely far ahead in the polls. In a world where the media daily preaches nothing but cynicism about politicians, honesty counts less than competence. But perhaps most important of all was Mori's finding at the end of 2003 that 78 per cent were 'satisfied' with their standard of living, compared with just three per cent who were feeling 'very dissatisfied'.

Labour's lead stayed undented by Howard's arrival on the scene. Despite a universal sense that at last the Tories had a leader to frighten the government with his rapier sallies in the Commons and that theatrical flash of his Something-of-the-Night electricity, the Conservative ratings barely budged. Howard did well at re-enthusing Conservative voters: he could boast a stronger plus rating among Tories than Blair has among Labour voters, but he pulled in no new voters to the Tory camp. The *Guardian*'s ICM poll continued to show Labour five comfortable points ahead. Even in the lead-up to Blair's 'worst week' – the double crisis over the tuition fees rebellion and the publishing of the Hutton report – ICM and MORI still had Labour as comfortably ahead as ever.

Seven years in power and several wars changes a man beyond recognition – and may leave him in a dangerous state of mind: hubris is the enemy now. His own party knuckled under sufficiently to avoid a crisis, but they still humiliated him in the vote over tuition fees. Now a large surly crew on the backbenches is likely to rebel if he tries their patience again with high-handed policy-making that goes against the grain of the party. Hutton may have exonerated Blair beyond his wildest hopes but it still leaves a large section of the public resentful over the lack of WMD he swore existed.

He is not the man he was back in 1997. He has lost many of his mainstays – Alastair Campbell, Peter Mandelson, Stephen Byers and Alan Milburn among them. There is a risk that Hutton's total vindication will make him more grimly confident of his own decision-making and even less inclined to listen to advice from colleagues. He could approach the next election as the Captain of the *Bounty*, with a mutinous crew in his own party. The man who benefited most over Iraq, Kelly and Hutton was, of course, the Chancellor. For the first time Gordon Brown's personal approval ratings have soared above Tony Blair's and remain there.

But for all that, voters still say they will elect Tony Blair and his government again – and the pollsters think they will – trust or no trust.

Appendix 1

Today programme, 29 May 2003 at 6.07am:
Andrew Gilligan's original report

John Humphrys: The government is facing more questions this morning over its claims about weapons of mass destruction in Iraq. Our defence correspondent is Andrew Gilligan. This in particular, Andy, is Tony Blair saying they'd be ready to go within 45 minutes.

Andrew Gilligan: That's right, that was the central claim in his dossier which he published in September, the main erm, case if you like against er, against Iraq and the main statement of the British government's belief of what it thought Iraq was up to and what we've been told by one of the senior officials in charge of drawing up that dossier was that, actually the government probably erm, knew that that 45-minute figure was wrong, even before it decided to put it in. What this person says, is that a week before the publication date of the dossier, it was actually rather erm, a bland production. It didn't, the, the draft prepared for Mr Blair by the intelligence agencies actually didn't say very much more than was public knowledge already and erm, Downing Street, our source says, ordered a week before publication, ordered it to be sexed up, to be made more exciting and ordered more facts to be er, to be discovered.

JH: When you say more facts to be discovered, does that suggest that they may not have been facts?

AG: Well, erm, our source says that the dossier, as it was finally published, made the intelligence services unhappy, erm, because, to quote erm the source he said, there was basically, that there was, there was, there was unhappiness because it didn't reflect the considered view they were putting forward, that's a quote from our source and essentially, erm, the 45-minute point er, was, was probably the most important thing that was added. Erm, and the reason it hadn't been in the original draft was that it was, it was only erm, it only came from one source and most of the other claims were from two, and the intelligence agencies say they don't really believe it was necessarily true because they thought the person making the claim had actually made a mistake, it got, had got mixed up.

JH: Does any of this matter now, all these months later, the war's been fought and won?

AG: Well the 45 minutes isn't just a detail, it did go to the heart of the government's case that Saddam was an imminent threat and it was repeated four times in the dossier, including by the prime minister himself, in the foreword; so I think it probably does matter. Clearly, you know, if erm, if it, if it was, if it was wrong, things do, things are, got wrong in good faith but if they knew it was wrong before they actually made the claim, that's perhaps a bit more serious.

JH: Andrew, many thanks; more about that later.

Appendix 2

Edited extracts from the transcript of a conversation between Susan Watts and Dr David Kelly, the day after Andrew Gilligan's report on the *Today* programme

Susan Watts: What intrigued me and which made, prompted me to ring you was the quotes yesterday on the *Today* programme about the 45 minutes part of the dossier.

David Kelly: Yep. We spoke about this before of course.

SW: We have.

DK: I think you know my views on that.

SW: Yes, I've looked back at my notes and you were actually quite specific at that time – I may have missed a trick on that one, but er ... (*Both laugh*).

* * *

SW: On the 45 minutes.

DK: ... I knew the concern about the statement ... it was a statement that was made and it just got out of all proportion ... they were pushing hard for information which could be released, that was one that popped up and it was seized on ... and it was unfortunate that it was, which is why there is the argument between the intelligence services and Cabinet Office/No 10, because things were picked up on, and once they've picked up on it you can't pull it back.

SW: But it was against your advice that they should publish it?

DK: I wouldn't go as strongly as to say . . . that particular bit, because I was not involved in the assessment of it . . . no . . . I can't say that it was against my advice . . . I was uneasy with it . . . I have no idea who debriefed this guy. Quite often it's someone who has no idea of the topic and the information comes through and people then use it as they see fit.

SW: So it wasn't as if there were lots of people saying don't put it in . . . it's just it was in there and was seized upon . . . rather than No. 10 specifically going against?

DK: . . . It was an interesting week before the dossier was put out because there were so many things in there that people were saying well . . . we're not so sure about that, or in fact they were happy with it being in but not expressed the way that it was . . . I don't think they're being wilfully dishonest I think they just think that that's the way the public will appreciate it best. I'm sure you have the same problem as a journalist don't you? Sometimes you've got to put things into words that the public will understand.

* * *

SW: OK . . . just back momentarily on the 45-minute issue . . . I'm feeling like I ought to just explore that a little bit more with you . . . So would it be accurate then, as you did in that earlier conversation, to say that it was Alastair Campbell himself who . . . ?

DK: No I can't. All I can say is the No. 10 press office. I've never met Alastair Campbell so I can't. But . . . I think Alastair Campbell is synonymous with that press office because he's responsible for it.

Appendix 3

The Hutton Inquiry on the internet

The official site:

the-hutton-inquiry.org.uk
The gateway official site.
the-hutton-inquiry.org.uk/content/evidence.htm
All the documents filed by interested parties to the inquiry.
the-hutton-inquiry.org.uk/content/report/index.htm
Lord Hutton's Report.
dracos.co.uk/hutton
Remodelled, easier to browse version of the Hutton site.

Hutton on *Guardian Unlimited*

guardian.co.uk/hutton
Gateway to the *Guardian*'s online Hutton coverage across its network of sites.
guardian.co.uk/hutton/keyplayers
Guide to the main players and their evidence.
guardian.co.uk/weblog/special/0,10627,1002839,00.html
Guide to Hutton and the Kelly affair online.

The media

timesonline.co.uk/hutton
Reports from *The Times*.
telegraph.co.uk/hutton
Reports from the *Daily Telegraph*.
ft.com/hutton
Reports and background from the *Financial Times*.
news.bbc.co.uk/1/hi/in_depth/uk/2003/david_kelly_inquiry/default.stm
Background and reports from the BBC.

Original documents

number-10.gov.uk/output/Page271.asp
The dossier: *Iraq's Weapons of Mass Destruction – The assessment of the British Government*, published 24 September 2003.
publications.parliament.uk/pa/cm200203/cmselect/cmfaff/813/81302.htm
Full text of the Foreign Affairs Committee report published 7 July 2003 entitled *The Decision to go to War in Iraq*.

Audio and Video

bbc.co.uk/newsa/n5ctrl/events03/uk/bbc/kelly_smil/kelly.ram
BBC audio and video reports on the Kelly affair.
news.bbc.co.uk/media/audio/39224000/rm/_39224884_gilligan06_29may.ram
Audio: hear Andrew Gilligan's original *Today* programme report, from the BBC.
news.bbc.co.uk/olmedia/cta/events03/ukpol/iraq/foreign15jul.ram
See Kelly giving evidence to the Foreign Affairs Committee, from the BBC.